Anti-racism in Work Practice

CRITICAL
APPROACHES
TO SOCIAL
WORK

Anti-racism in Social Work Practice

Editor:
Angie Bartoli

CRITICAL
APPROACHES
TO SOCIAL
WORK

First published in 2013 by Critical Publishing Ltd, St Albans

British Library Cataloguing in Publication Data
A CIP record for this book is available from the British Library

ISBN: 978-1-909330-13-9

This book is also available in the following e-book formats:
Kindle ISBN: 978-1-909330-14-6
EPUB ISBN: 978-1-909330-15-3
Adobe e-book ISBN: 978-1-909330-16-0

Cover design by Greensplash Limited
Project Management by Out of House Publishing
Typeset by Newgen Imaging Systems
Printed and bound in Great Britain by TJ International

Critical Publishing
www.criticalpublishing.com

FSC
www.fsc.org

MIX
Paper from
responsible sources
FSC® C013056

We would like to dedicate this book to Padare students at the University of Northampton who have challenged, taught and inspired us in many different ways.

Through the course of writing this book, my mother, Anna Bartoli (née Raia) left my side but not my heart.

Contents

About the authors

Angie Bartoli is a Senior Lecturer in Social Work and Teaching Fellow at the University of Northampton, where she has worked since 2006 and leads on a Master's programme. Her research interests include issues relating to race and gender, social work supervision, mentorship, child protection and inter-agency working. She is also a deputy editor for the internationally peer-reviewed journal *Practice Teaching and Learning* and a member of the National Steering Group of PIAT (Promoting Inter-Agency Training in Safeguarding).

Charity Chukwuemeka qualified as a social worker from the University of Northampton in 2010. She is currently a social worker within the statutory sector, working with children with disabilities. She is also a founder member of Padare, the Black African Social Work student support group at the University of Northampton.

Paul Crofts is an independent Equality and Diversity consultant and trainer. He has been providing training and consultancy for almost 30 years in race, community and race relations, discrimination law and practice, and hate crime to a range of public sector, community and private sector organisations. Paul is the Vice-Chair of Northamptonshire Rights and Equality Council.

Bernadette Curran is a Senior Lecturer in Social Work at the University of Northampton since 2010. With extensive experience within the statutory sector as a social worker, Child Protection Conference Chair and Independent Reviewing Officer, her research interests include asylum and immigration, childcare practice and service user participation.

Sue Kennedy as the Principal Lecturer is the Head of the Social Work Field and Teaching Fellow at the University of Northampton. Having worked in the statutory childcare sector for 25 years as both a practitioner and manager she has acted as an adviser to government departments and a leading childcare voluntary organisation. As a feminist, Sue's research interests include perceptions of risk within child protection, and issues relating to gender, culture and race.

Sukhwinder Singh is a Senior Lecturer and leads on the Social and Community Development undergraduate programme at the University of Northampton. His current doctoral studies include teaching and learning race issues. He has previously worked for the Home Office and provided training and consultancy on hate crime and social cohesion to a variety of agencies. He is also committed to enabling students to develop skills in evidence-informed practice.

Prospera Tedam is a Senior Lecturer, Programme Leader for the undergraduate Social Work course and Teaching Fellow at the University of Northampton, where she has worked since 2006. Her research interests include human rights with a particular focus on children, cultural competency and legal frameworks. She is also the chair of the voluntary organisation Afruca (Africans Unite Against Child Abuse). Prospera is also a member of the Independent Families Returns Panel for the UK Border Agency.

Introduction

ANGIE BARTOLI

I have come to believe over and over again that what is most important to me must be spoken, made verbal and shared, even at the risk of having it bruised or misunderstood.

(Lourde, 2007)

Anti-racism has a long history within the profession of social work and in social work education especially in the 1980s and 1990s. Following the launch of the social work degree in 2003, the anti-racist competency was replaced with the umbrella term of *anti-discriminatory practice*. This has diluted the emphasis of particular forms of discrimination and so obscures the impact of the appearance of specific forms of discrimination, including racism.

Why are we worried about anti-racism again?

Despite an agenda within higher education that promotes internationalisation, and social work practice that recognises diversity, racism has never disappeared. Within the political landscape race and racism have preoccupied the country and the media. Much of the most heated political debates leading to the formation of the Coalition government centred on immigration and asylum seekers. In January 2012, a verdict was finally reached on the racially motivated murder of Stephen Lawrence. Combating racism within football has become topical as high profile Premier League players have been accused of racism. The death of Victoria Climbié, an eight year old from the Ivory Coast, and the conviction for the murder of Kristy Bamu have meant that debates around faith-based child abuse and working with African families have resurfaced.

In November 2012, Rotherham Council made a decision to remove some children from foster carers due to the foster carers' membership of the political party UKIP, who the Council claim have 'racist policies' (BBC News, 2012). The *Daily Telegraph*, which initially covered this news item, instigated another provocative debate that questions social work decision-making based upon anti-racist paradigms. The Education Secretary, Michael Gove, in ordering an inquiry into the Council's decision, which he claims to be 'indefensible', has widened this debate further (Marsden, 2012).

The recently published Leveson Inquiry Report (2012) highlights the fact that women, minority ethnic groups, migrants and asylum seekers have been misrepresented and discriminated against within the media.

The legislation framework within the UK connected with issues of diversity has continued to grow within the last decade. The Human Rights Act in 1998 introduced a number of political and civil rights enshrined in 16 articles. Discrimination is covered in Article 14, which explicitly addresses race. The year 2010 saw the introduction of the Equality Act, which bans unfair treatment of people because of their protected characteristics including race. More recently (2012) the College of Social Work has offered the social work profession the Professional Capabilities Framework (PCF), which outlines eight domains with the third being:

DIVERSITY – Recognise diversity and apply anti-discriminatory and anti-oppressive principles in practice.

Immigration legislation is rapidly changing and has become more stringent in the last decade. On 29 November 2012, we saw a drop in the net number of migrants to the UK with the Immigration Minister claiming that *tough policies have taken effect* (Travis, 2012). This is part of a wider policy agenda that has seen a recent shift from examining issues of racial inequality and anti-racism to a focus on *community cohesion* and a return to 1960s policies of *assimilation*.

Why another social work text about anti-racism?

Many of the primary texts available for social work students focus on either the knowledge base of racism (see for example, Bhatti-Sinclair, 2011) or working in particular social work settings (see Dominelli, 2008). Books such as these, together with the work of Graham (2007), Laird (2008) and, more latterly, Sinclair *et al.* (2011) have a valuable place within social work education and practice. How does this text differ? The anti-racist knowledge within this book has been built upon and informed by black social work students and social work educators' experience of working alongside black students at the University of Northampton. The former regulator of the social work profession, the General Social Care Council (GSCC), claimed that students from ethnic minorities made up 21 per cent of enrolments on the social work degree, with African students being the second highest ethnic group after white students.

This book will be largely based upon the authors' experience as educators and their own research about and with black students' experience of racism and *otherness* within social work practice and education. A strong message within this book is that we consider the term *anti-discriminatory practice* has diluted the covertness of racism and students' understanding of the insidious and painful nature of its impact.

The primary motivation to write this book stems from two of the chapter authors (Prospera Tedam and Sue Kennedy) and myself as the editor. In 2008, as three women social work educators, we became curious. We had noticed that there were a growing number of black African students who appeared to have a different experience on their social work educational journey. Many of the chapters are highly influenced by the authors' deepened understanding of racism that has developed through professional and personal paths.

Who is this book for?

This book aims to be radical and honest in nature and re-visits the subject of anti-racism in a clear and accessible manner. Our intention is that this book will appeal to social work students as the content is original, containing empirical research and thinking that has been informed and shaped by students and social work educators' desire to share their understanding. It is our intention that this book appeals to all students regardless of their ethnicity, as the chapter authors reflect the diversity of the student population in terms of gender and ethnicity – which is not necessarily the case in other existing texts written about anti-racism and social work education.

The chapter authors' experience to date is that black social work students have found our research findings affirming, whilst other social work educators and practice assessors listening to us in presentations, workshops and international conferences have found our work informative, transformational and challenging.

How does this book work?

Each chapter addresses a critical question, and then offers readers reflective questions to pause and consider what they have read. Real case studies are a feature in each chapter, acting as a means of illustrating some complex concepts (for example Cultural Competence in Chapter 3) or theories (Critical Race Theory in Chapter 6). Case studies also include personal experiences shared with authors by students and colleagues (for example in Chapters 4 and 7). Reference to historical and contemporary research will be made throughout the pages that follow and each chapter will highlight a particular piece of research to highlight current thinking and ideas. Each chapter will conclude with a *Taking it Further* section where readers can further develop their knowledge and understanding by reading further texts, journal articles, research, or are signposted to Websites of interest.

Influence of history and legislation

As you read this book, you will become aware that the history of anti-racism thinking and practice has often provoked new legislation or is influenced by legislation. At times a brief historical overview of key events (eg immigration in Chapter 1) will be offered to provide a context to the ensuing legislation, national policy and the consequent impact on social work practice.

As social workers, we have a professional and ethical duty to apply knowledge within professional practice, which includes the law and is encapsulated within the new Professional Capabilities Framework (College of Social Work, 2012). A number of pieces of legislation will be referred to in the following chapters and the table below offers a summary of legislation and public enquires that have influenced anti-racist social work practice over the last five decades.

Immigration is a key feature of this book, as this is when race issues tend to be bought to the fore through popular media, politicians and the general public. Reactions, trends and attitudes to racial matters can be traced throughout the history of social work education through the demise of CCETSW and the explicit anti-racist requirements for social work training (see Chapter 2), and the internationalisation agenda within a wider higher education discourse (see Chapter 4).

For example, Chapter 1 will offer a historical overview of the legislation that has shaped and changed concepts in connection with immigration, asylum and citizenship. A timeline is offered in Chapter 2 that charts the history of anti-racist social work education, while Chapter 5 considers the shifting language of anti-oppression education and practice within an historical lens. The concept of Cultural Competence (in Chapter 3) is placed within historical and legislative frameworks to reflect the need and benefits of such a model in a multicultural and multiracial society. American history and the Civil Rights movement have been highly influential in developing deeper understandings of racial discrimination. Two concepts within this book – Cultural Competence (Chapter 3) and Critical Race Theory (Chapter 6) – have their origins in America but are just as significant within a UK context, as is demonstrated within these two chapters through the use of case studies.

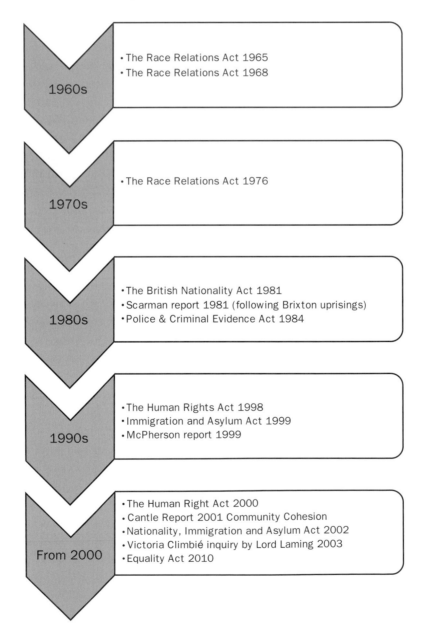

1960s
- The Race Relations Act 1965
- The Race Relations Act 1968

1970s
- The Race Relations Act 1976

1980s
- The British Nationality Act 1981
- Scarman report 1981 (following Brixton uprisings)
- Police & Criminal Evidence Act 1984

1990s
- The Human Rights Act 1998
- Immigration and Asylum Act 1999
- McPherson report 1999

From 2000
- The Human Right Act 2000
- Cantle Report 2001 Community Cohesion
- Nationality, Immigration and Asylum Act 2002
- Victoria Climbié inquiry by Lord Laming 2003
- Equality Act 2010

Chapter summaries

It is unlikely that you will read this book all in one sitting or sequentially. There are some overlaps between the chapters, which are highlighted, as policy and practice does not happen within a vacuum.

In Chapter 1, social work educator Bernadette Curran considers the challenges to social work students of putting the social work values emphasised within the Professional Capabilities Framework into practice when working in immigration, asylum and with refugees. Current UK legislation is considered in regard to opportunities, social and political inclusion surrounding citizenship. The case study outlined within this chapter has been kindly offered by solicitor Zubier Yazdani and is available via the Refugee Council website.

Sukhwinder Singh offers in Chapter 2 the preliminary outcomes of his research on how professional social work educational programmes prepare students to work with *cultural diversity* and *cultural difference*. The range of standards that promote awareness and recognition of diversity and difference in terms of legislative frameworks, policy and professional standards will be considered.

The conceptual model of Cultural Competence will be the focus of Chapter 3, which offers a practical tool, connected to the PCF, for addressing anti-racist practice in contemporary social work. By providing a brief historical overview of Cultural Competence, Prospera Tedam will focus on assessments of families where ritual and faith-based abuse might occur.

In Chapter 4, the black student peer support group at the University of Northampton, Padare, will be introduced by Angie Bartoli. By drawing on previous research and publications this chapter will provide a background to Padare, its aims and objectives as well as its strengths and weaknesses, achievements to date, current position and future ambitions.

Chapter 5 will explore racism through the dialogic experience between a white woman tutor on a social work programme and a black African woman social work student. Using a philosophical hermeneutic approach, Sue Kennedy will critically reflect on a specific event that brought the two women together and consider the student's lived experience as the platform for a dialogue that has challenged knowledge and an understanding beyond the arrangement of 'black' and 'white' to recovery and belonging for both women.

Critical Race Theory is introduced in Chapter 6 together with the socially constructed concept of 'whiteness' and its significant relationship to racism in the UK. Paul Crofts will challenge white readers to look at their roles and responsibilities to reassess their part in *either* promoting the continuation of racism and colluding with it, *or* taking an active part in opposing it in a variety of ways.

In Chapter 7, a black social worker and former graduate from the University of Northampton and a founder member of Padare will provide a reflective account. Charity Chukwuemeka will explore her understanding of anti-racism at the point of qualification and examine current awareness of anti-racist practice from her perspective as a black female social worker by using case examples and voices of other black colleagues.

The fact that election gains had been won on a blatantly racist ticket that was in direct opposition to anti-racist policies did however get heard and the focus moved to stemming disquiet on immigration rather than redressing the degradation of a racial climate.

The use of immigration policy to restrain the backlash of the perceived injustice of equality legislation to prevent immigrant communities experiencing racism has proven to be not only ideologically and ethically questionable but also pragmatically flawed. As with the omission of the police and social services, it has permitted attitudes to remain intact and for social systems to create categories of 'other' now most notably defined by their citizenship.

The popularity of the approach was initially demonstrated by the support provided to Enoch Powell following his now infamous Birmingham speech referred to as 'Rivers of Blood'. In this speech Powell alluded to an imaginary conversation with one of his constituents bemoaning the state of affairs in the UK and, with language reminiscent of a colonial period, the constituent warned Powell that soon the *black man will have the whip hand over the white man* (Powell, 1969).

Race relations

Powell focused on the Race Relations Act (1968), asserting that his constituents' concerns were legitimate and evidenced by the enactment of equality legislation:

Here is the means of showing that the immigrant communities can organise to consolidate their members, to agitate and campaign against their fellow citizens, and to overawe and dominate the rest with the legal weapons which the ignorant and the ill-informed have provided. He saw the enactment of equality legislation as the start of a preventable evil that filled him with foreboding. Like the Roman, I seem to see 'the River Tiber foaming with much blood'. (Powell, 1969)

Here Powell was forecasting 'Rivers of Blood' as a response to immigrants having the opportunity to be accepted as equal rather than to control immigration. He would go on to assert that immigration could continue, perhaps no surprise given that he had, in his guise of Health Minister, actively recruited people from Commonwealth countries to settle and work in Britain to meet drastic labour shortages.

This has nothing to do with the entry of Commonwealth citizens, any more than of aliens, into this country, for the purposes of study or of improving their qualifications, like (for instance) the Commonwealth doctors who, to the advantage of their own countries, have enabled our hospital service to be expanded faster than would otherwise have been possible. They are not, and never have been, immigrants. (Powell, 1969)

Powell (1969) was clear in what he saw as the solution, stating:

Granted it be not wholly preventable, can it be limited, bearing in mind that numbers are of the essence: the significance and consequences of an alien element introduced into a country or population are profoundly different according to whether that element is 1 per cent or 10 per cent. The answers to the simple and rational question are equally simple and rational: by stopping or virtually stopping further inflow and by promoting the maximum outflow.

The speech had no authorisation from the Conservative Party and it led to Enoch Powell being dismissed from the shadow cabinet, never to hold public office again. He was then, and is now, not without support. He and many others, without reference to the policing practice of the day, or inner city decline, would go on to assert that his foreboding about the 'rivers of blood' was proven to be correct when the widespread disturbances were displayed in simplistic 'racial' terms. The legitimacy of this discourse is questioned not only by the limitations of the equality legislation but also by the growing body of academic literature demonstrating that race relations are damaged not by the creation of equality but by the continuation of inequality (Hall *et al.*, 1978; Hall, 1992).

Powell's solution to what he perceived to be an ever consuming crisis has proved to be more prophetic with each successive government wishing to enforce his perceived solution to immigration:

granted it be not wholly preventable, can it be limited, bearing in mind that numbers are of the essence: the significance and consequences of an alien element introduced into a country or population are profoundly different according to whether that element is 1 per cent or 10 per cent. (Powell, 1969)

It was first frequently shown by Margaret Thatcher who, when she was leader of the opposition, spoke about the UK being

swamped by people with a different culture, and you know, the British character has done much for democracy, for law and done so much throughout the world that if there is any fear that it might be swamped people are going to react and be rather hostile to those coming in. You see, my great fear is now that if we get them coming in at that rate people will turn round and we shall not have good race relations with those who are here. Everyone who is here must be treated equally under the law and that, I think, is why quite a lot of them too are fearful that their position might be put in jeopardy or people might be hostile to them unless we cut down the incoming numbers. They are here. They are here. They must be treated equally. (Granada, 1978)

Her stated commitment to equality legislation did not prevent Enoch Powell from expressing his *hope and relief* at Margaret Thatcher's comments. No doubt influenced by her concluding comments, *If you want good race relations, you have got to allay people's fears on numbers ... We do have to hold out the clear prospect of an end to immigration* (Granada, 1978).

No doubt spurred on by the lead her party gained in the National Opinion Polls, one showing the Conservatives holding an 11-point lead over Labour (just before Thatcher's comments, Labour had led by two points in a poll by the same organisation), her first administration went on to enact another cornerstone piece of immigration legislation – the British Nationality Act (1981). This Act updated nationality codes, reclassifying CUKC into three categories, British Citizenship, British Dependent Territories Citizenship (BDTC) and British Overseas Citizenship. It also modified the application of *jus soli*, making it necessary for at least one parent of a UK-born child to be a British citizen or a permanent resident of the UK for a child to be granted British citizenship.

Restriction and exclusion

The restriction of entry to the UK has remained a prevailing feature of successive British governments' approach to immigration, including Blair's New Labour. Unlike their Conservative predecessors New Labour did present as willing to combat racism and promote race equality. They commissioned the official enquiry into Stephen Lawrence's death and passed the Race Relations (Amendment) Act 2000. They showed less willingness to combat the racism created by Immigration Policy, enacting a plethora of immigration laws that were all designed to impose not only forceful border controls but also stringent restriction internally such as the Immigration and Asylum Act 1999, Nationality, Immigration and Asylum Act 2002, and Asylum and Immigration (Treatment of Claimants etc.) Act 2004. This line of attack on immigration has been continued by the present Coalition Government, who have declared their immigration objective to *bring annual net migration down to the tens of thousands – rather than the hundreds of thousands we saw under Labour – by the end of this Parliament*.

The method of exclusion has prohibited a large population group from making a valuable contribution to society or benefiting from the resources within it. The exclusion is becoming ever more visible via declarations on passports that spell out No Access to Public Funds and the use of holding and detention centres to *house* those that have become classified as 'illegal', whilst they await their ultimate exclusion from society – removal, return or deportation.

Protecting the humanity of people

Operationally for those seeking to and protect the humanity of people subjected to immigration control, the options have become more restrictive, and more complex legal challenges against unfair treatment in the UK are not brought on the basis of domestic equality laws but on Britain's recognition of European and international law. Both forms of legislation have become increasingly concerned with the implementation of a human rights discourse, a discourse that any social worker practising with those subjected to immigration control needs familiarity and commitment to. The increased use of internal controls to monitor and manage people who want to immigrate to the UK has permeated every fabric of society and its impact is seen in areas such as employment and in the allocation of welfare provision.

The ever-increasing use of quotas to manage what is perceived or created to be a crisis of immigration also fails to acknowledge that people's decision to immigrate is most likely to be induced by push rather than pull factors. Indeed the international event James Callaghan cited as a haven spurred the need for immigration control. For example, Idi Amin's 'Farwell to Indians' campaign aptly demonstrated that immigration occurs due to global events and that British international policy and history can contribute to factors that push migration.

A lack of willingness to recognise this has a profound impact on the lived experience of anyone entering the UK. A popular discourse has emerged within which any immigrant group can be perceived not as an individual or person who wants to contribute but one who wants to take, and take something that is not theirs to have, such as housing, health care, welfare benefits or jobs. It fails to acknowledge the push factors that explain immigration and most perversely, whilst applied across the board, it seems it is most stridently preserved for those who have arrived in the UK in order to exercise their right to claim asylum under the auspices of the 1951 United Nation Convention. As Refugee Action state:

All too often, media coverage of asylum in the UK is negative, misinformed and one-sided. It frequently contains the kind of factual inaccuracies and misleading terminology which would not be tolerated in coverage of other sensitive issues. At worst, some sections of the tabloid press have waged what amounts to a concerted campaign against asylum seekers' most fundamental rights.

Why do you think people seeking refuge in the UK are not protected by domestic equality legislation?

Global conditions

The world's physical and political geography and the UK's international position have altered dramatically since the passing of the Commonwealth Immigrants Act (1968) and the Race Relations Act (1968). The British Empire has been overhauled as independent nations fought and gained national autonomy. The UK has become an active economic and social member of the European Union, a Union that has been dramatically expanded by the demise of the monolithic Soviet Union and its replacement with a number of independent states.

This geographic and political change has brought social disruption either during the struggle for independence or because of the pace of social changes following independence. Significant areas have also witnessed the heightening of tensions regarding *identity* that have resulted in war, persecution and human rights abuse within in a number of former colonies (Kenya, Uganda, Zimbabwe and Somalia) and Soviet states (Bosnia), culminating in the need to flee poverty, political unrest, human rights violations and armed conflict. These developments have had a profound impact upon the political, social and legal identities of the world's global citizens.

A major pull on many has been the development of the concept of European Citizenship – this is true both for individuals and nation states, especially those freed from Soviet control and centralised planning. Many of the former countries constituting the Soviet Union have chosen to embrace European Union (EU) membership. These countries are being gradually brought into the European Union. Their induction has being restrained by their own economic position during a period of unprecedented economic turmoil and their membership is staggered and managed to this end. The A8 countries (referring to the eight Eastern European countries) who become economic members of the EU in 2004 joined with various restrictions on their participation in labour markets. As full employment conditions were prevailing in the UK at this time Britain allowed A8 nationals to work under the terms of the Worker Registration scheme that outlined access to welfare support. From this period until 2007, 630,000 A8 workers migrated to the UK. The migrants were predominantly young: 83 per cent were aged 18–35 and they were accompanied by 50,000 children aged 0–17 (Home Office, 2007).

The data on migratory patterns concerning people arriving from Central and Eastern Europe confirm that they leave for a variety of reasons and with varied patterns of movement that suggest short-term to long-term residence. These patterns suggest that there will be expressions of need across the health and social care sector, needs that were not considered or addressed when the invitation to work in the UK was extended.

Without this consideration this group is likely to experience the same form of exclusion that previous immigrants to the UK have had – full or partial exclusion from health and social care services. This is a key issue for any social worker who wishes to promote inclusion and one that will require a culturally competent practitioner who can understand the political and social forces that produce migration and the changing nature of racism. In the UK the arrival of A8 migrants has been accompanied by the emergence of right-wing political movements whose discourse centres on UK sovereignty that displays a subtle racist agenda aimed at diminishing the rights based discourse of the European Union and free movement of people. Data by Ní Laoire *et al.* suggest that exclusion in other European Union countries has resulted in the children of A8 migrants selectively adapting to their host societies whilst retaining a group identity clustering in tight friendship groups within school, social and neighbourhood settings (Ní Laoire *et al.*, 2008). This demonstrates that, as with previous populations, a group's inclusion cannot be attained by a policy and practice geared towards assimilation.

For social workers the exclusion of those outside of the EU demonstrates an even greater need for Cultural Competence and commitment to social justice. For this group of people the world, or more specifically Europe, has become less accessible and inviting. Their entry to the UK is managed and directed by the UK Borders Agency. Their needs, whilst more starkly visible, remain largely unmet. The majority are frequently arriving from well-known conflict zones such as Iraq, Zimbabwe, Afghanistan and Somalia. They arrive to exercise their right to claim refuge in the UK under the terms of the United Nations 1951 Convention Relating to the Status of Refugees (CRSR). This key legal document, which Britain has been a signatory to since it was drafted by the United Nations (UN), defines who is a refugee, their rights and the legal obligations of states. It is the document that protects individuals fleeing war, repression and human rights by permitting them to claim sanctuary in another country.

As in the past refugees from around the world are often linked to wider regional or global struggles, such as war, repression and human rights abuses rather than poverty (Castles *et al.*, 2003). This correlation is frequently borne out statistically with applications for asylum increasing from countries experiencing conflict, so that in the year 2000, most refugees came either from Iraq or from Sri Lanka, and in 2001 Afghanistan was the country of origin of most refugees to Britain. Global conditions that generate these applications cannot be based on quotas. The cost to life and human rights has unfortunately been revealed by the experience of those who sought to flee Nazi Germany. Whilst there is a dominant perception that Jewish refugees were treated well in Britain, there is strong evidence for the view purported by Louise London that Britain did not view Jewish refugees in a humanitarian light, but through the eyes of self-interest. More could have been done in trying to assist Jews fleeing from Nazi Germany and also to permit the shattered remnants of European Jewry to enter post-Holocaust Britain. For, as Edie Friedman has asserted, the arrival of large numbers of Jewish refugees was regularly met with a less than rapturous welcome by the government, trade unions, certain newspapers and indeed sections of the Jewish community itself. Moreover, their arrival was the catalyst for the formation of several anti-Semitic groups, including, in 1900, the British Brothers League, in some ways a forerunner of the British Union of Fascists (Friedman, 2008).

As Knox and Kushner (1999, quoted in Karpf, 2002) state in their work:

Of all the groups in the 20th century, refugees from Nazism are now widely and popularly perceived as 'genuine', but at the time German, Austrian and Czechoslovakian Jews were treated with ambivalence and outright hostility as well as sympathy. People feel that the country should maintain asylum for genuine asylum seekers, but they're always in the past, never today.

And *never today* means that they are received into a climate of disbelief that views them as *bogus* applicants, *asylum seekers* who must have their claim for refuge examined rather than accepted. As with their predecessors the cost can be two-fold: refusal of entry or forced return. For example between 1990 and 2002, only 1.9 per cent of Sri Lankan asylum seekers were granted refugee status in Britain, 73.6 per cent in France and 80.9 per cent in Canada. The Refugee Council report highlighted the experience of those returned by the British government to a Sri Lanka racked by civil war, potential torture, arrest, detention and even death (Karpf, 2002).

As the statistics above reveal, the global forces that are producing these migratory patterns are reflected in other EU and non-EU countries. Indeed, those leaving the well-known conflict zones are far more likely to receive refuge and support in other countries outside of Europe. In 2002, 'developing countries' provided asylum to 72 per cent of the world's refugees. Within the EU, *the UK received the highest number of asylum applications ... but ranked fifth when population size was taken into account* (Shaw and Durkin, 2003, p 7).

The perception of Britain as a magnet for *bogus* refugees has encouraged the use of internal control of immigrants with methods being employed to prevent people from benefiting from resources that it is alleged they want to exploit and have not earned. No substantive evidence exists to support the claim that people arrive in the UK because of a desire to attain significant social and/or economic benefits. Yes, it is often to avoid direct economic hardship (a desire to work is inherent in this from the new arrival) but also because of a genuine fear of persecution.

Research from Robinson and Segrott (2002) suggests those factors that prompt people to seek refuge in the UK are not knowledge of welfare entitlement but the cultural and linguistic link established during the colonial era. They are for example influenced by having relatives or friends in the UK. There may also be an underlying belief that the UK is a safe, tolerant and democratic country, a view possibly enhanced if their country of origin had a colonial relationship with Britain. If such a relationship is evident then it is likely that an ability to speak English would also act as a further inducement for those seeking refuge in the UK. There is little evidence of any prior knowledge of UK immigration or asylum procedures, of entitlements to benefits or availability of work in the UK. There is even less evidence that asylum seekers have comparative knowledge of how these vary between different European countries. Most want to work and support themselves during the determination of their asylum claim rather than be dependent upon the state (Robinson and Segrott, 2002).

The simplistic explanations offered in popular discourse and media presentations frequently fail to recognise the legal and ethical complexity this group of people's circumstances creates and warrants. The question of having a government strategy that returns people to war and famine-torn countries has rarely been asked. As Chris Mullin points out, even the BBC flagship *Today* current affairs programme was not immune to raging hysterically about asylum seekers during a programme broadcast in March 2006:

John Humphries sounding more like Richard Littlejohn, ranted away at the immigration minister, Tony McNulty (who is already ruthless enough without being pushed into greater excess), demanding to know why we're not sending more home. No one mentioned that many of the worst offending countries – Iran, for example – won't accept back their citizens or that there is no government in Somalia to negotiate with (indeed there's a famine underway there at the moment). (Mullin, 2011, p 85)

For social workers, this experience is demonstrated in more immediate ways as opportunities to provide support and protection via the execution of legal duties outlined in the European Convention of Human Rights and domestic legislation that has afforded asylum seekers protection via different identity characteristics (such as being child) have become more restrictive. This restriction is most visible in Schedule 3 of the Nationality Immigration and Asylum Act 2002. This imposes restrictions on local authorities in terms of their duties to certain types of care leavers and presents them with a contradiction within different pieces of legislation. For example this is evident within Schedule 3 of the Nationality, Immigration and Asylum Act 2002 and the Children Act 1989.

The inequitable and unfair treatment of this group of children has been a feature of numerous local authorities, resulting in lengthy court hearings and rulings to prevent the two-tier system that frequently operates for an indigenous child or one seeking refuge. It is a practice that provides a poor experience for the refugee concerned, with emphasis given to legal duties without adequate consideration of the range of options and challenges available.

The failure of the organisation and the individual to examine the needs and options available to this group, and instead practice in a technocratic manner, provides credence to Lipsky's (1980) depiction of social workers as street-level bureaucrats and implementers of laws that are designed to be restrictive to those not considered to belong to the nation state. Such actions cannot be informed by social work values. To do this the social worker has to acknowledge the human rights of the person concerned, not implement decisions on the basis of nationhood, as this leads to the denial of services. This approach further stigmatises people and reinforces prejudice and preconceived ideas about immigrant populations. Invoking a practice that Gupta defines as *povertyism* denigrates people's self-esteem and respect and migrant populations are made to feel that they should be grateful for services: *beggars can't be choosers* (Gupta, 2004, quoted in Parrott, 2010). It also fails to recognise that in matters pertaining to social welfare the overriding legal principal of domestic and international law should be that the welfare principle (Children Act 1998) should dominate. Unwillingness or inability to do this will ensure that citizenship is a vastly different experience depending upon one's legal status. This is encapsulated by the Prime Minister of the Cape Colony and mining millionaire, Cecil Rhodes, who once allegedly asserted that whilst for some there is always first place, for others there is not:

Remember that you are an Englishman, and have consequently won first prize in the lottery of life.

CRITICAL QUESTION

How will you seek to ensure your practice with asylum seekers and refugees is ethical and informed by a human rights perspective?

CASE STUDY

Read the following case study (Refugee Council, 2012) and consider if the social work practice described advantages or disadvantages the individual concerned.

Consider what you might do to improve the situation for the person described.

Reza will be 19 years old on his next birthday. He came to the UK from Iran on a visitor's visa when he was 18 years old to stay with an uncle in London. He ran away from his uncle's house a year later and became *looked after* by the Local Authority as he did not want to return to his uncle's care under any circumstances. Reza does not have any formal Iranian ID documents. Reza's family, in Iran, were persecuted by the Iranian authorities. He had little or no contact with his parents but soon after becoming looked after he discovered that his stepbrother was in London and he began to visit him periodically. With the support of his social worker, Reza made an application for asylum, enrolled at school and did well in his studies. Reza's asylum application was refused but he was granted discretionary leave to remain in the UK until he was 17 and a half. His social worker helped Reza access formal legal advice by working with reputable refugee support organisations to help him find a solicitor. Reza obtained advice on submitted an application to vary his discretionary leave to remain in the UK (often known as 'an application to extend leave to remain'), which was submitted in time before his current leave ran out.

However, Reza suffers from post-traumatic stress. Just before his 18th birthday he revealed to his psychologist that he was sexually abused in Iran and that such abuse continued in London in his uncle's house (who was in fact not related to him). Reza confided that he was treated as a prisoner and domestic slave in his 'uncle's' house. The psychologist asked Reza if he could inform his social worker, with whom Reza had a good working relationship. He agreed.

After he turned 18, a number of negative things happened to Reza. His social worker was changed to someone who he did not get on with, his application to vary his leave to remain was refused and his subsistence payments were reduced to £45 per week. In addition to this he was given a week's notice to move to a room in a shared house far from his college and psychologist. Reza's new social worker called him for a meeting, informing him that he had just received notification from the UK Border Agency that Reza's application for leave to remain had failed two weeks ago. The Local Authority had to now consider whether it could continue to support him. The social worker informed Reza that he had already conducted a Human Rights Assessment and concluded that Reza could return to Iran using the voluntary assisted return and reintegration package. The Local Authority would support Reza for a further 28 days with a room and £30 per week.

Practice issues

Up until his 18th birthday Reza has benefited from some effective social work practice. Following this his experience appears to have been influenced by mechanistic practice that is not concurrent with the Professional Capabilities Framework as it does not appear to be guided by enforcing Reza's rights, seeking justice for him and promoting his economic well-being; such an approach would have used intervention and skills to provide support for him and to prevent harm, neglect and abuse. The practice described in the case study has not recognised the issues of diversity and anti-discriminatory and anti-oppressive practice. There is little evidence of the application of knowledge, critical reflection and analysis. Had a more effective approach been adopted the organisation and social worker may have considered:

- that the welfare principle dominates (Children Act 1989);

- recognising that Reza has not exhausted his appeal rights. He has 28 days from any refusal to appeal;

- appointing a Personal Advisor (s23C(3)(a) Children Act 1989);

- preparing an assessment of need and reviewing his pathway plan (s23C(3)(b) Children Act 1989);

- legal responsibilities in safeguarding Reza given the disclosure of sexual abuse by his 'uncle' (Children Act 1989 (s47));

- as his corporate parent assisting him to find legal advice.

Do you consider there to be another impediment that might prevent Reza from returning to Iran?

At the time of writing there is no Iranian consular presence in the UK. Therefore there is no way for Reza to get an emergency travel document. In such circumstances he cannot return home through no fault of his own and the failure to support him will be a breach of his ECHR rights.

How does research inform the social worker's understanding of meeting the needs of immigration?

This section of the chapter will focus on developing an understanding of how important it is for those working in the field of immigration to understand the merits and pitfalls of the research that can be used to inform understanding of service users' needs and interventions. The discussion will centre on the research completed by the Newcastle-based East Area Asylum Seekers Support Group, a charity that provides support to asylum seekers. The research was commissioned by one of the charity founders and supporters and was compiled by the University of Durham Centre for Social Justice and Community Action in 2009 by Dr Rachel Pain (Durham University) and Dr Peter Hopkins (Newcastle University). It sought to:

- explore the emotional geographies of unaccompanied asylum-seeking young men in their new communities;

- evaluate the emotional support and enhancement of well-being provided by the project;

- consider the extent to which Common Ground operates as a space of emotional well-being (Pain and Hopkins, 2009).

This research has been selected as it provides an example of how an ecological approach can at a personal and cultural level be used to simultaneously challenge discrimination whilst improving the day-to-day physical and emotional welfare of those subject to immigration control. Examining the refugee experience from this perspective is compatible with social work values and the second, third and fourth domains of the Professional Capability Framework. It therefore illustrates for present and future practitioners how central holistic practice is with this service user group, and provides an example of how it can be achieved. The research begins by providing a comprehensive definition of well-being. To this end the project and the report uses the conceptualisation of well-being from Gough *et al.* (2007): *the right every person has to a 'fully rounded humanity'* (Pain and Hopkins, 2009, Section 2.1). This recognises that well-being involves more than the fulfilment of subsistence needs – an approach that is well matched with a desire to engage in practice that is informed by a human rights perspective.

This and the report's findings demonstrate the central place that the skills, knowledge and values of the practitioner have upon the nature of the experience that marginalised individuals and groups have.

The positive benefits of service provision are difficult to pin down; it is about an ethos that is built through interactions, personalities, caring work and social relations in particular spaces, and as it is subjective, shifting and personal and it cannot be easily quantified. (Pain and Hopkins, 2009, p 5)

Or as one of the young people interviewed by the project summarised:

When asylum seekers see somebody – anybody – smiling at them – especially the English – asylum seekers love English person to smile at them ... they feel at home, and they feel safer.

Interviewer: What about outside Common Ground, do people smile at them?

Well they do smile at them. But the smile at Common Ground is different to the smile outside. At Common Ground they don't feel sorry for him, they want to help him. (Ashur). (Pain and Hopkins, 2009, p 10)

As the report recognises data of this nature is difficult to quantify and qualify. As with all research that can be used to develop knowledge and understanding to organise service provision to ensure equity and social justice for any of the newly arriving population groups to the UK, research methods that employ a qualitative approach will be most effective. Pain and Hopkins (2009, p 5) reported that *intensive qualitative methods are required to gain purchase on how this ethos is experienced and felt, and what its effects are.* The qualitative approach is reflected in the methods employed by the two researchers who examined the services offered at Common Ground, including:

- a number of visits to the project;

- a discussion group with eight young men;

- in-depth interviews with five young men and one young woman;

- shorter interviews with staff members and volunteers;

- observations of daily activities and interactions at Common Ground;

- informal conversations with staff, clients and visitors (Pain and Hopkins, 2009).

The methods used examined the needs of one of the most marginalised newly arriving immigrant populations, namely young unaccompanied asylum seeking people in the UK. This report also challenges the potential effectiveness of current models of service design and delivery, which further excludes this group of people from being given a voice. As discussed within the chapter tighter internal and external immigration control has restricted the means by which newly arriving populations can have their needs met. This has occurred alongside equality legislation that has resulted in an official need to incorporate the *voice* of the service user at the heart of service provision, health and social care education (Department of Health, 2006).

Practice that is informed from a service user perspective recognises the benefits that experiential knowledge can create to improve social work practice. However, if this is restricted to provisions that are made available, it will fail to acknowledge the discrimination the population group being researched experience as a consequence of not being offered a service in the first place. This potential restriction is particularly relevant to a population whose legal identity is continually classified and reclassified and to whom the exclusion from public resources is identified by the classification of 'No Recourse to Public Funds'. Such a mechanism places the population outside of formal service provision and as such open to being discriminated against again. Addressing this situation requires the service user and practitioner to develop the research process beyond the mechanistic to the meaningful.

The danger of this occurring according to Pain and Hopkins (2009) is reduced by a number of factors. Firstly the project meets the needs not only of those legally defined as refugees but also those who are classified as an asylum seeker, those granted *Exceptional Leave to Remain*. Secondly the service has been created to meet needs not currently catered to by statutory services. The project, Common Ground, was set up in 2001 as a community response to asylum seekers arriving in the area following dispersal. Its premises are a drop-in centre that houses a shop where clothing and household items are donated and given away to those in need; a meeting place; facilities such as internet, phone and interpretation; a hub for accessing various services; and advice provided by the staff. Thirdly, its ethos has always been to welcome newcomers and members of the existing community, partly to aid the integration and acceptance of asylum seekers, and partly because the project is located in a socially and economically deprived area of the city where British-born residents also have a high level of need for services and basic resources. The approach therefore seeks to prevent the maligning and marginalisation of asylum seekers in the immediate and wider society, encouraging the longer term residents to *realise that asylum seekers are real people, human beings with real stories too* (Pain and Hopkins, 2009, p 11).

As with previous studies completed with this population group the researchers identified that the young people's emotional well-being was challenged not only by the pre-flight experiences but also the obstacles and hostility encountered once having arrived in the UK. The young people spoke of the negative impact that the complexity of the asylum application process and the climate of disbelief embedded within it has upon their well-being. The impact from the physical and verbal racial attacks encountered, recollections of being *verbally abused in the street, physically removed from nightclubs or bars and provoked whilst travelling on public transport* were provided to the researchers (Pain and Hopkins, 2009, p 7). The young people spoke about the sense of isolation and suicidal thoughts, with Common Ground providing a place to discuss issues safely.

The young people's response to Common Ground is positive as highlighted by Abel (research participant) in the following quotation: *The people who work here are very important as they help me and they help people* (Pain and Hopkins, 2009, p 11). It is possible that this positive feedback arises more from a fear that criticism might result in the loss of the minimal service (frequently the only service being received). However, the parallels between what the young people valued in the project, and the paid and unpaid staff, have a striking similarity. What appears to be the most striking difference in affecting the outcome for the children involved with Common Ground is the lack of attention given to ensuring their welfare needs are met at a national policy level.

Conclusion

The reasons for immigration are many and varied but whatever the motivation to leave one geographic and/or political border to enter another, the treatment that the group or individual receives when they reach an alternative destination has profound implications upon their life chances and opportunities. The history of immigration to Britain indicates that it has been shaped and marred by racism. It would therefore seem logical that social work as a profession that purports to tackle disadvantage and discrimination has a role to play in improving the opportunities and life chances of immigrant populations. Social work does not however operate in a vacuum and practice is *conditioned by and dependent upon the context from which it emerges and the context from which it engages* (Harris, 2008, p 663). Historically and currently social work practice has not always effectively questioned the racism of the context from which it has emerged as evidenced by the ongoing underrepresentation of black and ethnic minority communities in preventative children and adult social care settings. The social work discourse that has emerged to challenge the direct and indirect discrimination that has contributed to this experience has emphasised the importance of adopting an anti-racist approach. This requires social workers to be able to think about wider concepts, and critically reflect and analyse the society they practice in and their professional and personal values (Thompson, 2007; Dominelli, 2008).

Taking it further

Briskman, L. and Cemlyn, S. (2005) Reclaiming Humanity for Asylum Seekers: A Social Work Response. *International Social Work*, 48(6): 714–24.

Crawley, H. (2010) *Chance or Choice: Understanding Why Asylum Seekers come to the UK*. Available at: www.refugeecouncil.org.uk.

Dominelli, L. (1997) *Anti-Racist Social Work*. Basingstoke: Palgrave.

Doyle, L. (2009) *I Hate Being Ideal: Wasted Skills and Enforced Dependence among Zimbabwean Asylum Seekers in the UK*. Available at: www.refugeecouncil.org.uk.

Friedman, E. and Klein, R. (2008) *Reluctant Refuge: The Story of Asylum in Britain*. British Library.

Humphries, B. and Hayes, D. (eds) (2004) *Social Work Immigration and Asylum: Debates, Dilemmas and Ethical Issues for Social Work and Social Care Practice*. London: Jessica Kingsley.

Knox, K. and Kushner, T. (1999) *Refugees in an Age of Genocide*. London: Frank Cass.

Kohlu, R.K.S. (2007) *Social Work with Unaccompanied Asylum Seeking Children*. Basingstoke: Palgrave Macmillan.

Williams, F. (1989) *Social Policy: A Critical Introduction. Issues of Race, Gender and Class*. Cambridge: Polity Press.

2 Anti-racist social work education

SUKHWINDER SINGH

Chapter aims

This chapter will provide you with some of the conceptual building blocks for understanding and mapping a way forward across a terrain that is highly contested and politically challenging.

CRITICAL QUESTIONS TO BE ADDRESSED

Does the spectrum of approaches encompassed under anti-racism have any usefulness for working with *culturally encapsulated students* and social workers (Lacroix, 2003, p 23), and enabling them to move beyond *liberal white guilt* (Hugman, 1996)?

Introduction

This chapter will explore the relevance of anti-racist social work education and practice and consider how it encompasses a broad combination of emancipatory perspectives committed to challenging racism in all its different forms and guises. In order to do this we firstly need to consider what we mean and understand by terms we use to think about and describe anti-racist practice and how these relate to different approaches to 'race', racism and ethnicity. A range of cross-disciplinary and literature considered to be seminal will be looked at to identify different theorising around anti-racism and its academic relevance for social work practice. This will include discussion about the implications of the eventual retrenchment and appropriation of anti-racist social work into a broad 'anti-oppressive practice' model (Williams, 1999). The chapter concludes by exploring research on the use of a critical incident technique to promote transformative learning.

By focusing exclusively on 'race' issues my intention is not to give the impression of race being privileged over other forms of social oppression or to inadvertently suggest that there exists a 'hierarchy of oppression' (Williams, 1999). On the contrary, a focus on cultural issues should be interpreted as working for a more inclusive and holistic understanding of the *multidimensional nature of diversity* (College of Social Work, 2012), and the interlocking nature of the *various forms and expressions of oppression* (Macey and Moxon, 1996, p 309).

It is important to recognise that in social work education there is a very clear requirement on qualifying social work students to demonstrate an informed practice awareness of diversity issues. The Professional Capability Framework for social work states that qualifying students should develop an appreciation of *oppression, marginalisation and alienation as well as privilege, power and acclaim*; it also requires students to *recognise the importance of diversity in human experience* and *apply anti-discriminatory and anti-oppressive principles* (College of Social Work, 2012). These areas of the framework consolidate existing standards; for example the Quality Assurance Academy (QAA, 2008), Benchmarking Statements for Social Work requires students to demonstrate 'knowledge and understanding of the processes of discrimination' and The Department of Health (2002) Requirements for Social Work Training place emphasis on the 'principles of valuing diversity and equalities awareness'. In essence these standards provide us with a mandate to embed in our learning more awareness and practice competence in understanding, evidencing and challenging racism.

Authorial identity

Before proceeding it is important that I declare to you my *theoretical and social position, substantive interests and biography* (Dunne *et al.*, 2005, p 46). I have decided to declare my partiality as an author and recognise how my positioning has led me to *take sides* (Becker, 1967). What I have decided to write about as Black British South Asian in this chapter has been shaped by personal, institutional and group experiences of racism for the past 30 years. By situating self in this chapter and making myself visible to you I am questioning the neutrality of knowledge production and whether it is possible for any of us to write or speak from *nowhere*. The explicit position taken in this chapter is that *we cannot speak [or write or practice] from nowhere, but from where we are positioned, socially, culturally and politically* (Gray, 2003, p 33). Where I am positioned socially, culturally and politically will influence how I experience the social world and the types of theories and literature I draw upon to explain and make sense of it. Gray suggests that in order to avoid becoming *disembodied arbiters of truth and knowledge* we need to adopt the partial view from *somewhere* that professionally and politically for social work has more credibility than the relativist view from *everywhere* or the abstract view from *nowhere* (Gray, 2003, p 33). My *somewhere* can partly be found in my experiences and active resistance of racism.

Stuart Hall makes an important observation when he states that

we all speak from a particular place, out of a particular history, out of a particular experience and a particular culture. (Hall, 1992, p 258)

CRITICAL QUESTION

Where do you speak from? How would you describe your *somewhere*?

Understanding and conceptualising *race*

When thinking about anti-racist social work practice we often use language and concepts that have complex and contested meanings, whether it be in academic, political or public discussions (Goldstein, 2008). These terms refer to how 'race', racism and ethnicity are conceptualised and help explain how the difference of *others* is sometimes *conceived, represented and encountered* (Sharma, 2006). Given the importance of these terms for anti-racist social work education and practice it is important to comment upon each of these separately. Dominelli suggests that the language we use to think about and describe race issues matters and is important because:

Words indicate understandings of reality, shape interactions within discourses that produce them, and expose specific conceptualisations of power and people's place in the world ... Words both reveal and construct ways of knowing, exposing the epistemological and ontological assumptions that underpin thoughts and behaviours. (Dominelli, 2008, p 8)

Race is an extraordinarily difficult and problematic term to define, it has certain elusiveness, but one way or the other we all know what it means (Balbo, 1998). Turney (1996) suggests that *a deconstructive approach acknowledges the presence of this category in our thinking, accepting that, while technically 'empty', we nonetheless use this term to mean something on our cultural map. We deploy the language of 'race' as though it does indeed signify and as though we know what it means* (Turney, 1996, p 13).

Stuart Hall (2000), drawing upon the work of Derrida, also cautions against the use of the term *race* and suggests that it should only be used *under erasure ... as it is no longer good to think with* (Hall, 2000, p 15) because of its problematic and artificial nature. He argues that 'race' and related concepts such as ethnicity, identity and culture are so 'discursively entangled' (incapable of pure meaning) that they should only be used 'under erasure' (Hall, 2000, cited in Gunaratnam, 2003, p 31). 'Race' is therefore often enclosed in inverted commas to indicate its lack of validity as a descriptive and analytical tool (Woodward, 2003); this also indicates its contested and socially constructed rather than biological nature (Spencer, 2006). However, despite being devoid of any scientific value, 'race' retains a central position in public consciousness (Ratcliffe, 2004; Law *et al.,* 2004) and has been used in sociological work as a metaphor to describe, explain and develop academic theorising into the processes of representation, exploitation and domination (Downing and Husband, 2005). The concept rests on the assumption that humans can be divided into distinct types based on biological and phonotypical differences. 'Physical markers' (Pilkington, 2003), such as skin pigmentation, hair texture and facial features are drawn upon to attach different meanings to different 'races'. *These meanings often involve hierarchies and hostility, which is where racism is involved* (Woodward, 2003, p 16).

Within this discourse of 'race', *colour symbolism* is very significant, with *blackness* being historically associated as the opposite of everything European, Christian and civilised (Dwyer, 2004). Three distinct phases in 'race' thinking encompassing the fourteenth, seventeenth and twentieth centuries can be identified in the literature to help make sense of how understanding about 'race' has evolved (Singh, 2002). Gurnam Singh, a writer and researcher on anti-racism practice and social work education, suggests that the 'scriptural phase' in 'race' thinking was characterised by quasi-religious explanations that viewed black people as heathens without souls and that associated skin colour to symbolic representations of black and white, with white portrayed as signifying purity, goodness and spirituality, and black as representing evil, sin, dirtiness and death. The *biological phase* was characterised by literature and provided pseudo-scientific explanations to justify oppression and slavery based on the supposedly evolutionary inferiority of the Black 'race'. The *sociological phase* was initially driven by a structural analysis of power and the search for observable and identifiable discrimination, but has now increasingly become occupied with cultural analysis and theorising (Black 2004). This brief historical overview suggests that thinking and theorising about 'race' has been a constant feature throughout time (Fryer, 1984), and that as a social construct it continues to be linked to relations of power and processes of struggle (Graham, 2007).

Rattansi (1999, p 80), suggests that *the legacy of the 'scriptural and biological phase' has been the enduring nature of the 'racialised hierarchy', which has been drawn upon* to reduce *'non-white' populations to the lowest rungs of the racial ladder.* These *racial hierarchies* have legitimised slavery, the policy of forced labour, and justified Britain's imperialist and colonialist past (Fryer, 1984). Modood (2007) argues that the continuing relevance of this hierarchy for ordering contemporary social relations and life opportunities can be evidenced through the fact that the more distant an individual or group is in terms of their '*class, culture and colour*' from the 'white mythical norm' the greater their marginality or exclusion (Singh, 2002; Tomlinson, 2002).

Racism and the relevance of social theory

What we mean and understand by the term 'race' and racism is sometimes difficult to comprehend and explain. The Stephen Lawrence Inquiry simply viewed racism as a system which either *advantage[s] or disadvantage[s] people because of their colour, culture or ethnic origin* (Macpherson, 1999, p 20). The term has also been used to refer to and describe the processes by which certain groups are stereotyped, discriminated against and subjected to unequal positions and outcomes (Solomos, 2003; Fredman, 2002).

It is important to recognise that we do not just have one single form of racism that remains bounded and anchored to a particular set of racialised beliefs. Racism appears in different guises and is *constantly renewed and transformed* (Fanon, 1970, p 41). Anthias and Lloyd (2002, p 8) suggest that the political, economic and ideological condition in which racism operates *is always a fluid and shifting one.*

Miles (1989) also views racism as essentially a fluid and open process rather than something that is fixed around a given set of beliefs and practices. He draws upon the concept of 'racialisation' to argue that racism is an ideological process in which 'race' is given the status of an *apparent truth.* Miles suggests that racism is promoted through *a representational process whereby social significance is attached to certain ... characteristics* (Miles, 1989, p 74). He suggests that certain 'social signifiers' give rise to certain racist beliefs and that these do not necessarily need to be related to a person's skin colour. Instead these 'social signifiers' may be related to other physical features or certain cultural and behavioural traits that are thought to be innate, as with anti-Semitism and anti-Irish racism (Connolly, 2000). What is important here is the way in which under given historical circumstances:

An arbitrary signifier – a colour, a body, a religious creed, a social arrangement/custom, or a set of cultural practices – comes to be associated with particular meanings; that is, it becomes a 'certain kind of difference' etched within asymmetrical power relations with specific outcomes and effects. (Brah, 2007, p 138)

An understanding of language and the role it plays in constructing the world, and the way in which we experience it, is also of central importance to understanding the role of discourse in reproducing racism. Discourse refers to forms of thought and knowledge that we may hold about the social world. The language we draw upon to talk about racism both produces and reflects dominant ideas. The French philosopher, Foucault, refers to this as 'forms of thought' or 'regimes of truth', which are taken for granted but are in fact always being resisted and challenged (Fook and Askeland, 2006, p 10). Humphries (1999) suggests that Foucault's ideas relating to discourse were *an attempt to understand the relationship between language, social institutions, subjectivity and power* (Humphries, 1999, p 121). Within this discourse particular perspectives gain authority whilst others are suppressed, hence the dominant discourse, which suggests that 'race' and cultural issues have no place in fostering and adoption childcare work, will carry more power than the suppressed one, which argues to the contrary.

These 'forms of thought' and 'regimes of truth' are reproduced and influenced according to Derrida by the binary oppositions that operate in language. Derrida argues that language and the use of binary oppositions play a critical function in obscuring issues relating to dominance. Singh (2002) suggests that

the operation of binary oppositions performs a key function in the construction of dominant and subjugated identities within western culture. Thus concepts such as rational/irrational, good/evil, white/black, man/ woman, straight/gay, objective/subjective, moral/immoral, modern/primitive ... in which the first is regarded as superior and the second a threat to it, play a critical role in the production and reproduction of oppression. (Singh, 2002, p 73)

This analysis of 'racialisation' and 'discourse' signals a shift away from viewing racism as simply relating to colour of skin. Modood's (2008) ongoing work on 'cultural racism' and the experiences of Britain's Muslim communities is further evidence of this shift away from the grand narrative of 'skin colour' and towards other social signifiers for understanding the contemporary nature of racism. Modood (2007) usefully draws upon the concept of 'Islamaphobia' to explore the hate encountered by British Muslims and the stereotypes they face in terms of belonging to a backward culture that is not compatible with Western values.

Although there is complete rejection of 'race' as anything apart from a category that is socially constructed and constantly changing (Gillborn and Ladson-Billings, 2004), it is important to recognise that:

'Race' like gender and sexual orientation, is real in the sense that it has real, though changing effects in the world. It has tangible and complex impacts on people's sense of self, experiences, and life opportunities. Thus, to assert that 'race' and racial difference are socially constructed, is not to minimise their social and political reality. It is, rather, to insist that their reality is precisely social and political rather than inherent and its meanings and functions change over time. (Van Soest and Garcia, 2003, p 13, cited in Graham, 2007, p 33)

Whilst the overarching concept of 'colour racism' remains an important one for understanding the ways in which *ethnic groups are conceived, responded to* in terms of *inclusion and exclusion in the UK* (Platt, 2007, p 18), it is important to move our gaze away from simply viewing racism as solely to do with individual prejudice and individual pathology (Lloyd, 2002). It is important to understand that trying to explain racial discrimination in terms of individual prejudice ignores and fails to recognise the issues of power within institutions and society (Downing and Husband, 2005).

Porter (2002) suggests that the naming of racism as a social structure that is both constraining and resisted is an important one. Porter goes on to suggest that the existence of structural racism does not necessarily mean that all interactions between white and Black individuals will be characterised by racism. Individuals have 'agency' and the ability to resist and challenge these forces through developing 'criticality' and anti-racist understandings.

The contemporary emphasis on ethnicity and culture

Pilkington (2003) suggests that whilst 'race' entails distinguishing people on the basis of 'physical markers', ethnicity entails distinguishing people on the basis of 'cultural markers'. These 'cultural markers' include a shared language, a shared history, belief in common ancestry, attachment to a real or imagined homeland, a shared religion, social customs and group memories (Pilkington, 2003; Karner, 2007; Brah, 1996). These cultural markers have been linked to positive psychological well-being; research has reported that *individuals secure in their ethnic identity act with greater autonomy, flexibility and openness* (Banks, 1999, p 38).

However, Sharma (2006) states that the identity category of 'South Asian' has been specifically 'othered' in terms of being steeped in an excess of culture and that it is important to avoid a simplistic understanding of religion and other cultural markers as if they were bounded, unchanging and unchangeable.

CRITICAL QUESTIONS

Can you identify your cultural markers? What do they tell us about your identity?

How are these cultural markers perceived and experienced by others?

Culture is always connected to ritual and can be found in social exchange and in behaviour; its impact on everyday life can be understood through the rules defining religious observance, permissible and prohibited types of food and drink, and the organisation of time and space. Rules concerning bodily posture and control, concepts of shame and honour (*izzat*) and strong cultural expectations as to who you should marry are also strongly associated with culture (Karner, 2007).

O'Hagan (2001), drawing upon the work of O'Riagáin, also recognises the important role of language in culture:

Language is in the first instance a means of communication ... a communal tool, developed and refined by its users to express their ideas, their beliefs and their feelings. It reflects a people's development, their shared historical experience and their sense of community. It is a receptacle where a people's most intimate and finest thoughts can be recorded, stored and transmitted, not only to other contemporary members of the community, but even from one generation to the other. It is the mainstream of culture. (O'Hagan, 2001, p 153)

Religion, theology and prayer also play an important role in how ethnicity and culture are constructed, shared and celebrated (Gilligan and Furness, 2006; Crabtree *et al.,* 2008).

For many ethnic minority service users religion is a basic aspect of human experience (Al-Krenawi and Graham, 2000). Religion is central in the self-definition of the majority of South Asian people as many tend to define themselves by their religion, which has been reinforced by research (Modood, 2001).

Despite the importance of faith in the context of many cultures, social work's uncomfortable relationship with religion (Pierson, 2008) has made it reluctant to embrace a more informed understanding of religious differences and their implications for practice (Zahl *et al.,* 2007; Pierson, 2008).

Ahmad suggests that it is important not to view culture as *a rigid and constraining concept, which is seen to somehow mechanistically determine people's behaviours and actions* (Ahmad, 1990, p 190). Fernando (1989) also warns against an over-emphasis on culture, which he suggests may lead to a racist approach in practice as it may encourage the promotion of 'cultural sensitivity' issues without understanding the nature and dynamics of racism. Cultures are not simply relative; *power relations exist between cultures, resulting in some being valued more than others* (Dominelli, 2002, p 66).

The postmodern challenge

Postmodernism requires us to critically reflect upon and recognise the nature of identities and comprehend their fluidity. It warns of the dangers of reifying the dynamic and situated meanings of lived experiences by exclusively focusing on one aspect of a person's identity. Hall (2000) suggests that identities are always fluid, incomplete and always in the process of becoming. However postmodernism has been strongly criticised for its emphasis on fragmenting individuals, which tends to suppress and exclude the collective experiences and histories of Black people (Graham, 2002a). Postmodernism's self-declared purpose of opening up and enabling different ways of knowing does not necessarily hold true for those of us who seek to recognise the continuing importance of ethnic identity-making situations and the realities of racism in the lives of many Black communities (Mason, 2003). Clearly the need to recognise the importance of 'colour and culture' and the different socio-economic profiles of Black communities enables social workers to demonstrate sensitivity and competence in working with cultural, linguistic, religious and social differences (Mason, 2003). Recognition of the realities of racism and structural disadvantage does not necessarily mean adopting a rigid perspective that views identity and experience as fixed and determined and culture as ossified (Dominelli, 2002).

Anthias (2002) suggests the need for a reflexive critical multiculturalism to move beyond this apparent deadlock between postmodernism and anti-racism. She asks for a multiculturalism that recognises the fluid nature of cultural identities as well as their location within racialised social structures, stating that:

The existence of multiple identities does not mean that individuals do not have different investments in different identities at different times ... they are not like cloaks that we can don and then discard but like different layers that can be worn, some on top and some below at different times. (Anthias, 1999, p 6)

Anthias (2002) also recognises the need to acknowledge issues of intersectionality between and across multiple fields of power and this is taken up in the work of Healy (2005), who suggests that in social work practice we need to understand how other categories of social oppression such as disability and sexuality intersect and differentiate racial and ethnic *identifications and experiences* (Healy, 2005, p 198).

CRITICAL QUESTION

What do you understand by the term intersectionality? How does intersectionality challenge a mono-dimensional view of identity?

The relevance of these terms ('race', 'racism' and 'ethnicity') for social work are significant and remind us of a not too distant past when this type of theorising had no real meaning or practice relevance for the profession. Indeed, up until the mid-1970s, social work in the UK was an exclusively white profession. It was not until Barbara Solomon's (1976) groundbreaking text *Black Empowerment* and Ahmad's (1990) seminal text *Black Perspectives in Social Work* that the social work profession began the slow and uncomfortable journey of reflecting upon its past practices and representations of Britain's ethnic minority communities.

The remainder of this chapter charts the nature of this journey and maps out the history, tenets and relevance of British 'anti-racist social work' practice.

Social work's historical conceptualisations of working with culture and colour

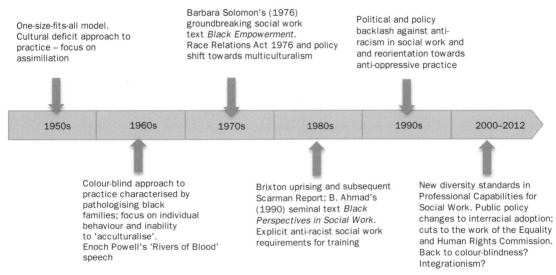

One-size-fits-all model. Cultural deficit approach to practice – focus on assimiliation

Barbara Solomon's (1976) groundbreaking social work text *Black Empowerment*. Race Relations Act 1976 and policy shift towards multiculturalism

Political and policy backlash against anti-racism in social work and and reorientation towards anti-oppressive practice

| 1950s | 1960s | 1970s | 1980s | 1990s | 2000–2012 |

Colour-blind approach to practice characterised by pathologising black families; focus on individual behaviour and inability to 'acculturalise'. Enoch Powell's 'Rivers of Blood' speech

Brixton uprising and subsequent Scarman Report; B. Ahmad's (1990) seminal text *Black Perspectives in Social Work*. Explicit anti-racist social work requirements for training

New diversity standards in Professional Capabilities for Social Work. Public policy changes to interracial adoption; cuts to the work of the Equality and Human Rights Commission. Back to colour-blindness? Integrationism?

Figure 1 Social work education anti-racism timeline

In many respects social work's arduous journey in recognising and working with cultural and 'race' differences has mirrored prevailing 'race' relations policy, which since the 1960s has tended to be either *culturalist* or *racism blind* (Barn, 2007, p 1436). The current changes to same-race fostering and adoption policy are reflective of the how the *colour blind* paradigm has gained dominance in public policy and enabled a sustained media attack around the over-zealous and politically correct concerns of social workers in unduly identifying, resisting and challenging racism.

In the post-Second World War era social work practice with new and established ethnic minority communities was characterised by assumptions that minorities needed to assimilate and *fit in* with the majority. Another way of looking at this is seeing people from minority groups through a 'cultural deficit' model of practice (Ahmad, 1990). This approach had its roots in the ideologies of slavery and colonialism that Barn (2007) suggests placed white European cultures at the apex. This approach pathologised the lifestyles and structures of black families, who were viewed as dysfunctional, culturally deprived and in need of government intervention. Owusu-Bempah (2005) suggests that in this period of social work, professionals grossly misinterpreted child-rearing practices. For example, South Asian children, especially girls, were viewed as *overprotected, over-controlled or oppressed*, whilst the opposite was believed about black children, who were seen to be 'out of control' and 'delinquent' (Owusu-Bempah, 2005, p 180). This period of public policy and social work practice was also highly critical of black women's abilities as mothers, who were seen to be abandoning their children (Williams, 1989).

In this period personal and social difficulties were viewed as a reflection of individual failure and the inability to acculturalise (Fernando, 1989) and therefore fit in with the norms and values of British society. Enoch Powell's infamous 'Rivers of Blood' speech in 1968 was reflective of this concern about the inability of immigrant communities to integrate.

As we moved into the 1960s race relations policy was characterised as the so-called colour-blind approach (Husband, 2007). This approach was highly influential in social work and entailed treating all service users with equal respect and promoting their individual rights and choices. Colour of skin was considered to be irrelevant: even the basic dietary and skin care needs of Black children taken into care were often neglected and not considered as relevant due to the professional perception that these children were no different to their white counterparts.

The colour-blind approach – the product of liberal universalism – eschews difference in its search for a universal formula. It suggests a standard of good practice can be established which fits all. Despite being consistently pilloried as naïve, assimilationist and downright oppressive, this approach represents a powerful and tenacious paradigm within social work, both nationally and internationally. (Williams and Soydan, 2005, p 903)

The shift to multiculturalism and the push for integration

Public policy criticisms of the '*colour* makes no difference' approach in the 1970s led to a policy reorientation towards multiculturalism (May, 1999). Unlike other European countries, the UK enacted in 1976 a significant and groundbreaking piece of race equality legislation that for the first time made unlawful direct and indirect racial discrimination. This new era of progressive race relations thinking and policy change also required social workers to move away from its universal and generic approach to practice and work with the cultural specificities of practice. This multicultural phase was also a reflection of increasing community grassroots mobilisation in ethnic minority communities and many social work departments during this period employed specialist Black Section 11 workers to work specifically with their respective communities of interest.

The policy shift towards multiculturalism was also a reflection of the inner-city riots that took place in Brixton and other Black communities in 1981 and the subsequent recommendations of the Scarman Report that suggested the entrenched social and economic problems affecting Britain's inner cities could be addressed through a policy that embraced multiculturalism and tackled racial disadvantage (Pilkington, 2003).

Tolerance was also frequently used as a term to describe the virtues of multiculturalism and was viewed as the polar opposite of prejudice. However, *for tolerance to be necessary, there must be a prior belief that the person to be tolerated has an intrinsically undesirable characteristic* (Downing and Husband, 2005, p 197). The shift from assimilation to multiculturalism was also promoted by the highly influential Swan Report (1985) *Education for All*, as a strategy for better meeting the educational aspirations of Britain's ethnic minority children (Gillborn and Ladson-Billings, 2004).

In general multiculturalism has resulted in better services through recognition of difference and the need to move away from a universal *one-size-fits-all* approach (Modood, 2007).

This period witnessed the growth of autonomous black and ethnic minority groups, for example black mental health organisations, housing movements, black refuge groups and women's projects. This period also witnessed the development of minority representation in local areas, the strengthening of the Black Caucus within the British Labour Party, and in social work itself the setting up of specialist services for Black and South Asian communities (Ahmad, 1990; Bonnet, 2000). In wider areas of public policy racial disadvantage continued to be tackled through positive action employment initiatives, inner-city urban renewal and ring-fenced funding (Bonnet, 2000). It has been argued that those who benefited most from multiculturalism were black middle-class professionals, as they were absorbed into state institutions and inadvertently used to police and appease the 'black' communities they had apparently left behind (Sivanandan, 1983).

However, multiculturalism has been criticised for lacking a *robust and committed exchange of ideas* (O'Donnell, 2006, p 254), and for never going beyond a superficial exchange of festival and food. Mirza (2003), has been critical of the inability of multiculturalists to address and recognise particularly sensitive issues for fear of being labelled racist.

A sustained attack against multiculturalism has also come from the far right in British politics, which has promoted the urban myth that multiculturalism has resulted in a policy of positive discrimination in favour of black communities, at the expense of the white majority and that the threshold of British 'tolerance' has been exceeded (McGhee, 2008). The resulting white backlash, particularly associated with the electoral gains of the far right racist British Nationalist Party and emergence of the English Defence League, has recently led to a greater public policy focus being given to the marginality and exclusion of some white communities. The view is that the concerns of disadvantaged white communities may have been sidelined and neglected in mainstream equality work due to an over-emphasis on 'race' issues (Commission on Integration and Community Cohesion, 2007).

Multiculturalism has therefore come into serious disrepute and has been displaced by the ideas associated with the politics of a new integrationism (Johnson, 2007). Clearly there is a concern that cultural differences, as part of the British cultural mosaic, are resulting in non-integration in the form of cultural polarisation and excessive intra-community bonding (Parekh, 2000).

This is best seen in the findings of the Cantle Report, which was set up to review the causes of the disturbances in a number of northern towns and cities in 2001. These disturbances were characterised by racially motivated rioting between South Asian and white communities in Bradford, Leeds, Oldham and Burnley and were considered to be symptomatic of prevailing British race relations policy that had resulted in racial segregation and hatred rather than a *melting pot* of different cultures living together in harmony. The Cantle Report (2001) was highly critical of the type of communities multiculturalist policies had helped to create and sustain.

The team was particularly struck by the depth of polarisation of our towns and cities.

The extent to which these physical divisions were compounded by so many other aspects of our daily lives was very evident. Separate educational arrangements, community and voluntary bodies, employment, places of worship, language, social and cultural networks, mean that many communities operate on the basis of a series of parallel lives. These lives do not seem to touch at any point, let alone overlap and promote any meaningful interchange. (Cantle, 2001, p 9)

Trevor Phillips, then Chair of the Equality and Human Rights Commission, also raised similar concerns when he suggested that we were *sleepwalking into segregation* (Johnson, 2007); and these echoed the sentiments of Lord Herman Ouseley, the former Chair of the now defunct Commission for Racial Equality when he raised concerns about communities living monocultural and 'parallel lives' (*Guardian*, 24 October 2005).

What both race relations thinkers are referring to is not only the 'ethnic enclaves' that result from South Asian communities, in particular, choosing to live with their own kind (Kumar, 2008; Modood, 2008), but also the excessive loyalty and commitment to cultural traditions and ethnic identity of particular groups that is considered to be detrimental to inter-racial contact and wider participation (Wetherell, 2007, p 8).

The public policy response to these concerns has been to develop a community cohesion strategy that tackles the excesses of 'bonding capital', often associated with inward-looking forms of association and an exclusive identification with culture and religion (Wetherell, 2007), to one that builds 'bridging capital' and is more outward looking, encouraging contact between and across groups (Putman, 2000, cited in Khan, 2007). The intention of this policy is to loosen community ties and a sense of belonging to a particular identity.

Fixed social identities should be de-emphasised as they become the sites of polarisation and non integration between groups. (McGhee, 2008, p 126)

What is also being challenged here is a person's 'habitus', referred to in the work of the sociologist and philosopher Bourdieu as a set of 'dispositions' that influence thought and behaviour by shaping an individual and constraining their behaviour (Spencer, 2006).

What is being proposed here is the breaking down of the social capital associated with insular and defensive behaviour, and instead developing a different type of habitus that engages in intercultural dialogue and exchange.

The principal consequence for many minorities … will be the enforced loss of their own, ethnic, cultural and linguistic habitus as the necessary price of entry into the civic realm. (May, 1999, p 31)

Burnett (2007, p 355) suggests that this policy is tantamount to a move towards cultural uniformity and that 'community cohesion' should best be understood as a *euphemism for integration; and integration a euphemism for assimilation.* Other writers have criticised this direction in policy for failing to recognise racism, discrimination, racial violence and for over-emphasising cultural factors to the detriment of social exclusion and economic marginalisation (Bourne, 2007). The new policy emphasis on 'culture' rather than 'structure', on internal rather than external factors, has also been criticised for its 'neo-liberal' policy emphasis on individuals and their communities, rather than the role and responsibilities of broader societal institutions and the state (Alexander, 2007).

CRITICAL QUESTION

What do you think are the advantages and disadvantages of the concept of community cohesion?

From a social work perspective *social bonding* capital, often associated with a strong sense of cultural identification, belonging, self-identity and religion, is also linked with positive resilience factors in professional social work practice (Goldstein, 2005).

McGhee (2005, 2008) argues that the British state is now moving towards a policy of 'monoculturalism' and 'cultural homogenisation', through managed integration strategies. These integrationist strategies, based on a programme of cultural and linguistic assimilation, can be seen as being played out in citizenship classes and ceremonies, which seek to address the patriotic deficits in some communities (Sirna, 1996). They have also increasingly infiltrated populist debates that have called for all foreign spouses to be tested for their English language proficiency skills as a condition of entry into the UK (McGhee, 2008). The wearing of the 'veil' or niqab has also been attacked and has been seen as a symbol of backwardness and self-imposed segregation, often associated with the oppression of an archaic patriarchal culture (Spalek, 2005).

However the surfacing of these debates has raised some highly relevant questions in relation to forced marriage, the policing of young women's sexuality and their general *invisibility and silencing in communities* (Patel, 2002, p 130). These issues have been related to the rise of religious fundamentalism, in not only Islamic but also Christian and

Hindu contexts, and have often been associated with inflammatory, homophobic, sexist and anti-Semitic views of radical preachers (Women Living Under Muslim Laws, 2006). This rise of these phenomena has been understood as relating to an attempt by some religious and community leaders to assert the old certainties of tradition, by rejecting the uncertainties and advances of reflexive modernity (Bhatt, 1997). The rise of religious fundamentalism has also been associated with the radicalisation of young British Muslims, especially in some British universities, around a politics of identity centred around Islamic faith and the 'Ummah', which refers to an exclusive allegiance to the community of Islam (Taher, 2008).

The value of British anti-racist social work

In many respects a focus on *identity* is also a central preoccupation of anti-racist social work practice. It is considered to be a politically committed form of practice (Tomlinson, 2002), and a radical practice that emphasises the need to actively identify and resist racism (Bonnett and Carrington, 1996).

The usefulness of anti-racist perspectives for social work can be identified in a number of areas that

- identify and name racism (Goldstein, 2005);

- identify its valuable and transformative role in education (Singh and Cowden, 2010);

- focus on the social construction of 'race' and its ever-changing political and social meanings (Dominelli, 2008);

- transform unequal social relations, shaping intercultural encounters into equal ones (Dominelli, 1988, 2008);

- draw attention to asylum seekers who find themselves vilified, detained, dispersed and deported (Humphries, 2004);

- identify the complexities of everyday personal, cultural and institutional racism (Bhatti-Sinclair, 2011);

- challenge representations of Black people in popular culture (Downing and Husband, 2005), and the social construction of Black people as 'dangerous' (Keating et al., 2002), which may lead to inappropriate and oppressive social work interventions;

- raise awareness of differential treatment, racial inequalities and the processes associated with racial oppression, racial marginalisation and racial exclusion (Pilkington, 2004);

- critically examine the dynamics of power relationships, the processes of disempowerment and the interlocking nature of social oppression (Heron, 2004);

- entail raising self-awareness of prejudices, biases and stereotypes in individual interpersonal relationships (Husband, 2000);

- challenge the attitudes and values of individual students and practitioners (Bhatti-Sinclair, 2011).

Singh suggests that the overall effect of this learning enables social work students to realise that:

The wider struggles against state sponsored racism, against the asylum, immigration and nationality laws, against deaths in police custody, against stop and search, against racism in the judicial system, against school exclusions, against the premature deaths of black people due to health inequalities, and against the economic policies leading to the devastation of inner cities where the vast majority of black people live are always relevant to worker-client interactions. (Singh, 2002, p 77)

The role of Black perspectives in anti-racist social work

Graham (2004, 2007) proposes that Black perspectives and creating alternative ways of knowing, which she refers to as *Afrocentricity*, are also key components of anti-racist social work. Graham draws upon *Afrocentricity* to refer to African-centred worldviews grounded in the philosophy of traditional African cultural systems and suggests that these challenge *the hegemony of Eurocentric social theories in demanding equal standing across the spectrum of human knowledge* (Graham, 2000, p 424). Graham is highly critical of how Eurocentrism ultimately privileges the voices and perspectives of white social work academics and practitioners, and drawing upon the work of Hilliard, suggests that:

Anti-racism in social work education must engage in multiple ways of knowing in order to advance the course of social work knowledge. Thus, what is required therefore is a balanced model of anti-racist social work where alternative worldviews are a legitimate strategy for social work education. Based upon the assumption that 'human culture is the product of the struggles of all societies', African-centred knowledge becomes relevant to the anti-racist discourse. (Hilliard, 1992, p 13 cited in Graham, 2000, p 426)

Black perspectives play a pivotal role in the conceptualisation of anti-racist social work practice and in the evolution of social work education (Graham, 2002b; Singh, 1996). The use of a capital letter 'B' in Black perspectives denotes the term as a noun, to identify a politically defined group that has been visibly and politically racialised as the 'other', rather than the term implying an adjective based on skin colour (Banks, 1999; Mirza, 2003).

The term Black perspectives has operated as an attempted representation of a particular shared experience and a particular construction of unity around those experiences (Brah, 2005). Goldstein (2008) suggests that these shared experiences relate to a common history of colonialism and a collective memory of the British Empire, the existence of immigration and nationality legislation and contemporary experiences of racism. Robinson (1995, 1999) has also drawn upon Black perspectives to explore the processes associated with 'nigrescence', which refers to the process of developing a positive Black identity. Ahmad (1990) has also suggested that a Black perspective is a symbol of Black resistance and Black empowerment, and states that

The circumstances that shape a Black perspective stem from the experience of racism and powerlessness, both past and presented. The motivation that energises a Black perspective is rooted to the principle of racial equality and justice. The articulation that voices a Black perspective is part of a process that is committed to replacing the white distortion of Black reality with Black writings of Black experience. (Ahmad, 1990, p 3)

Closely aligned to Black perspectives work in anti-racist social work theorising is the increasing tendency to explore the social construction and power associated with *white culture and 'Whiteness'* (Butler *et al.*, 2003, p 276). (This is explored further in Chapters 3, 5 and 6).

Anti-racist social work is therefore a broad combination of a range of different perspectives concerned with actively identifying and resisting racism. However it has been reluctant to embrace a form of practice often associated with a discussion and recognition of 'cultural issues' and cultural awareness training, which is explored further in Chapter 3.

This resistance has often been associated with a professional and political concern that an over-reliance on cultural explanations may distract attention away from the more pressing structural issues associated with power, discrimination, poverty, marginalisation and social exclusion (Penketh, 2000).

The focus for anti-racist work remains on the institutional and structural nature of racism and how it is reproduced in state institutions, including social work educational and practice contexts (McLaughlin, 2005). In contrast to the liberal character of the terms used by multiculturalists, such as equality, culture, competence, prejudice, customs, ignorance, fairness and opportunity, anti-racist practitioners and academics have tended to draw upon more hard-edged politicised terms concerned with struggle, structure, power, exploitation and resistance (Gillborn and Ladson-Billings, 2004).

The rise and fall of anti-racism in British social work education

Within British social work education anti-racism gained ascendency in the late 1980s. The shift towards this politically committed form of practice was associated with the influential work of Central Council for Education and Training in Social Work (CCETSW), Black Perspectives Committee, comprising both white and Black academics, concerned about the failure of social work educational programmes to address anti-racist issues. The 'Requirements and Regulations for the Diploma in Social Work', Paper 30 (CCETSW, 1991), put in place mandatory anti-racist learning requirements for students undertaking social work training to address issues of 'race' and racism, and demonstrate competence in anti-racist practice. CCETSW's Paper 26.3 also charged practice teachers with the responsibility of facilitating anti-racist teaching in practice placement contexts (Penketh, 2000). CCETSW's Paper 30 stated that:

Racism is endemic in the values, attitudes and structures of British society including that of social services and social work education. CCETSW recognises that the effects of racism on black people are incompatible with the values of social work and therefore seeks to combat racist practices in all areas of its responsibilities. (CCETSW, 1991, p 6)

Paper 30 articulated the need for social workers to be able to work in a society that was multiracial and multicultural, and stipulated learning requirements in relation to anti-racist work, which included:

- recognising the implications of political, economic, racial, social and cultural factors;

- upon service delivery, financing services and resource analysis;

- demonstrating an awareness of both individual and institutional racism and ways to combat both through anti-racist practice;

- developing an awareness of the inter-relationships of the processes of structural oppression, race, class and gender and working in an ethnically sensitive way (CCETSW, 1991, p 6).

CRITICAL QUESTION

Compare and contrast these learning requirements with the Professional Capability Framework standards for diversity. Can you identify similarities and differences?

CCETSW's requirements went beyond a concern with individual prejudice and culture and sought to expose the structural and institutional nature of racism in British society. However its period of authority in the social work academy was short-lived; it was attacked and sometimes ridiculed by a right-wing Thatcherite government and also faced a number of genuine concerns from social work itself in relation to:

- silencing students (Macey and Moxon, 1996);

- marginalising issues of class and gender difference (Mirza, 2003);

- encouraging a superficial adoption of a *politically correct perspective* (Macey and Moxon, 1996, p 309);

- failing to recognise white-on-white or black-on-black racism (Modood, 2007);

- encouraging a false assumption that Black cultures are free from exploitation and oppression (Keating, 2000);

- having no practice relevance because of its focus on macro-political issues (Macey and Moxon, 1996);

- erasing any differentiation in the experiences of racism between different ethnic groups (Ballard, 1992; Modood, 1992);

- highlighting 'Blackness' and encouraging the homogenisation of different histories, cultures, needs, aspirations and trajectories of migration and settlement, implied in the use of the singular category Black to describe all ethnic minority communities (Lorenz, 1996);

- marginalising the racialisation of other British minority communities, for example, Jewish people, Turkish and Greek Cypriots, by not enabling them to find a voice within a political and cultural space marked out as Black (Rattansi, 2005);

- lacking clarity and analytical inadequacy, for example, *which black perspective and whose black voice?* (Macey and Moxon, 1996 p 302);

- maintaining the invisibility of anti-Irish racism (Mac an Ghaill, 1999);

- inferring that whiteness was a marker of privilege, failing to recognise that many white people have, in fact, very little social, political, economic and cultural power (Turney *et al.*, 2002);

- being overly obsessed with ideological concerns at the expense of developing reflexive practice and practical solutions to meet the needs of black and ethnic minority service users (Williams and Soydan, 2005);

- reducing the totality of black experience to a response to white racism, thereby conferring a *victim status* on black people (May, 1999);

- being *theoretically inadequate, being informed by neither sociological, political nor economic theory or research on racism in Britain* (Macey and Moxon, 1996, p 297).

These criticisms, together with a vehement attack by a right-wing media, led to the anti-racist learning requirements being dropped by CCETSW and subsequent learning requirements make no explicit reference to race and anti-racism. CCETSW's Black perspectives committee was also disbanded and this period marked social work's abandonment of the anti-racist project. The revised learning requirements promoted a different type of social work education, one that recognised and embraced different areas of social oppression, and one that no longer supposedly privileged *racial identity* and *race* issues over other forms of oppression. For Macey and Moxon:

The shift from anti-racist to anti-oppressive social work education is radical rather than reactionary. It moves from the narrow, exclusive focus on racial oppression to a broader, more inclusive understanding of the links between various forms and expressions of oppression. (Macey and Moxon, 1996, p 309)

Reflecting on the shift from anti-racist social work to anti-oppressive practice

Anti-oppressive practice (AOP) embraces a spectrum of social justice discourses and

requires critical reflection on the ways in which social structures associated with capitalism, patriarchy and imperialism contribute to, and interact with, the personal and cultural levels of oppression. (Healy, 2005, p 180)

AOP draws upon a range of practice theories that includes feminist, postmodern, anti-discriminatory and post-structural frameworks (Thompson, 2012; Healy, 2005). Key social work practice principles include: the rooting of AOP in a human rights-based legislative framework, which endorses equality (Braye and Preston-Shoot, 2006); ongoing critical self-reflection on one's historical, social and political positioning (Fook *et al.*, 2006); assessment of service user experiences of social oppression (Thompson, 2012); empowering practice (Dalrymple and Burke, 2006); working in partnership; and minimal intervention (Burke and Harrison, 2002; Danso, 2007).

The shift associated with the movement of anti-racist work practice into a multi-oppression, anti-oppressive practice paradigm (AOP) has been criticised on a number of levels. Williams (1999) suggests that anti-racist social work practice issues have become diluted and that there has been a reluctance to recognise *major differences in the understanding of the causes and natures of oppressions expressed and experienced by different groups*

(Williams, 1999, p 227). She also suggests that a broad approach to learning about social oppression has rendered anti-racism politically sterile and opened the way to avoid talking about race.

Concern has also been expressed that the academically and practitioner driven nature of AOP fails to incorporate or provide space for *ground-up knowledge* (Sakamoto and Pitner, 2005), that relates to service user views and perspectives.

Anti-oppressive practice is dependent upon service users' knowledge of their oppression(s). The dominant role of social work academics and practitioners places limits upon what they can know or understand of service users' oppression; they are not therefore best placed for claiming expertise in anti-oppressive theory and practice. (Wilson and Beresford, 2000, p 566)

These authors are also critical of the tendency to combine the different oppressions included within the concept of AOP (Wilson and Beresford, 2000, p 565). Singh (2006) also suggests that AOP overly focuses on processes that draw attention away from the individual and the *specificities of lived Black experience* (Singh, 2006, p 94).

Butler *et al.* (2003) believe that rather than encouraging the integration of anti-racist practice considerations into the whole breadth of social work education and practice learning, anti-oppressive practice tends to lead to its compartmentalisation as a standalone and discrete area of teaching.

Heron (2004) has proposed that the shift towards anti-oppressive practice can be construed as a political ploy designed to redefine anti-racism as something less threatening.

Replacing anti-racism with the terms anti-discrimination or anti-oppressive not only removes anti-racism from the agenda ... it also distorts the very meaning of racism. This distortion limits students' ability to construct a logical way to understand 'race'. (Heron, 2004, p 290)

The limited research that has been published on *race* issues in a UK social work education context suggests that that there are questions about the way students learn about racism and that it remains largely *invisible and insignificant* and therefore not a core pillar of social work training (Heron, 2004, p 289). Research has also reported that in assessed student written work only minimal reference is made to anti-racism (Heron, 2006, 2008). In practice, learning contexts studies demonstrate that practice teachers/assessors do not feel supported or confident in addressing *race* issues (Collins *et al.*, 2000). They lack familiarity with key *race* terms and only have a limited understanding of race equality issues, thus restricting their capacity to provide effective practice teaching (Penketh, 2000). With the exception of a handful of British research studies it is difficult to identify other published research undertaken in a UK context that focuses exclusively on social work education. This dearth of work clearly echoes Williams *et al.*'s (2009) call to develop research capacity and evaluate the outcomes of anti-racist social work education.

Research summary: 'how students make sense of anti-racism'

This research was carried out with a group of second year undergraduate social work students. The aim was to investigate how these students experience this new learning and

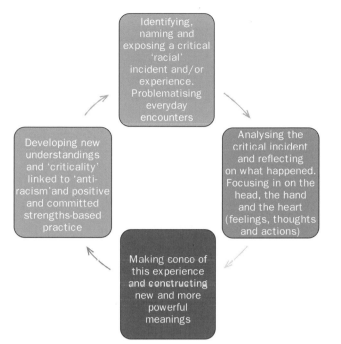

Figure 2 Critical incident reflection model

whether it enables them to develop confidence and competence in their practice learning encounters with different groups and communities.

One component of the research involved the use of a critical incident technique to explore how student learning in both the classroom and in practice learning settings can be transformed through the analysis of a critical incident. My research suggests that this technique, followed up with group discussion, can be a powerful and useful educational strategy to develop awareness and practice learning.

A critical incident technique involves the description and analysis of critical incident and is considered to be *the first stage of a critical reflective process* (Fook *et al.,* 2000, p 231).

CRITICAL INCIDENT ANALYSIS MODEL

In this model critical reflection is a process and learning is constant; it goes beyond 'benign introspection'. (White, 2006, p xiiii)

A group of 30 social work students were encouraged to draw upon this model and write about an incident that had prompted reflection and then share this experience in a group.

The critical incident technique enabled most students who participated in this research to identify and evidence important areas of learning. Students wrote and spoke about the following incidents that had transformed their learning and praxis.

- Recognising and finding the confidence to challenge stereotypical views about Black service users.

- Reflecting on the apparent lack of engagement from Black service users.

- South Asian students being pigeonholed as 'race' and cultural experts.

- Responding to hostility and overt racism from white service users.

- Recognising and dealing with 'internalised racism' through critical Black feminist perspectives.

- Thinking about the lack of contact or exposure to working with Black clients and recognising the absence of this experience for my learning.

- Taking my shoes off!

- Recognising lack of agency commitment to addressing 'racism'.

- Reflecting on lack of culturally competent and culturally congruent care.

- Exposure to the testimonies of Black service users.

- Developing cultural awareness and questioning culture as normative.

- Naming and understanding personal experiences of racism (Black students only).

- Learning about Black perspectives.

Some of the critical incidents reflected upon above may be considered to be obvious or not of any exceptional intrinsic value other than for the students concerned; at this stage of their professional development, the learning accrued from these critical moments was transformative and out of the ordinary. These critical moments were the first tentative steps towards committed and positive practice.

A particular concern for students was their apparent lack of familiarity and confidence in working with South Asian communities. These students were reflecting on their lack of cultural encounters and suggesting that the practice wisdom and tacit understandings that are accrued from multicultural practice should not be undervalued and are evidently important for developing culturally competent practice (O'Hagan, 2001; Walker, 2005).

This point was further reinforced when one student in a critical incident group analysis context passed around the following postcard (see Figure 3), which had been given to her by a young Bangladeshi child she was assessing with a view to arranging respite care for. Many members of the group were visibly moved when they read the contents of this postcard; the student who shared this critical incident commented:

I had to think hard about why this young person felt the need to provide me with this postcard ... but I get it now ... I probably would have neglected her cultural needs. I wouldn't have expected this postcard from a white service user.

My name is Anita Chowdury

I do not drink beer, wine or alcohol, I am a Muslim.
I do not dance with boys or when boys and men are in the
same room. I do not go out with boys or have boyfriends and
kiss them.

I do not eat pork, ham, bacon or anything else with pig's meat in it.
We try to eat halal meat. This is meat from the muslim shop.
We always wash our bum when we do a pee or a poo. I need a special jug for this.

We say our prayers five times a day, (Fajar-Zuher-Azer-Magrib-Eysh)
(Wake up-Afternoon-afterschool-Evening-Night)
We do wudhu everytime before prayer
(wash 3 times nose, mouth, hands, face, head, ears and feet).
We read the Holy Quran (Book of God) everyday if we know how to.

We do not wear rude cloths that show our body and be naked.
We do not tell, or be rude or nasty.

Place
Stamp
Here

Postcard template by www.craftideas4kids.com

Figure 3 An example of a critical incident: a postcard from service user Anita Chowdury (pseudonym)

CRITICAL QUESTION

Draw upon the critical incident analysis model to identify and analyse a 'race' incident that has challenged and developed your thinking.

To complete this reflective task, firstly identify a recent incident either from a practice learning encounter or from a university teaching context that you believe unsettled you, made you feel uncomfortable, sensitised you or just simply prompted you to think about a 'race' issue that you had not considered to be important. Was this incident a 'light bulb moment'?

Carefully describe the nature of this incident. Was it a regular occurrence or atypical? Think about what happened, why it happened, who was involved and how it made you feel. Now analyse this incident from different standpoints and perspectives. Try to draw upon your reading and interpretations of this chapter and the teaching and learning you have been exposed to as part of your social work training. Think about the different types of theories and explanations you can identify to make sense of this incident and identify which explanation has more credibility. Finally reflect upon how this incident has led to new learning and developed your practice awareness of 'race' issues.

Conclusion

This chapter advocates that anti-racism is a key component of anti-oppressive practice and is useful for developing emancipatory practice. The principles and values it draws upon mirror the concerns of social work with justice and fairness. As an approach to practice anti-racism develops critical thinking skills and enables social workers to problematise everyday practice encounters. It enables us to understand the personal dimensions of racism and how they are played out in the lives of service users whilst also providing us with a critical insight into the processes associated with structural exclusion and cultural marginalisation.

It is unlikely that we will ever return to an explicit set of regulatory anti-racist learning outcomes for social work training; therefore it is imperative that we focus attention on the policy, legal and value frameworks that drive and influence educational activity in this area of professional training. The Professional Capabilities Framework has a set of tiered diversity standards that we should now be better placed to appraise and evidence in relation to our understanding and practice around racial diversity.

Taking it further

Websites

The nature and origins of diversity (part of the RCN Transcultural Health Care Practice materials written by Professor Charles Husband).
www.rcn.org.uk/development/learning/transcultural_health/politics/sectionone

The UK's leading independent race equality think tank.
www.runnymedetrust.org/

Independent statutory body established to help eliminate discrimination, reduce inequality and protect human rights.
www.equalityhumanrights.com/

Key journal references

Butler, A., Elliot, T. and Stopard, N. (2003) Living up to the Standards We Set: A Critical Account of the Development of Anti-Racist Standards. *Social Work Education*, 22(3): 271–82.

Williams, C. (1999) Connecting Anti-Racist and Anti-Oppressive Theory and Practice: Retrenchment or Re-appraisal? *British Journal of Social Work*, 29(2): 211–30.

Specific book chapters

Singh, G. (2002) The Political Challenge of Anti-Racism in Social Care and Health, in Tomlinson, D.R. and Trew, W. (eds) *Equalising Opportunities, Minimising Oppression:*

A Critical Review of Anti-Discriminatory Policies in Health and Social Welfare. London: Routledge, pp 72–81.

Singh, G. (2006) Postmodernism, Anti-Racism and Social Work, in Farrar, M and Todd, M. (eds) *Teaching 'Race' in Social Sciences: New Context, New Approaches*. (C-SAP), The Higher Education Academy Network, University of Birmingham, pp 72–109.

3 Developing Cultural Competence

PROSPERA TEDAM

Chapter aims

This chapter will focus on the concept of Cultural Competence by using a 'cultural web' as a practical tool for addressing anti-racist practice in contemporary social work. The chapter will provide a historical overview of Cultural Competence, its origins and development within social work as well as its application. In line with recent events in England, this chapter will also explore the links between Cultural Competence and the Professional Capabilities Framework proposed by the Social Work Reform Board and implemented by the College of Social Work. It will propose ways in which Cultural Competence and the 'cultural web' can support practitioners in their assessments of families where ritual and faith-based abuse might occur.

CRITICAL QUESTION TO BE ADDRESSED

What do you understand by the term culturally competent social work practice?

Introduction

Social work as a profession and academic discipline espouses the values of non-discrimination, equality, fairness, social justice, inclusion, human rights and empowerment. Whilst these are fairly easy to discuss and open to interpretation they tend to be more difficult to apply in practice with service users from a range of backgrounds, life experiences and cultures. In order to fully grasp the meaning of Cultural Competence, it is useful to provide readers with some idea of what the two keywords, 'culture' and 'competence', mean.

Defining culture

Reaching an agreed definition of 'culture' will be no easy achievement within this chapter. This is because, like many other concepts and terms, what constitutes culture is often contested and open to interpretation. Culture is that part of a person that adds to their identity and is by no means what constitutes the whole person. Culture can include: ethnicity, religion and faith, attitudes, beliefs, taboos, diet, language, history and so on. One useful definition of culture originates from America and, in particular, the National Association of Social Workers, which asserts that culture is an:

Integrated pattern of human behaviour that includes thoughts, communications, actions, customs, beliefs, values and institutions of a racial, ethnic, religious or social group. (NASW, 2001)

This definition encompasses all groups and includes gay, lesbian, transgender cultures, disability cultures and so on. Cross (2008) argues that diversity has began to extend and broaden and includes the social and cultural experiences of a range of people of different social classes, sexual orientations, genders, ages, and physical and mental abilities, religious and spiritual beliefs and faith. Given the scope of this book, a focus on Cultural Competence linked to ethnicity and race will be explored with a specific focus on Cultural Competence as an anti-racist tool/concept.

Historical overview of Cultural Competence

The concept of Cultural Competence began to appear in literature in the United States in the 1980s and it has been argued that this was as a result of the civil rights movement in the 1950s and the migration of people into America (Gutierrez *et al.*, 2004).

The civil rights movement in America, which lasted from 1955 to 1968, was a turning point in the lives of America's black population. In 1964, the Civil Rights Act was passed, making it illegal to discriminate against people based on race, colour, religion or national origin (Gutierrez *et al.*, 2004).

Migration to America saw the emergence and growth of different ethnic and racial groups, with different cultural, religious, linguistic and health needs that were further complicated by their experiences of displacement, violence and political aggression. These differences meant that people had to be treated differently but fairly, based on their backgrounds and circumstances and a colour-blind approach would not be appropriate. Consequently, healthcare professionals and later social workers were required to work with a range of service users using methods of intervention that were fair, non-discriminatory and non-oppressive especially when working with people whose backgrounds are different from the professional's.

In the United Kingdom, some of the earliest calls for Cultural Competence came in the 1980s and specifically within the healthcare profession as a framework for understanding the needs of a diverse population and for assisting in the identification of the types and levels of intervention needed (Sue, 1981).

In addition to this, the UK's membership of the European Union and the virtual borders across the 18 member countries has resulted in an increased movement of people into the UK and subsequently the increase in cultural diversity in the population. Furness (2005) has argued that this change in the demographics has led to governments implementing policies and frameworks to enhance race relations and to assist newly arrived immigrants. She argues for a more inclusive and systematic process for working with cultural diversity.

In England Cultural Competence is receiving growing recognition in the helping professions such as in nursing, mental health social work and counselling (Holland and Hogg, 2001).

Defining Cultural Competence

In social work, there is increasing acknowledgement that it is a useful concept and can positively inform social work practice here in England and worldwide (O'Hagan, 2001). Laird (2008, p 159) asserts that Cultural Competence is *one of the greatest challenges in the social work profession* primarily because it requires social workers to step outside the comforts of their own culture and cultural knowledge in order to not only show sensitivity but also to demonstrate competence in working with service users from a range of backgrounds. Participants in a study by Maiter and Stalker (2010) identified insensitivity and ignorance of cultural issues as one of the main barriers to effective working between social workers and families from the South Asian community. One respondent in their study put it thus:

If I'm an Asian, definitely a South Asian woman knows my culture better than a Canadian, or Italian or Polish. I mean … we had an Italian social worker. She did not know a thing about the culture back home, she knew nothing about it. (p 145)

This perceived disregard of cultural issues has the potential to sabotage and undermine effective working relationships between social workers and service users, from the outset, with little opportunity to remedy the situation in order to progress interventions. In addition, implicit in the statement above is the view that a practitioner from a similar cultural background will possess a better understanding of the culture in question. This is not necessarily the case.

Cultural Competence is difficult to define and as such a range of definitions have been proposed, such as those by Norton (1978), Cross (2007), Boyle and Springer (2008) and Harrison and Turner (2011). These definitions range from specific focus on the 'minority and majority groups' to encompassing the many aspects of difference within our identities.

Walker's definition of Cultural Competence is one that is used extensively in social work literature in the UK. He suggests that it is *a set of knowledge-based and interpersonal skills that allows individuals to understand, appreciate and work with families of cultures other than their own* (Walker, 2005, p 31).

An understanding of culture is central to the development of Cultural Competence and an understanding of culture can shape practitioners' worldview in terms of their understanding of service users' problems and circumstances and can also shape their responses to these problems and the allocation/provision of resources and support. Knowledge therefore is a prerequisite to culturally competent practice and social workers must 'know' about cultural biases and stereotypes that hinder sound social work practice as well as the skills that are needed to engage effectively with service users from a range of backgrounds. Despite the global and local variations in definitions about what constitutes Cultural Competence, the idea of social work practice with a service user whose cultural heritage is different from the practitioner's is a common theme permeating the definitions provided.

Why is Cultural Competence important in social work?

The International Federation of Social Work in 2001 defined social work as follows:

The social work profession promotes social change, problem solving in human relationships and the empowerment and liberation of people to enhance well-being. Utilising theories of human behaviour and social systems, social work intervenes at the points where people interact with their environments. Principles of human rights and social justice are fundamental to social work. (IFSW, 2001)

Inherent in this definition is the undertone of Cultural Competence in that users of social work services will belong to 'social systems' and 'environments' that could be different to social workers' and/or what is familiar to them. The understanding of and ability to work within these social systems presents social work students and practitioners with the rationale for developing Cultural Competence.

For some, developing Cultural Competence may be a moral and/or ethical consideration, whilst for others it may be driven by a sense of commitment to political and stated norms of the era. Working therefore from this, the importance of Cultural Competence in social work practice cannot be overstated; indeed, it provides a baseline of how we should be working with people across a spectrum of difference and how we would expect to be engaged if we were to be users of social work services.

Benefits of becoming a culturally competent social worker

For social workers who are in training or are practising in the workplace, there are many benefits to being culturally competent in their work with vulnerable children and adults.

1) Anti-discriminatory, anti-oppressive and anti-racist practice

For students of social work, anti-discriminatory, anti-oppressive and anti-racist practices are concepts they will become familiar with and develop an understanding of their application to the field and work scenarios. Once students have understood these concepts, their ongoing practice should result in the development of Cultural Competence. The benefits of developing Cultural Competence suggests students are comfortable drawing upon anti-discriminatory and anti-oppressive methods of intervention. Lum (2007) argues that Cultural Competence has roots in social justice, social action and advocacy, all useful concepts towards enhancing anti-oppressive practice.

2) Organisational/agency duties

Organisations and agencies employing social workers will have a requirement or a number of requirements about how practitioners support the larger organisation to meet their equality duties (Equality Act 2010).

3) Reflective practice

Becoming culturally competent is a process that social workers will have to go through. The procedural nature means that social workers will have to engage in good levels of reflection and reflective practice in order to be fully able to appreciate the benefits of Cultural Competence. In this regard, Connolly *et al.* (2006, p 41) propose a 'culturally reflective' approach, which they argue constitutes:

reflecting on cultural thinking can challenge unhelpful attitudes and practices that have the potential to create cultural misunderstandings ... using critically reflective process can help to dislodge beliefs underpinning assessments when they are no longer relevant to the changed practice environment.

Yan and Wong (2005) further suggest that cross-cultural social work provides opportunities for social workers and clients from different cultures to co-create new relationships, meanings and understanding by communicating and negotiating. For example, had the social worker involved in the Victoria Climbié case engaged in this level of practice, mutual learning could have occurred resulting in different and possibly non-fatal outcomes.

4) Better decision-making

Decision-making is a crucial component of social work practice and intervention with service users. Decisions are reached after careful, thorough, evidence informed assessment of people's circumstances and situations. In the not too distant past, social workers have been in the spotlight for failings in relation to poor assessments and decision-making that have resulted in undesirable consequences. These failings were blamed on varying degrees of cultural (in)competence on the part of social workers and their managers. An example of this is the Victoria Climbié case where the Laming Enquiry concluded that the social worker's view that Victoria stood to attention in the presence of her great aunt was a sign of deference and respect was erroneous and not based upon any evidence (Laming 2003). One can conclude therefore that the absence of culturally competent skills and knowledge contributed to the poor decision-making in this case.

5) Outcomes for service users

Outcomes for service users are more likely to be effective and appropriate when they are designed to meet the specific needs of a family, group or community. Examples of the success of this can be found in mental health services where clinicians' levels of Cultural Competence had a positive impact on the outcomes for ethnic minority users of the service (Thyer *et al.*, 2010).

Parrott (2009), referring to a study on women who experienced domestic violence, suggests that social workers had the tendency to attribute the violence to cultural norms, which resulted in them becoming overly scrutinising of women from Asian, African, Irish and Jewish cultural backgrounds. The outcomes for service users could be improved with the understanding of culturally competent practice.

Barriers to becoming a culturally competent social worker

Although Cultural Competence is presented as a progressive and positive force to challenge racism and discrimination, there are a number of barriers that make it difficult to implement and achieve in practice for the social worker and employers.

1)   A lack of awareness

Even the best intentioned motivation can result in poor outcomes for the recipients due to a lack of awareness of what is required. It will not be surprising to find that individual social workers, teams and organisations pose a barrier to Cultural Competence because of their lack of awareness of what it is, its relevance and benefits to practice. Mama (2001, pp 374–5) proposes the use of a framework to enhance awareness of Cultural Competence. This model comprises three elements, which are:

- Facilitating an awareness, understanding and acceptance of one's own culture in relationship to the culture of others.
- Gaining a knowledge and appreciation of other cultures.
- Recognising diversity as normative and the outcomes for service users.

2)   Poor organisational commitment

Another barrier to becoming a culturally competent social worker lies in organisational and managerial commitment. Cultural Competence can leave social workers feeling that it is an individual responsibility without fully considering the fact that structural systems (organisations) can and should be held liable for failings in this regard.

3)   Negative perceptions and disrespect

Perceptions and views held by social workers and other professionals may result in negative and uncooperative attitudes towards developing Cultural Competence. There is no hierarchy of cultures in the sense that no one culture is better or more important than the other. The key here is that cultures are different.

4)   Racism

Racism is a form of slavery. This may appear to be a very serious assertion to make and can leave the reader feeling anxious, hurt and uncomfortable. The intention behind this statement is to encourage social workers to challenge this statement and to reflect on it before reaching their own understanding about what racism means in contemporary society. The sentiments of superiority, disrespect, suspicion, misunderstanding, prejudice, oppression, segregation, colonialism and discrimination all reflect the undertones of slavery, now abolished. Careful consideration of these sentiments mirrors the underlying causes and effects of what we know now as racism.

5)   Cultural incompetence

Cultural incompetence, by implication, is the opposite to being culturally competent and refers to not possessing the skills, knowledge, expertise to work with people from different backgrounds and ethnicities. This would be preferable as the starting point of a continuum and not as the end result. It is hoped that through ongoing reflective practice and training, social workers move from this dangerous and potentially oppressive and discriminatory position.

In the discussion to follow, the cultural web is introduced as a tool to aid the assessment and provision of services for people from a range of cultures.

CRITICAL QUESTION

Racism is a form of slavery. What are your views on this statement?

The cultural web

The cultural web is adapted from the culturagram developed by Congress (1997) and used by Parker and Bradley (2010). I have used the term 'web' as a preferred word to describe the complex, interlocking and intricate links between people and their cultures. Misunderstanding of a family's cultural web can leave professionals tangled, confused and ineffective. The domains of the PCF have also been connected to the various parts of the web.

The cultural web is one of many tools and frameworks to support the development of culturally competent social workers. It is recommended for use by social workers to develop and extend their understanding of service users' unique, complex and often ignored cultural and spiritual positions and perspectives. The assumptions made by the social workers involved with Victoria Climbié contributed to poor analyses and evaluations of her circumstances. The cultural web provides additional lines of enquiry that may otherwise remain invisible to social workers.

Cultural Competence should be viewed as a process and not a fixed state of being (Hoopes, 1979). This is because becoming culturally competent involves an examination of one's worldview, alongside trying to understand, respect and appreciate other worldviews and perspectives. It is impossible to become culturally competent by reading academic books alone or attending a workshop. An ongoing healthy combination of practice and theory is recommended for social workers seeking to develop Cultural Competence. This view is captured below in the discussion of the Cultural Competence Attainment Model (CCAM) by McPhatter (1997).

McPhatter (1997) proposed the Cultural Competence Attainment Model with three main components which are linked and provide a holistic conceptualisation. Each component should be viewed as a part of a bigger picture and no one dimension on its own can transform a social worker into a culturally competent practitioner. The components are grounded knowledge, enlightened consciousness and cumulative skill proficiency. A grounded knowledge base is one that critically questions and challenges existing knowledge about human development,

Figure 1 The cultural web

family structures and functioning as well as other aspects of the lived experiences of service users. McPhatter argues that many schools of social work drew largely upon discourses that were Eurocentric and so social workers training in this type of circumstance would be disadvantaged.

The enlightened consciousness is the widening of one's perspectives and worldviews to incorporate the worldviews of others. McPhatter (1997) argues that this widening of perspectives or shifts of consciousness can be frightening and exposing as it has the potential of stripping away beliefs and attitudes that are no longer in line with current reality.

A social worker whose life experience has been restricted to groups and communities of similar cultures is more likely to feel anxious or incompetent when working with service users from different cultural backgrounds.

Skill proficiency, according to McPhatter (1997, p 272), is *focussed, systematic, reflective and evaluative*. These skills involve communication and rapport building skills and influence the type and depth of information social workers will need to extract for the purposes of assessment. Poor skill proficiency can lead to poor outcomes for service users. A social worker who is striving towards Cultural Competence will acknowledge the value of, and will possess, the skills challenging discrimination, oppression and racism on behalf of their service users.

Cultural Competence continuum

Cultural Competence can be understood as being on a continuum comprising six stages. These stages, according to Cross *et al.* (1989), can relate to individuals and also to groups, teams and organisations. They argue that social work practitioners will have to go through these stages in order to reach the final stage of cultural proficiency.

In this stage, individuals, groups, teams and organisations work to policies, structures and programmes that are designed to undermine, disrespect and oppress particular cultural groups. An example of this is the Apartheid policy that existed in South Africa.

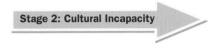

This second stage recognises some cultural groups as undeserving of services and unwelcome. Organisational and other policies are not tailored to meet the needs of a culturally diverse society. This stage mirrors one of institutional racism as recently defined by the McPherson Report. Following the stabbing of the teenager Stephen Lawrence in 1993 and the subsequent inquiry into the handling of the case by the Metropolitan Police, Sir William McPherson in 1999 coined the phrase 'institutional racism' to describe the

Collective failure of an organisation to provide an appropriate and professional service to people because of their colour, culture or ethnic origin. It can be seen or detected in processes, attitudes and behaviour which amount to discrimination through unwitting prejudice, ignorance, thoughtlessness, and racist stereotyping which disadvantages minority ethic people. (McPherson, 1999, 6.34)

At this stage, social workers or other practitioners provide a 'one size fits all' service to everyone, without the recognition or acknowledgement that specific cultures require different approaches to intervention and support.

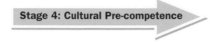

Stage 4: Cultural Pre-competence

At this level, a developed understanding of the importance of diversity in the workforce is achieved as is the view that service delivery should be able to cover a wide range of cultures, ethnicities and backgrounds.

Stage 5: Cultural Competence

At this stage, social workers feel confident and knowledgeable about working with diverse service user groups. Their teams and organisations are well resourced and staff reflect the diversity of the locality within which they work and practice. Social workers engage with training and ongoing professional development that is aimed at improving their Cultural Competence and confidence.

Stage 6: Cultural Proficiency

This final stage is one in which social workers, through their teams and organisations, actively promote and advocate for cultural groups to access resources and services to meet their needs.

The stages discussed above provide one framework for understanding Cultural Competence and serve as a useful tool against which social workers might measure their own levels of Cultural Competence.

Critique of Cultural Competence in social work practice

This chapter has thus far provided a positive and empowering analysis of Cultural Competence as a useful tool for social workers who want to work in an anti-oppressive and anti-discriminatory way. It would be unfair, however, to omit an examination of some of the limitations of Cultural Competence both in terms of its concept and its application to practice. Some critics have argued that Cultural Competence is impossible to achieve (Armour *et al.*, 2006; Johnson and Munch, 2009). This, they argue, is because no one can really ever achieve Cultural Competence because it is a process and therefore a journey with no end. Armour *et al.* (2006, p 26) suggest that *there is no end stage of having arrived at cultural competence*. Such a conclusion can leave social workers feeling anxious about what it means to be culturally competent if there is no sense of ever reaching the final destination. This is why I would question how social work educators, managers and organisations assess, measure and appraise social workers and students for culturally competent practice. This dilemma could be addressed in part by what Geron (2002) proposes, which is that Cultural Competence requires more stringent models and tools for measurement. The Social Work Reform Board (SWRB) have declined the use of the word 'competence' in the development of their Professional Capabilities Framework in favour of the word 'capability'. This, they argue, will move away from a tick-box process to a broader application of skills, knowledge and practice expertise (College of Social Work, 2012).

Another criticism is that by claiming to understand, respect and be sensitive to service users' culture, social workers could be privileging group characteristics over individuality and the individual's right to self-determination, thus leaving open opportunities for stereotyping and labelling (Johnson and Munch, 2009). They further argue that any prior learning and understanding of service users' cultures robs service users from telling their own story, making a mockery of the service users as the experts of their lives and narratives.

Cultural Competence has also been berated for implying that a service user's culture can be understood by social workers asking questions and reading about different cultures. Knowledge is always partial as it evolves, changes and develops over time. It also assumes that all service users are knowledgeable about their own cultural heritage and are therefore in a position to inform the social worker. Again, Johnson and Munch (2009) propose an openness and willingness to learn on the part of the social worker, and also recognition of the sub-cultures that exist in families, groups and communities.

CRITICAL REFLECTION

Reflecting on what you have been reading so far, can you think of additional advantages and disadvantages of Cultural Competence for your own practice?

Cultural Competence and the Professional Capabilities Framework

The Professional Capabilities Framework for social work (PCF) was proposed by the Social Work Reform Board (SWRB) in 2010 with the view to being adopted in social work education from 2012. This is currently being implemented and will have wide-ranging implications for the future of social work practice, pre- and post-qualifying. The PCF replaces the National Occupational Standards in social work, which were used to determine a student's safety, competence and readiness to practise. The PCF advances nine areas of professional practice that social workers will have to demonstrate competence in as part of their professional development and in order to progress from newly qualified practitioner to advanced practitioner.

In this section, an examination of the components of PCF will be undertaken and the links made with Cultural Competence as a model of effective and anti-racist practice. For ease of access, this will be tabulated.

Professional Capabilities Framework	Links to Cultural Competence (CC)
Professionalism	Social workers as accountable members of a registered and protected profession; CC will affirm their commitment to the principles of the profession and any breach of this is dealt with by the appropriate regulating body.
Values and ethics	CC will support social workers in using appropriate partnership strategies to work with people of different cultures to understand their circumstances, whilst challenging their own personal values.
Diversity	Understanding and respecting difference in culture results in social workers who are likely to challenge discrimination and oppression. Understanding one's own culture is a prerequisite for understanding others.
Rights, justice and economic well-being	The foundation of culturally competent practice is one of promoting equality and respect working from a human rights and social justice perspective. This mirrors social work practice, which is steeped in principles of empowerment and advocacy of service users
Knowledge	Social workers will require knowledge of a range of perspectives to enhance their Cultural Competence. These include cross-cultural sociological and psychological theories, Afrocentric theories and the impact of discrimination, oppression and prejudice.
Critical reflection and analysis	Using Cultural Competence as a means to critically reflect on practice, social workers can highlight any gaps in knowledge and rationale for decision-making. Multiple sources of information may be required for this analysis, including formal supervision.
Intervention and skills	Social workers are required to use their authority, whilst promoting service users' independence. Cultural Competence requires the use of skills and knowledge that is evidence based, effective and non-oppressive. The use of the cultural web and other models of Cultural Competence will support this practice.
Contexts and organisations	Specific organisational and team procedures and policies that enhance Cultural Competence by social workers must be visible, understood, regularly reviewed and audited.
Professional leadership	Management, supervision and educational processes must draw upon Cultural Competence frameworks and models, ensuring that the cultural minorities are not disadvantaged.

The table above has identified all nine domains of the PCF and has made links to the main tenets of culturally competent social work practice. This is by no means exhaustive, but seeks to provide a snapshot of the relevance and contemporary nature of culturally competent practice.

In addition to the above, the Health Care Professionals Council (HCPC), which succeeded the now abolished General Social Care Council (GSCC), has mapped the domains of the PCF to the Standards of Proficiency for Social Workers (SoPs). Of these standards, a number of them have a direct bearing on culturally competent practice. These are:

- To be aware of the impact of culture, equality and diversity on practice (5.0).

- To be able to reflect on and take account of the impact of inequality, disadvantage and discrimination on those who use social work services and their communities (5.1).

- To understand the need to adapt practice to respond appropriately to different groups and individuals (5.2).

- To understand the impact of different cultures and communities and how this affects the role of the social worker in supporting service users and carers (5.4).

- To be able to exercise authority as a social worker within the appropriate legal and ethical frameworks (2.6).

- To be able to use practice to challenge and address the impact of discrimination, disadvantage and oppression (6.2).

- To be able to practise in a non-discriminatory manner (6.0).

(Adapted from 'Standard of Proficiency-Social Workers in England', accessed online at www. hpc-uk.org/publications/standards/index.asp?id=569.)

CRITICAL REFLECTION

Reflecting on the links between Cultural Competence and the Professional Capabilities Framework, consider how you might apply these ideas in practice.

Using the Cultural Competence framework when working with faith and ritual abuse

Between 2000 and 2010, approximately six children died in England as a result of what is now referred to as beliefs in witchcraft and spirit possession (Obadina, 2012).

Year	Child and age	Nature of accusation by parents/carers	Nature of abuse
2000	Victoria Climbié Eight-year-old female	Possessed by evil spirits	Praying and fasting without food or water, beaten with bicycle spokes, belts, etc., slept in wet bathtub, no heating, slept in her own urine and excrement.
2001	'Adam' Four–Seven-year-old male	Unclear (This case remains the only unsolved case of child murder despite police efforts)	Torso found in the River Thames. Stomach allegedly contained ingredients used for African ritual magic.
2005	Samira Ullah Three-month-old female	Possessed by evil spirits	Cigarette burns to face, lips and breasts.
2005	Child 'B' Eight years old	Accused of being a 'witch'	Beaten, cut, chilli rubbed into her eyes.

Year	Child and age	Nature of accusation by parents/carers	Nature of abuse
2008	**Khyra Ishaq** **Seven-year-old female**	Accused of being possessed by 'jinn' (evil spirits)	Withdrawal of food, physical chastisement, having cold water poured over her.
2010	**Kristy Bamu** **Fifteen-year-old male**	Accused of being a 'witch'	Starved, punched, kicked, beaten.

The table above depicts children who died between 2000 and 2010, following accusations that they were either possessed by evil spirits or that they possessed witchcraft, and is by no means representative of the scale of this form of abuse perpetrated towards children (Obadina, 2012). The majority of children who are accused of witchcraft or spirit possession do not lose their lives, but suffer the consequences of the actions or omissions linked to the abuse (La Fontain, 2009)

Stobart (2006) highlights complex family compositions as a key similarity in the cases above and argues that the gender of the child was of little significance in these cases. It may be tempting to think that issues of faith should remain in the religious sectors and not the more secular areas of society. However with a growing recognition that places of worship host a range of people of different ages including children, it has become necessary to ensure that children are safe wherever they are, whether that be in school, in hospital, in play and holiday schemes and also in places of worship. In 2007, the government published the *Safeguarding Children from Abuse Linked to a Belief in Spirit Possession* report following concerns by child welfare professionals that this area of child abuse was growing and hidden. Due to its invisibility, social workers were unlikely to be inundated with similar cases in their practice; however, it has been recognised as an area inadequately taught on qualifying social work programmes (Department for Education, 2012) and therefore misunderstood in practice. By implication then, any contemporary writing about the importance and value of Cultural Competence in social work practice needs to address some of the unfamiliar forms of abuse that have been labelled under the umbrella of cultural practices.

Few will have forgotten the death of Victoria Climbié in 2000 and the subsequent enquiry chaired by Lord Laming from 2001 to 2003. Among some of the behaviours and attitudes witnessed and documented by many adults who came into contact with Victoria were that she (Victoria):

• was the cause of their unemployment and poverty;

• was possessed by evil spirits;

• required exorcism to 'free' her from the evil spirits.

CRITICAL REFLECTION

As already discussed, utilising the three aspects of the cultural web ensures that consideration is given to its use and relevance when working with cases involving faith and ritual abuse.

Health beliefs

Understanding a family's health beliefs is an important area to be incorporated into any assessment of children and vulnerable others. In at least two of the most tragic child deaths mentioned above – Victoria Climbié and Kristy Bamu – bedwetting was viewed by their carers as caused by evil spirits and not as a health and/or emotional need. In addition, it is important that a family's understanding of health and ill health is explored, alongside patterns of health seeking behaviour for adults and on behalf of children and minors.

Contact with cultural and religious institutions, food and holidays

The role of the church, faith and religious groups in the lives of many families is well documented (Gilligan and Furness, 2006; Furness and Gilligan, 2010; Raghallaigh, 2011). Using the Ghanaian community in the UK as a specific example, Fumanti (2010) asserts that Methodist Ghanaian families in the UK rely on church membership to minimise social isolation and loneliness and also gain support, encouragement and many forms of assistance. In church, families are not judged and not ill-treated; they have the opportunity to worship and to be 'British' and 'Christian', irrespective of their immigration status and situation. As a result, significant time is spent engaging in church-related activities and meetings. Using the cultural web presented earlier in the chapter, a family's contact with a faith organisation is significant and should inform the assessment and any future involvement and intervention. Victoria's great aunt sought guidance and advice from her church about Victoria's bedwetting and other issues (Laming, 2003). She highlighted some patterns of behaviour that then led the pastor to conclude that Victoria was indeed possessed. With the benefit of hindsight and research we can now acknowledge the role for the social worker to have focused on the place of spirituality in the lives of Victoria and her aunt and also any faith groups or churches they may have been members of.

Values about family myths, rules, structure and power

The 'family', according to McKie and Cunningham-Burley (2005), continues to be a dynamic concept, experienced, defined and perceived variably. Families are perceived as flexible social categories and include: nuclear families, step families, lone parent, same-sex, extended families and adopted families. Family dynamics can be complex and this complexity, according to Stobart (2006), increases the risk for children's well-being and safety. A thorough understanding of the relationship between Victoria Climbié and her great aunt may have shed some light on the case as well as provide the social worker with some understanding of the power dynamics within the relationship.

Impact of trauma and crisis events

Individuals, families and groups respond to crises and trauma in different ways and to different magnitudes and it is crucial that a culturally competent assessment examines the nature of these responses to crisis events and trauma. Social workers should explore, for example: the impact of unemployment, bereavement, ill health and isolation on family members. There is some evidence to suggest that, in many cases, the source of such crises have been blamed on children and young people.

Key legislation for safeguarding children, where there is a risk of harm arising from a belief in spirit possession, is reflective of the wider safeguarding agenda for all children. These include:

- The Children Act 1989

- Education Act 1996

- Housing Act 1996

- Human Rights Act 1998

- Housing Act 2004

- The Children Act 2004

- The Equality Act 2010.

For the purposes of this chapter, a few of the pieces of legislation highlighted above will be discussed. One of the main principles of the Children Act 1989 requires professionals to take into account a child's race, culture, religion and language in decisions that affect them. Article 14 of The Human Rights Act 1998 prohibits discrimination in all its forms.The Equality Act 2010 also identifies nine protected characteristics including race, gender and disability and prohibits the unfair treatment of people who possess these characteristics (Laird, 2010).

CASE STUDY

Mansa is an 11-year-old girl of Ghanaian heritage. Born in London, Mansa has just started secondary school and lives with her father, mother and younger brother.

Last year, Mansa's father was made redundant from his £25,000 a year job and the family now has to rely on his wife's salary of £17,000 a year from her work as a healthcare assistant. Earlier this year, Mansa's brother (Nana, aged nine) began to display challenging behaviour at school and has had a series of exclusions from school. Nana's teacher explained that Nana loses concentration easily, distracts his peers and gets into fights during breaks. In addition, Nana appears to have lost weight and has been seen on occasion to have only an apple in his lunch box.

Mansa's behaviour is not of concern. However, she too has been overheard telling her friends that she is 'not allowed' to have a meal until evening and that she feels exhausted most of the time.

You are a final year social work student on placement in the school and a teacher has referred Nana and Mansa to you for support. You arrange to undertake a home visit to see the family.

Questions:

1) What would be the main areas of concern when you meet with the family?

2) How might you collate and present a culturally competent assessment to the head teacher?

3) Which agencies/organisations might you seek advice/guidance from and why?

Research summary: Laird – anti-oppressive social work

To assist students and social workers in making sense of the theory and practice of Cultural Competence, Laird's book, *Anti-oppressive Social Work* (2008), is recommended for further reading and analysis. Laird provides a brief history of migration to the UK by various ethnic groups and highlights the key immigration legislation and policy frameworks that existed from the 1940s. She presents an overview of racial disparities in the areas of education, health, employment, criminal justice and housing.

Using Thompson's PCS analysis, Laird traces the move from anti-racist practice to anti-oppressive practice and begins to explain concepts such as ethnicity and culture. Models of Cultural Competence are proposed, and practice standards for Cultural Competence highlighted, as are the problems caused by a lack of Cultural Competence on the part of practitioners. Some of these have been discussed within this chapter. The rest of the book provides analyses of Indian, Caribbean, Bangladeshi, Pakistani, African and Chinese communities; their migration histories, family structures, child rearing and gender roles, religious observances, health and disability, older people and social networks. Case studies are used to encourage students to apply the knowledge they have gained from their reading of the cultural knowledge provided.

Conclusion

This chapter has sought to explore Cultural Competence as a means to developing and enhancing anti-racist practice in social work. A brief historical overview of the concept was provided followed by an examination of various definitions, advantages and challenges, and a model for understanding Cultural Competence in practice was explored. The chapter also provided links between Cultural Competence and the Professional Capabilities Framework, and new standards for social work by the HCPC.

A unique feature of this chapter is the introduction of child abuse linked to belief in spirit possession and witchcraft and how Cultural Competence models might assist social workers in working with unique but growing cases of this nature.

Developing Cultural Competence in social workers must begin with the social work student on social work qualifying programmes. Social work educators, many of whom will be aware of the value of culturally competent practice, will be the first ports of call for students who have only just encountered Cultural Competence in their academic studies, and should feel confident about sharing their own strategies and experiences of Cultural Competence to students of social work. Encouraging students to work with and among diverse student groups is a useful strategy for the development of sensitivity, understanding and respect for difference. Long (2012), with reference to nursing students, proposes a range of ways to enhance students' appreciation and development of Cultural Competence. These include, not only through standard lectures, but also through group work, seminars, written assignments and reports, role-play, oral presentations, lived immersion, practice learning and guest speakers to name but a few. There is no reason why these strategies cannot be applied to social work education.

A useful conclusion by Dean (2001, p 627) is provided here:

Our goal is not so much to achieve competence but to participate in the ongoing processes of seeking understanding and building relationships. This understanding needs to be directed toward our selves and not just our clients. As we question ourselves we gradually wear away our own resistance and bias. It is not that we need to agree with our clients' practices and beliefs; we need to understand them and understand the contexts and history in which they develop.

CRITICAL QUESTIONS

How have I previously worked with service users whose backgrounds are different to mine?

How might my understanding of Cultural Competence enhance my work with service users from different backgrounds?

Taking it further

Laird, S. (2008) *Anti-Oppressive Social Work: A Guide for Developing Cultural Competence.* London: Sage.

La Fontaine, J.S. (ed) (2009) *The Devil's Children: From Spirit Possession to Witchcraft.* Farnham: Ashgate.

Africans Unite Against Child Abuse (AFRUCA) online at www.afruca.org.

4 Padare: a meeting around a tree

ANGIE BARTOLI

Chapter aims

This chapter will consider how group work can offer BME, and in particular black African students, support during their educational journey.

CRITICAL QUESTIONS TO BE ADDRESSED

Social work training is academically and personally challenging. What types of support strategies are effective for students from black and minority ethnic backgrounds?

Introduction

This chapter will look at the benefits and challenges of being a black student on a social work programme, and in particular being an African student. This will be achieved by exploring the student support group at the University of Northampton, Padare, which was formed in 2008 by the black African social work students as their response to a need for support and friendship outside of regular teaching and study. I will examine previous work undertaken by the university with black African students by exploring the background to Padare, its aims and objectives as well as its strengths and challenges. You will be invited to consider group work theory, contemporary issues relating to peer support and mentoring within a higher educational setting. A number of metaphors will be used to illustrate different ways of thinking and to further develop well-known concepts such as collectivism.

Background

Together with two colleagues (Prospera Tedam and Sue Kennedy), we undertook a study to try to understand the educational journey of African social work students (Bartoli *et al.*, 2008). Our collective teaching experience at the time was that it appeared that African social work students were experiencing more difficulties (both academically and whilst on practice learning) compared to other students on the programme. Our black students' experience mirrored that being reported nationally, which strongly indicates that students from Black and Ethnic Minority groups (BME) take longer to complete their studies (GSCC, 2009; Hussein *et al.*, 2006, 2008, 2009).

We become curious as to *why* this might be the case for our students and what, if anything, we could do differently. In an attempt to learn *from* and *with* the students, a focus group was set up to which all the African social work students studying at the university at the time were invited. The purpose was to enable academics to better understand the students' personal and collective stories, *to learn about black perspectives; and build alliances with black people by agreeing common objectives to create egalitarian partnerships* (Dominelli, 2008, p 33).

The General Social Care Council (GSCC), the former regulatory body for social work, has indicated that since 2007 black African students are the second largest ethnic group enrolling onto social work programmes in England and Wales.

The students involved in the study came from a range of countries within the African continent, including Ghana, Zimbabwe, Cameroon and Nigeria. The study sought to gain a better understanding of the students' experiences and perceptions, which included:

* gaining low grades;

* failing aspects of assessment;

* achieving high grades in familiar assessment strategies (ie law examination);

* struggling in practice learning environments;

* the need for a support group.

The practice learning experience has been explored and written about elsewhere, but will be referred to within this chapter (Bartoli *et al.*, 2008).

Definition of terms

The term *international student* within a higher education (HE) context is defined within a narrow category, which describes a student's fee-paying status. Many of the Padare students are not deemed international students, but *home* students, due to the number of years they have lived in the UK.

To consider all international students as one homogenous group without recognising differ-ence is unhelpful and furthermore it ignores diversity of experience, heritage, culture, language and history (Hyland *et al.*, 2008; Trahar, 2007). It also undermines different approaches to learning (Brown and Joughin, 2007). It is not my intention to somehow categorise all African students as one singular group or suggest that they are *all* the same. However, some similarities in experience have been shared and this will be commented upon, usually in the student's own words. It is important to remember that culture is not merely positioned within a geographical location; instead it weaves within and across cultures – none more so than in a continent as vast as Africa (Welikala and Watkins, 2008).

Defining the word *internationalisation* is complex and parallels can be drawn between defining this term within an educational context and discourses within social work (Bartoli, 2011) in terms of professional identity (Cree, 2003), and what international social work looks like (Gray and Fook, 2004; Nagy and Faulk, 2000; Razack, 2009). Defining *internationalisation* within higher education is problematic and subject of much debate. The definition is far from precise as it has a number of meanings, approaches and interpretations (Koutsantoni, 2006). This is because the definition largely depends on the individual, political and national context or organisational perspective. Similarly, *social work is always subject to competing claims of definition and practice and cannot be separated from the society in which it is located* (Cree, 2003, p 4). Despite these discrepancies, both the approaches and definitions of the internationalisation of higher education and global social work have been accused of being based upon Western educational and social ideologies, which are then imposed upon others with little regard to diversity or curricula relevance (Gray and Fook, 2004).

The birth of Padare

Within the aforementioned study (Bartoli *et al.*, 2008), all of the students and lecturers recognised the benefits of being together and openly discussing both the high and low points of the educational journey. A bond was formed, which, from a student perspective, until this point had been formal. The study, whilst deliberately bringing together a specific group of people, had inadvertently promoted the concept and realisation of the benefits of such a group.

After listening carefully to students, as academics, we concluded that the black African students' experience and journey through the social work programme was diverse and complex (Bartoli *et al.*, 2008). The students' starting point was at a different place to that of their white student peers and therefore it was necessary to create and support a particular space to meet this need within their educational journey. It demanded us to not necessarily do anything *more* but to do something *different* to support the student in adjusting to the transition of higher education (Carroll and Ryan, 2005).

Within the original focus group, a number of strategies were discussed and one was the need for a support group. This was instantly and aptly named *Padare*.

PADARE: Pronounced pa-dar-ay, this is a Zimbabwean (Shona) term for a 'meeting place', where ideas are generated and exchanged. Traditionally, the concept of Padare is one of an open communal discussion, typically gathered around a tree, where people feel safe but are prepared to take risks, gather new ideas and share stories.

A tree

Padare began as a support group run by and for black African social work students. The essence of setting up the Padare group was to initiate a forum to provide encouragement and sharing of information. The outcome of this approach to supporting black African students was hugely embraced by the students. The forum has not only empowered black African students, but also has resulted in the promotion of their academic performances, including verbal contribution in lectures, attaining higher educational grades and progressing successfully in their practice learning.

The icon that has become synonymous with the Padare group at the University of Northampton is that of a tree. This is fitting with both the origins of the meaning of the word (a meeting around a tree) and the elements of the tree. A tree is multi-purposed and can be used for shelter, furniture, paper, transportation (such as boats) and even toys. Padare offers different students different things, including: support, knowledge, structure and a sense of identity. The branches and leaves, known as the *crown*, have the job of making food for the tree. The monthly Padare meeting is the place where students are sustained and nourished. The trunk of a tree is covered in bark, which acts as a protection from danger and exposure to extreme weather. Students often refer to Padare as a safe space where views can be expressed in a non-judgemental environment. The roots of a tree, although unseen, act as an anchor and nourish the tree through water.

Why a group?

Given that people universally connect and operate in and via groups within any society, it is hardly surprising that one of the outcomes for the students was to form a support group (Mayadas *et al.,* 2006). A collective solution to a collective problem does make sense. Collectivism is based upon the principle of ownership by a group as opposed to individuals. However, it would appear that this was more than just a logical response by the black African students. The Padare group members when describing their *home* experiences talk of being part of community, tribe or village. The students use the word *family* to include more than those with whom they share a household or blood-tie. In essence the students' knowledge and familiarity is in living and working within a group. Individualised-based cultures are on the whole associated with *western industrialised and technologically advanced nations* (Mayadas *et al.,* 2006, p 48) where self-improvement is gained at times at the cost of others, usually those with less power and more vulnerabilities (Dominelli, 2008).

CRITICAL QUESTIONS

Make a list of all the different types of groups you have been a part of (either formally or informally) throughout your life (this might include nursery, church, hobbies, education, etc.). What does it mean to you to be part of these groups?

Who do you consider to be your *family*? How are these *family* members connected to you?

Group work with principles in shared goals and objectives encompasses what Dominelli refers to as *egalitarian relations* (2008, p 33). In other words, the commonalities felt in belonging within a group can generate a more balanced and fair platform. Thus Padare has become a place and space where individual and group empowerment can be achieved but within a collective gathering.

The Padare group meets regularly every month. A key discussion is academic progress, and achievements are celebrated and peer support is offered to those who experience disappointment with their grades. The goals of most meetings are to articulate possible answers to students' questions and to also establish a common ground for further developments. The forum provides black African students with the opportunity to discuss their experiences and presence at the university. The students also feel that the forum has provided a space for suggesting ways in which they can use their personal resources for their common goal, both as students and at the point of qualification.

Padare can be categorised as a support group. Self-help groups can defy categorising in that they can be global, national, regional or local in scope (Kurta, 2006). Support groups can exist independently or be part of another organisation or totally dependent (either financially or morally) on another organisation. Padare can be described as being semi-dependent in that it relies upon lecturers for support and encouragement but the students continue to meet in their absence, such is their enthusiasm. The terms *self-help* and *support* groups are often used interchangeably (Kurta, 2006). Self-help groups tend to have an aim of effecting change and rarely have a facilitator. On the other hand, support groups meet with the purpose of providing support, often in the form of affirmation or information to others in a similar predicament and are often linked to larger organisations. Due to the collective nature of Padare, with its focus on mutuality rather than individualism, *support group* is the preferred term used to categorise and describe it.

Significant similarities can be noted between self-help and support group in that they rely on some form of external support. This is also the case for the Padare group, who rely upon the lecturers as a link to their organisation, in this case, to a university, in terms of booking rooms for meetings, *spreading the word*, circulating information and being a channel of communication between the group and its members.

CASE STUDY

Vimbai was a mature student and her country of origin is Zimbabwe, where she grew up and went to school. She described coming to university:

It was like a dream come true. I could not contain my excitement about coming to university but little did I know that having been away from school for 20 years and educated abroad made such a difference.

However, Vimbai found the academic aspects of her degree course very demanding and failed her first assignment. Not unlike many of her peers returning to formal education after a significant gap, Vimbai was unprepared for the challenges of her new academic voyage. Yet, unlike many of her peers, Vimbai had additional barriers to overcome. English was her third language and her formative education was based in a different system to the one in which she now found herself. By the time Vimbai embarked on her social work degree, the Padare group had been set up. In her own words she describes her first introduction to the group:

As soon as we embarked on our studies we were introduced to Padare, where we met with other social work students who were then in their third and second years. We were given a briefing and then we went into discussions. These discussions ranged from how to approach an assignment, how to organise yourself, time management and many others. Padare became a revelation in my life that I needed others for discussion purposes and people who had similar problems. Then I was realising that I was struggling academically. Our lecturers were there to provide direction but we literally ran the group. Since we met on our own we had a free forum to share openly as students where we were falling short academically. Feedback was then given back to our course leaders to enable them to provide us with help with our studies. Together with the other Padare students we improved academically. We took time to analyse all the tutor comments, which we received when our assignments were returned. We looked at our situation positively.

Not only was Padare a significant source of support for raising Vimbai's confidence in her written expression and academic work, she also grew in personal confidence, which she was able to apply into her practice with service users.

Padare gave me an identity and an opportunity. Knowing who I was and what I wanted to achieve also prepared me for my placements. Taught modules laid the foundation such that when I went on placements I was well equipped. Thanks to Padare, I am now the proud holder of a degree in social work.

CRITICAL QUESTION

Consider yourself in Vimbai's shoes. How do you think that her social work education would have been different without the support of Padare?

Where is Padare now?

The ethos of the Padare group is a positive approach to learning, one that openly acknowledges and celebrates difference, whilst building upon achievement by focussing on what works as a *liberating force* rather than deficits (Aymer and Bryan, 1996, p 2).

This concentration on the negatives, as has been done so far, and identifying black students as victims could create an 'ain't it all awful' culture. (Aymer and Bryan, 1996, p 2)

With an emphasis on drawing upon the strengths of groups and collectivism, the Padare group is working towards eliminating the notion of black people as victims and under-achievers (Aymer and Bryan, 1996). The tangible outcomes from the inception of Padare have been improved student retention, attainment, significant improvement in National Student Surveys, employability and alumni involvement.

Another outcome of the Padare group, which is less tangible but nevertheless important and real, has been the candid discussions about the perceptions of racism on a personal, institutional and professional level. Whilst necessary to discuss, this is not something that everyone finds comfortable, including students and lecturers from *all* ethnic backgrounds. However, the Padare group offers the opportunity to minimise any suspicion that might surface about the existence of such a group, and provides an honest platform that has the potential to make a difference to both the learning and teaching experience. Padare, as a support group, continues to flourish within the social work programme. Its success, in terms of providing mutual support, has been shared at international, regional and local events. Since its formation, the group membership has grown to include more students from new cohorts and other African countries, for example Uganda, Kenya and the Ivory Coast. On the whole, the Padare group is viewed by the students and the university as a positive contributing factor in enhancing the student experience. The only negative comments about the group are associated with frustration at the infrequency of meetings; this is due to a lack of time when students are on placements rather than lack of commitment. During these times students tend to remain connected through telephone and e-mail correspondence.

Through discussion, informal evaluations and observation, some themes have emerged in terms of the effectiveness of the group, which have included:

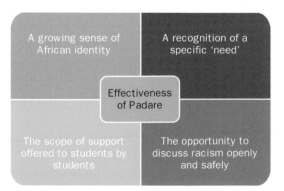

African identity

The overwhelming message that students give is of the contribution that belonging to the Padare group has made to their sense of confidence and self-esteem. Many of the students talk of the group contributing to their African and/or black identity, which is steeped in pride as well as difference. In the words of one of the students:

The Padare group has given me the confidence to identify myself as an African student.

It is well documented that group work brings with it the benefits of members experiencing a common bond and sense of togetherness (Brown, 1994; Coulshed and Orme, 2006; Doel and Sawdon, 1999; Doel, 2006). The Padare group is no exception. As one member put it:

Padare has given me a celebration and acknowledgement of African identity. I am no longer alone. I have an identity. (Former Padare student)

The above quote reflects how the Padare group has created a community where isolation is being eradicated and in its place a growing identity has formed. Yet the group has gone beyond a uniqueness merely formed by racial and cultural identity. They are not merely a group of black Africans within an academic setting. Their additional connectivity is that they are soon to be part of a professional group with a protected title – social workers.

Recognition of *'our need'*

The variation in educational attainment both at school and at university level dependent on ethnicity has been a persistent and growing concern (Singh, 2011). This wide variation of completion of degree rates is commonplace within the higher education sector of the UK (Singh, 2011) and is considered problematic within social work educational programmes (Bartoli *et al.*, 2008; Bernard *et al.*, 2011; McGregor, 2011; Stevenson, 2012). This is not a new phenomenon; previous studies have highlighted similar problems within the former Diploma of Social Work (Hussein *et al.*, 2006, 2008) and it has been reported in other professional programmes such as nursing (Stevenson, 2012). A recent study reports that the number of UK domicile BME students studying in higher education is statistically higher than that of white students (Stevenson, 2012).

The *mismatch* between student and university expectation is not an uncommon experience for a number of students. For international students or those who have lived and been educated outside of the UK, the experience is exacerbated due to the unfamiliarity of assessment strategies and academic expectations in higher education. Our approach to learning is imbedded in our formative experiences and is largely culture specific (Carroll and Ryan, 2005; Brown and Joughin, 2007). The majority of Padare students are considered *domicile* or *home* students, in terms of their fee-paying status, as many have lived in the UK for more than two years. However, their experience of the UK system is new, with university being the starting point, and everything can feel *foreign*, bewildering and different. Padare students have described feeling that they are disadvantaged due to their unfamiliarity of UK academic expectations and this has been confirmed in other research (Bernard *et al.*, 2011; Bartoli, 2010; Singh, 2011). The Padare students consider the recognition of their educational experience as being different, and so requiring a support group, as a positive contribution to their learning and development.

The scope of support

One would expect a support group to do just that – offer support. It is the scope of the support offered and gained by the Padare group members that is worthy of comment. Each Padare student has learnt a significant amount from previous students or those in other cohorts, which ensures that former graduates or those nearing the end of their studies can pass on advice, strategies, resources and reading recommendations to those at the beginning of their studies.

The support offered within the Padare group to one another is multi-faceted. As mentioned, a number of the Padare students, whilst not deemed *international* students, are fairly new to the UK and hence have little lived experience of the history of local politics. For some black students it can feel uncomfortable to ask questions within a large cohort for fear of appearing ill-informed or unaware. Padare meetings offer a safe place to express such knowledge gaps:

When I started my social work training, I did not know much about legislations and policies in England and their related historical and political background. However, due to the Padare group's harmony and supporting attitude, I was supported immensely and was signposted to relevant learning materials to increase my knowledge in order to enhance my learning. (Former Padare student)

A significant amount of learning occurs within the Padare group monthly meetings; this enhances the lectures and other student discussions in a non-judgemental manner. As one student eloquently stated:

Padare is a place where I can share my learning deficits, talk about my fears and get the confirmation that my feelings are normal without being judged. (Former Padare student)

The scope of support is at an academic and personal level in an environment where commonality, both in terms of being black students and on a professionally qualifying programme, is the key to the effectiveness and attraction of the Padare group.

I believe that people who have been through or are experiencing a similar circumstance can relate to, sympathise with and support each other very well. Therefore, Padare is a community that understands me as a black student on a social work training course in supporting me to achieve my full potential. (Former Padare student)

The emotional rapport offered through Padare is a feature of the group that students regularly comment upon. Through the work of the original study it transpired that all of the black African students on the social work programme had experienced at least one bereavement during their studies (Bartoli *et al.*, 2008). This is often complicated by the time and financial burden of having to either send money (for medical treatment) or return to countries of origin (for funerals). Needless to say, this has an impact on the students' emotional well-being. Padare offers a place to share these painful experiences with others who need little explanation and offer much understanding.

Discussing racism openly and safely

The development and continuation of Padare has created an openness to discuss and analyse racism, both on an individual and an institutional level for *all* students and the academics. International students within universities are often viewed as *difficult*, stereotyped as being plagiarists, rote learners and time consuming for educators (Carroll and Ryan, 2005). In my experience this is not confined to international students, but also to students whose formative education has been outside of the UK but within the educational system are categorised as *home* students due to their residency in the UK. In the original study the Padare students talked candidly of their perceptions of being treated differently by some students, academics and Practice Educators. Whilst on placement some Padare students were supervised more and assessors appeared to have lower expectations of them (Bartoli *et al.*, 2008). Often the Padare students have been reluctant to suggest that this might be due to racism, and often do not use the word *racism*.

Through the development of the Padare group, the academics involved have entered into open and at times painful dialogues about overt and covert racism. An illustration of this as narrated by the members of the Padare group is the division that often occurs in the teaching environment. They talk of white students having a *special* place to sit within classrooms or lecture theatres and the black students sitting at the other end of the room. This observation is also noted in the Bernard *et al.* study (2011, p 47) where student participants *described a form of 'segregation' taking place in the classroom; whereby students tended to occupy the physical space in the classroom around racial lines*.

Some of the factors identified by the Bartoli *et al.* (2008) study and supported by Bernard *et al.*'s later study (2011) have contributed to the academic performance amongst black social work students, including:

- gender;
- overseas family commitments;
- financial responsibilities in UK and at 'home';
- part-time employment.

A number of the Padare students have expressed concerns that if they do not achieve well academically this would confirm the negative stereotype about their intellectual ability as a racial group. This promotes a major source of additional stress to black students, which Padare can alleviate through mutual support and understanding.

CRITICAL QUESTION

Where do you sit within a social work lecture/teaching environment? Are you aware of any apparent divisions within the student group? If you are, what could you do to change this?

Challenges faced

Kurta (2006) identifies a significant growth of the self-help and support group movement over the past three decades. However financial support is decreasing due to central government cuts. It could be argued that face-to-face groups may decrease or even cease on occasions and more *virtual* support is available, made increasingly more possible by the growing popularity of social media networking sites such as Facebook.

It is further suggested that there are a number of challenges in support groups in terms of the potential for dispensing inaccurate information, inability to contain emotions and being offputting and intimidating to newcomers (Kurta, 2006; Garvin *et al.*, 2006). This, to date, has not been the experience of the Padare group; in fact, the evaluation of the first 12 months of its existence would suggest the opposite.

As mentioned, there is a frustration expressed by the Padare group members that meetings have not occurred as regularly as planned due to the structure of the degree programme where different cohorts are taught on different days or students are off campus and on placements. A way of dealing with this has been to set up a page on the university interactive website as a means of encouraging participation that is not reliant on geographical location for communication, information and a sense of connectivity.

CRITICAL QUESTION

Do you belong to any form of support group? What are the advantages/disadvantages of a 'real' (face-to-face) group as compared to a 'virtual' one?

RESEARCH SUMMARY

Bernard, C., Fairlough, A., Fletcher, J. and Ahmet, A. (2011) *Diversity and Progression among Social Work Students in England*. London: Goldsmiths University of London.

This is first national qualitative study undertaken to consider the diversity and progression on social work programmes in England. The report considers black and ethnic minority, disabled and lesbian, gay and bisexual students. The research methods used included:

• focus groups with black, disabled, and lesbian and gay students;

• semi-structured interviews with black, disabled and lesbian and gay and bisexual students;

• semi-structured interviews with academic staff, practice learning co-ordinators, and learning support staff, such as disability officers/co-ordinators, mental health co-ordinators, and senior members of staff responsible for diversity and widening participation initiatives within the higher education institution (HEI) sites.

The analysis of the data was influenced by techniques adapted from grounded theory. This *analytical approach to data analysis offers a set of procedures and techniques for developing categories, organising the data, and identifying themes* (Bernard et al. 2011, p 23). The software package NVivo was used as a tool to code and group the data into themes and emerging patterns.

For the purposes of this chapter, issues relating to black and ethnic minority students will be considered, of which 66 participated in the study. However, it is important to note that the study emphasises the particular vulnerability of students *negotiating multiple intersecting disadvantage*, for example black students with dyslexia (Bernard *et al.*, 2011, p 42). Congruent with other qualitative research (Hussein *et al.*, 2006, 2008, 2009; Singh, 2011) and smaller studies (Bartoli *et al.*, 2008) this study confirms that there are variations of progression rates for black and ethnic minority students on social work programmes.

This research has been specifically selected as it confirms some of the findings of our smaller scale study here at the University of Northampton. In particular the two studies correlate in the following areas:

- reluctance amongst BME students to directly discuss race issues;

- physical divisions within the classroom environment;

- BME staff offering positive role models and inspiration;

- preference for smaller group discussion;

- BME students face particular challenges in placement settings;

- programme level initiatives (such as support groups) improve outcomes for BME students;

- students with intersecting disadvantage (such as race, gender, additional caring responsibilities) were vulnerable to poor academic progression rates;

- disadvantaged educational backgrounds;

- growing up in poor communities and family backgrounds;

- experiencing adversity was a motivating factor to study social work;

- high expectations from family members;

- additional financial pressures experienced by international students;

- BME students' determination to succeed despite adversity;

- experiences of racism whilst on placement;

- BME students' accent seen as a difficulty by themselves and placement providers.

A full copy of this report is available at: www.kcl.ac.uk/sspp/kpi/scwru/dhinitiative/projects/bernardetal2011diversityfinalreport.pdf.

Spreading the word

The formation of Padare at the University of Northampton has generated a number debates, which have been articulated in journal articles (for example Bartoli *et al.*, 2008 in relation to practice learning; Bartoli *et al.*, 2009 in enhancing the student experience within a higher educational setting; Bartoli, 2011 in the assessment of international students), and also presented at regional and national conferences. This has often included Padare students and it has provoked discussions about support groups for black and/or BME students within higher education. As put by one Practice Educator:

As a white practitioner it enabled further consideration of the educational process, diversity and difference. I have been able to share the paper [Bartoli et al., 2008] with a number of social work and practice educator colleagues to help and enable further learning and also as a point for debate.

The membership of the Padare group is ever changing as students graduate and new students enrol. Academics promote the group to new students within the first few days of induction within the academic year. However, it would be fair to say that the academics who proactively *champion* the group are the three who were instigators of the original study. In September 2011, a former student was employed to act as a co-ordinator for the group, which has given the Padare students a point of reference within the teaching staff. The Padare group has also extended to other students within the Social Work Division at the university who, whilst not studying social work but social and community development, share similar issues. Hence now the Padare meets as a larger group, encompassing *all* the BME students across the two programmes, but also separately to address more professional issues such as black social work identity.

A journey with a pit stop

In our original study and subsequent journal article, we used the metaphor of a road to describe the social work educational journey for Padare students (Bartoli *et al.*, 2008). The destination of this journey is similar for *all* students regardless of their ethnic origin, age, gender or ability – a social work degree and qualification. The road travelled however is different and unique for each learner. No one single path is the same, or better or inferior than the other. For already disadvantaged students who might be manoeuvring between *multiple intersecting disadvantages*, the educational journey can be unfamiliar and bumpy at times and they might need assistance and support along the way (Bernard *et al.*, 2011, p 42). These intersections of disadvantage might be, for example, being a black student with a disability (Bernard *et al.*, 2011).

I would like to extend this metaphor and invite you to consider the route taken in motor racing where pit stops are commonly used. This is where a car stops in the pits during a race for refuelling, change of tyres, mechanical repairs or any combination of these things. During these pit stops the driver is surrounded by a team who provide assistance immediately. Pit stops are essential for drivers to complete races safely and as competently as possible. They are not haphazard or incidental, but strategic in nature and planned. As students, you will develop your own learning strategies dependent on your learning style and needs. At times you may need additional or different types of support or pit stops. A student support group, like Padare, offers a unique pit stop where students can be surrounded by people in similar situations to assist.

Within motor racing every member of a pit stop crew has a specific task and role. Due to being a male-dominated sport and activity, many of the roles are gender-specific in title. The main roles include:

Comparison between pit stop crew members and the Padare group	
'Lollipop' (man) Person	**Padare Co-ordinator**
The main mechanic who guides the incoming car into the pit	The academic staff member who co-ordinates and supports Padare activities
Wheel (men) Persons	**Year Rep**
Crew members assigned to each wheel	Each cohort has a nominated year representative
Refueller	**Padare meetings**
Attaches nozzle to the car for the refuelling process	Serve as a safe place to gain support and knowledge
Support (man) Person	**Personal Academic Tutors**
Holds the refuelling hose within the car	Available for support
Extras	**Padare members**
Extra crew members available to remove debris and prevent blockages	Offering mutual support at key points within the educational journey
Fire (man) Person	**Head of Division**
Standing by with breathing system and fire extinguishers	Playing a peripheral but vital role in terms of supporting and promoting the group

Similarly within motor racing there are specific parts of the car that are considered essential to *winning the race*. Below is a table of essential requirements for a car and for the effective running of a mutual support group such as Padare.

	In order to start a race, a motor car is an essential requirement. However, there are a number of different types and models of cars. Padare offers students from all BME backgrounds a starting point in their educational journey.
	Like good high performance tyres, Padare can enhance students' overall academic performance and sense of well-being.
	Padare students experience many pressures due to having ongoing commitments to family members overseas. The group can alleviate such pressure, which like a car needs to be just the right amount in order to operate effectively and smoothly.
	Being part of Padare has provided students with tools and resources that have enhanced their classroom learning.

	Like motor racing, *all* students can feel like they are 'racing against the clock'. Padare offers student a protected time and space to share successes and concerns.
	Refuelling is an essential aspect of a pit stop. Without fuel the car would not be able to race or win. Padare has been described by students as a place to *refuel* and *recharge* their batteries in a reflective and safe space.
	The finishing line for students is graduation. Students at each graduation ceremony explicitly cite the support and friendship of Padare as being the main motivating factor in their educational journey.
	The finishing block is the main prize for students and for social work students it is an opportunity to enter a profession with a protected title. Since the formation of Padare the retention and progression of BME students has been enhanced.

CRITICAL QUESTION

If you had to enter a 'pit stop', what support would you find helpful? What strategies can you put into place to ensure that you have the support you need to fulfil your academic potential?

Listening to students

Padare has now been running since 2008 and over the years, as educators, we have had the privilege to deepen our understanding of the educational and personal journey for BME students on a social work programme. My understanding is that Padare offers a safe environment to:

- develop critical thinking skills;
- offer and be offered support that is non-judgemental;
- promote, deepen and transfer learning;
- be student focussed;
- be involved and participate actively in learning;
- enhance networking skills;
- develop a personal and professional racial identity;
- make long-lasting friendships;
- allow quieter students the safety to voice their concerns and fears;
- celebrate successes;
- listen to alternative ideas and perspectives;

- share resources, tips and strategies;
- practice essential social work skills such as listening, decision-making, problem solving, negotiation, networking and team working.

Developing a support group such as Padare has been a successful venture for students at the University of Northampton. Rich and, at times, painful stories have been shared and lessons learnt. There are implications for *all* students and educators if we are to be truly inclusive and supportive of BME students.

Implications for educators

- It is incumbent upon educators to be aware of the dynamics within the 'classroom' in terms of sitting arrangements and when offering smaller group activities.
- Set up and encourage small group discussions that are respectful and inclusive.
- Consider, together with students, the potential benefits of setting up a Padare type support group within your establishment. What will your role as educator be?
- Encourage *all* students to recommend texts written by authors who reflect global perspectives of social work issues and concerns.
- Make no assumptions about *any* student – ask about their formative educational experiences.
- What role do you play within the journey and pit stops of your students?

Implications for students

- Does your university offer a support group for BME students?
- Consider, together with the support of your tutors, setting up a Padare group.
- White students can support BME students by understanding the need for a separate 'space' such as Padare offers for minority groups.
- BME students can support white students in their understanding by having open discussions.
- Ask former students, or students in other cohorts, for tips, strategies and advice.

Ubuntu **as a conclusion**

Concerns about the academic under-achievement of BME students have long been documented in both children and adults within the educational system (DfES, 2003; Connor *et al.*, 2004). Arguably the gap between the academic performance of white and BME students can be attributed to the portrayal of black people as under-achievers (Tomlin and Olusola, 2006). However, Stevenson (2012) argues that under-achievement amongst BME students is more connected with a lack of preparedness for higher education (such as lack of experience, poverty, class and prior educational opportunities) rather than racism, ethnicity or culture. This disproportionate and unhelpful focus on black under-achievement in the literature not only distorts the image of the BME community but it also creates and perpetuates a lower set of expectations for black students. Whilst much has been debated about the issues, this chapter serves to offer a contribution towards a solution in the form of a support group by and for black students.

The value of and continued need for a black student support group should not be overlooked or considered passé. Most black African students within the Padare group have been at the receiving end of negative stereotypes and daily racism. Remember that racism does to have to be intentional for it to *exist* and *feel* real (hooks, 2010). Appropriate support groups, rather than segregation, serve as primary venues for black students' engagement in their studies. Without such groups, some of the students may not have found a place for the expression and development of their black identities and academic achievements. Padare offers a platform through which to address black perspectives and initiate dialogue with academics devoid of fear or recriminations.

Lastly, when I asked the Padare students to describe their experiences of Padare in one word, they concluded with *Ubuntu*. This is an African proverb and ideology that means *I am, because you are*.

As individuals we are reliant upon one another. In other words, *Ubuntu* signifies humanity. Padare has pioneered a sense of community within our university as signified by the term *Ubuntu*.

In the words of a former student, support groups can create a

sense of belonging. It made us more confident and, as such, we became more able to challenge and think analytically.

Taking it further

Websites

Equality Challenge Unit – works to support equality and diversity for staff and students in higher education: www.ecu.ac.uk.

Chapters in books

Brown, S. and Gordon, J. (2007) Assessment and International Students – Helping Clarify Puzzling Processes, in Jones, E. and Brown, S. (eds) *Internationalising Higher Education*. London: Routledge, pp 57–72.

Books

hooks, b. (2010) *Teaching Critical Thinking: Practical Wisdom*. London: Routledge.

Ryde, J. (2009) *Being White in the Helping Professions: Developing Effective Intercultural Awareness*. London: Jessica Kingsley.

5 White woman listening

SUE KENNEDY

Chapter aims

This chapter aims to explore the role of anti-oppressive social work in social work education and practice. The reader will be asked to consider whether or not anti-racism has become lost in a language that does not help social workers to be clear about their own position or support professional development and awareness of racism. How professional development is achieved will be examined through acknowledging how the needs of black African students enrolled on a social work programme were met. The chapter will examine the impact of institutional racism on Akua, a black African social work student, her white woman Practice Teacher and a white woman academic through the study of events that took place during a practice placement experience. Using feminist theory in partnership with hermeneutics as a method of critical inquiry (Freeman, 2011) the chapter will take the reader through specific events as narrated by Akua and Jane, providing opportunities to consider the importance of communication, relationships and interactions in each narrated event.

CRITICAL QUESTIONS TO BE ADDRESSED

Can an understanding of the role of white privilege in the debates about racism provide new knowledge that adds to intra-personal professional development supporting the finding of self, place and position? Can this lead to a better understanding about what is meant by anti-racist, anti-oppressive and anti-discriminatory social work practice?

Introduction

Anti-oppressive social work

Social work is about change and built upon an accepted commitment to social justice. This brings together how emancipatory approaches and social justice inform how social workers engage and intervene in the lives of those who become involved in services (Dominelli, 2002). This demonstrates that there are inherent tensions in the nature and practice of social work. Social workers are expected to move in and out of people's lives using a range of interventions based upon a value base that asks them to recognise social inequalities while being mindful of their organisational role that requires them to act within a legal framework to keep service users and the community safe (Jordan, 2004). This is a challenging landscape that social workers have to navigate. Whether your approach is politically driven or from an individual *culture of experience* (Webb, 2006, p 30) these contested sites of political and cultural are both informed by human interactions aimed at helping (Dominelli, 2002).

Anti-oppressive social work was a response to the changing face of social work practice. Dominelli (2002) provides valuable insight into the changes that took place in the early 1970s as a political response to class and race. Social workers based in the community began to challenge the accepted societal structures of class alongside emerging black activist groups. This development in social work was influenced by radical social workers, feminists and in particular black feminists who recognised the interconnectedness of gender, race, disability, age, class and sexuality in the personal lived experience (MacDonald, 2006; Wilson *et al.,* 2008). Central to the thinking of the time was the role of power and the way in which oppression is socially constructed. The intent was to ensure inclusivity and an engagement with the social and political agendas of the day. The challenge to social work was to understand the complex nature of oppression by the promotion of anti-oppressive practice that challenged disadvantage (Jones *et al.,* 2008).

It was this work by social workers on the ground that led to challenges and changes within the academic world. The Central Council for Education and Training in Social Work (CCETSW) Paper 30 was first published in 1989 in response to the challenges set out in a policy statement on equal opportunities that social work students will *learn how to counter unfair discrimination, racism, poverty disadvantage and injustice in way appropriate to their situation and role* (CCETSW, 1991, p 8). Dominelli (2002) argues that this was a direct response to those social work activists who identified that social work education was out of step and that the inclusion of racism was a much needed expansion in the debates around inequality, oppression and discrimination.

However, the language of the anti-oppressive approach became hugely influential in social work and social work education. It emerged as an umbrella term aimed at addressing the multiplicities of inequality (MacDonald, 2006) and social work programmes were endorsed by regulatory bodies that required evidence of teaching and learning based on principles of valuing diversity and an awareness of inequality (GSCC, 2002). The meaning of this sentence is and has been open to interpretation in terms of how this is applied in teaching. The lack of specificity about what is meant by diversity and equality has raised concerns and some criticism. Fook (2004) argues that this lack of specificity has afforded opportunities for students and social work practitioners to engage on a superficial and comfortable level rather than one of challenge and criticality in the debates about oppression, discrimination and inequality. Vague terminology and in particular the use of anti-oppressive as a generic phrase have been condemned by Humphries (2004), who argues that it helped social workers come to terms with their statutory role, and Jones *et al.* (2008), who believe that it has been used by students to demonstrate that they have met the professional standards rather than a deeper understanding of inequality, oppression and discrimination.

Oppression and discrimination are done through fear, suspicion and lack of understanding. In the case of racism it will be that *whites have something of value that is denied to others simply because of the groups they belong to* (Curry-Stevens and Nissen, 2011). It is a side of humanity that is uncomfortable and, in some ways, it is understandable that social work education and practice finds it difficult to find the words that effectively translate the full meaning (Flax, 2010). For social work students and qualified social workers grappling with the range of inequities in society it is understandable that there has been a retreat into an easy practice that uses the term anti-oppressive as a catch-all phrase. Unfortunately, this approach does not deal with the specifics and has contributed to the disempowerment of social work students and practitioners. It has also led to a skills deficit and a level of complacency in social work that needs to reconnect with the radical intentions of the anti-oppressive approach to confront inequalities and oppression (Pon, 2009; Singh, 2011).

Anti-oppressive social work practice was built upon legislation and the promotion of equal opportunities (GSCC, 2002). The anti-oppressive discourse made links to the personal and political context of the lived experience (MacDonald, 2006) and was a term that met the needs of social work at that particular time. The need to refine the discussions around anti-oppressive practice to help students and social workers place themselves firmly in the centre of the debates is overdue. The term anti-oppressive has become too generic and has encouraged a short-hand phraseology that does not describe the concrete details of the lived experience of racism, sexism, disability, age, sexuality and gender. It has also supported what Flax (2010) refers to as *fabricating subjectivity*. That is that social work students and social work practitioners can take up certain positions that claim to be responding, or not, to oppression without critically reflecting upon their own position or defining what anti-oppressive practice looks like. The prefix of 'anti' may have supported this situation. Students and social workers may believe that by using the term 'anti' they are demonstrating a position that is against oppression and discrimination and therefore an explicit stance against social structures that create inequalities. The challenge for social work education is to support a move beyond the potential hiding places of words that have constructed a barrier to deeper learning and created a range of a fixed binary positions in which race becomes the problem of black people, just as gender is understood as the *woman problem* (Flax, 2010, p 78), and positions of *them and us* (Boyce *et al.*, 2008, p 6).

This move has already begun with calls for social work education to make a specific reference to anti-racist practice in the teaching and learning for social work students. In a review of the anti-racist standards within anti-oppressive practice Boyce *et al.* (2008) identified that social work students demonstrated a general lack of understanding about the impact of racism on individuals, groups and communities or were holding the belief that racism did not need attention any more. In this review there was a call for social work education to adopt *new frameworks* to support student learning (p 6). Singh (2011) also refers to social work education as having unfinished business in challenging the powerful systems that support a black and white arrangement whereby each of us looks at the other in a subsumed abstract of generalities that loses the real detail of this lived experience. With significant changes to social work education, practice and regulation through the introduction of the Professional Capabilities Framework (PCF), the Standards of Proficiency for Social Workers from the Health and Care Professionals Council (HCPC) and curriculum content advice from the College of Social Work (TCSW), it is a timely opportunity to engage with the expectations of the frameworks and standards that helps us to move from the range of fixed positions that have led to a form of segregation and denial that racism exists (hooks, 2009) to one that promotes anti-racist social work.

Anti-racist social work

How we promote changes to a framework of learning that helps students think beyond terms and phrases will be the challenge. By substituting one phrase or term for another, because one may be considered more explicit about what the debate is, could be considered too simplistic. This is a point that Boyce *et al.* (2008) refer to, pointing out that changing language may not always bring about *real change* (p 5). It is the intentions (actions) that lay within the words and the positioning (political or cultural) of the social work profession in a discourse and definition based on principles of human relationships and human rights (IFSW, 2004). To be anti-racist and/or anti-oppressive is about taking a position and signing up to a value base that sets out clearly the intentions of professional social work practice. However, all terms and adjectives can be hotly contested. Humphries (2004) and McLaughlin (2005) both challenge the use of the term anti-racist 'approach' in social work, arguing that such intentions are impossible to achieve in organisations that are inherently racist or have led to a rigid stance that has fostered division and exclusive debates.

The profession of social work and social work education has experienced a range of regulatory changes in the past ten years. The demise of the General Social Care Council (GSCC) as a regulatory and professional body and the transfer of registration to the Health Care Professional Council (HCPC) have brought a new set of professional frameworks and standards. The Professional Capabilities Framework (PCF) sets out the professional framework of expected practice for social work students and practitioners. One of the expectations is that social workers will recognise diversity and apply anti-discriminatory and anti-oppressive principles in practice. Within this expectation there is an acknowledgement that diversity is multi-dimensional and includes race (SWTF, 2010). The Standards of Proficiency for Social Workers (HCPC) identify the expectations for social workers in becoming aware, recognising and understanding the impact of *culture, equality and diversity on practice*, alongside being able to *practise in a non-discriminatory way* (HCPC, 2012, p 7). The use of the term non-discriminatory, which is often used alongside anti-oppressive, reflects the intention to ensure that social work practice is inclusive, referring to the range of multi-political aspects of equal opportunities. This is also a demonstration of the challenges we face in finding a language that can engage students in the realities of the social world (Clifford and Burke, 2009), which supports moving beyond positions that may have led to denial, critical paralysis and the 'other territory'. hooks (2009) refers to the need to keep moving rather than loiter or linger in one place. It may be that social work and social work education need to move beyond the language. However, before moving in any direction we need to stay with the terms and language of anti-racist, anti-oppressive and anti-discriminatory and explore these further in a way that helps to explain the human experience that leads to a better understanding.

The contention in this chapter is that before social work students can become involved in the lives of service users they need to understand their own social, political and cultural positioning and how this experience will have influenced their understanding of diversity and equality. More importantly, how will this experience influence their intentions to practice social work in a way that is anti-racist, anti-oppressive and anti-discriminatory? For many students and academics this is a big claim that needs to be critically examined in a space that nurtures critical reflection and focuses on the social interactions of those involved – service user, student, academic, practice teachers and employers within the professional context of social work in which they participate (Clifford and Burke, 2009). Lorde (1984) explains the nature of the complexity in her statement *there is no such thing as a single-issue struggle because we do not live single-issue lives* (p 28). This is a helpful statement to consider because it provides a frame of reference that is not one-dimensional. Lorde (1984) acknowledges, as does Jordan (2006), that we are all located within a range of *social systems, social interactions and social groupings* that we try to make sense of through the nature of the lived experience (p 77). I propose that through learning about the lived experience of racism in a way that helps to connect with each other's fears, histories, narratives and interpretations this can lead to a better understanding that racism harms us all (Nakagawa, 2012). Before considering events that led to changes within one social work education programme it may be helpful to explore, through the following framework, an understanding of the terms anti-oppression, anti-discriminatory and anti-racist social work practice and for you to critically think about where you would position yourself:

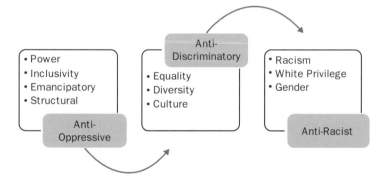

CRITICAL QUESTION

At first glance where do you position yourself? Is this position political or cultural? Is there a position that you do not feel able to take? Consider why this is and what has influenced your decision.

Meeting the needs of black African social work students

Transforming learning and understanding about the impact of racism came about at the University of Northampton through the experience of a specific moment that can be compared to the work by hooks (2009) that identified the need for education institutions in America to respond to the needs of African American students by providing an education that affirmed a history and culture. Black African students enrolled on the social work degree at the University of Northampton assumed that the literature they should draw upon in assessments should be UK based (Bartoli *et al.*, 2008). This experience challenged the programme thinking about the messages that had been given to the students. While individual tutors (black and white) quoted what they believed was a range of 'global' literature for students to draw upon, the feelings and actions of this interaction had been felt differently. Students were unsure and to some degree suspicious about what to read and use. This experience demonstrated the powerful colonial epistemology of knowledge that pervades thinking (Ackerly and True, 2010) and the lack of social work literature from a black perspective in the UK. That this even occurred pointed to the fact that there had been a suspension of critical thinking and awareness by all of those involved. In this interaction the understanding and interpretation of the reality had been very different. This particular event triggered further inquiry and research with black African students about their social work education experience (Bartoli *et al.*, 2008). The inquiry and research outcomes provided the programme team and all students with a range of new knowledge and understanding.

The black African students said they felt more confident in their identity and that there was now a sense of openness between the tutors and student group (Bartoli *et al.*, 2008). The learning developed through a dialogue (*narrative*) of individual experiences that explored the feelings attached. These feelings were validated through the connection with others and while a difference of culture, identity and ethnicity were acknowledged there was a coming together of the group through a lived and shared life experience (Jordan, 2000). This was evident when the women shared the common experience of sexism and the burden of the gendered division of domestic labour and childcare responsibilities and how these placed extra pressure on them as students trying to meet the academic and professional requirements. At this point there needs to be some clarification and a note of caution to the approach. I firmly adopt the view that providing opportunities to talk with and to each other is an important way of gaining insight into life's realities and this is not a new approach in social work. In fact social work is all about 'talking' and Hall (1997) argued that dialogue is a vehicle for change. In this experience there was a change in the confidence of the black African social work students and the way in which learning was approached by the tutors. Through team meetings that debated what constitutes a diverse social work reading list, and whether or not writers such as bell hooks can help students understand theory to practice, came agreements to review current reading lists and explore a range of different literature and how these can be used in the teaching. The talking captured imaginations and inspired a range of different initiatives such as the Beyond Horizons 'Black African Social Work Students Look to the Future' (Padare, 2012).

However, the caution is linked to concerns about learning from the black African students' lived experiences of racism. The writings of Lorde (1984) have posed questions about the role of black *people* in helping educate white *people* about 'their' racism given the emotional energy that is used up in this process with little to show in the way of outcomes for black people. As one student stated, she was *tired of being defined by a history of slavery in anti-racist education* that she had experienced. *I have to explain who I am and why I do not accept this as part of my black identity. This does not go down well with white people* (Mutokori, 2012). There have been further criticisms of an approach that does not include the role of white privilege in the teaching and learning process, posing a powerful argument that there has been an over-reliance and focus on the black experience of racism that has let white people off the hook (Curry-Stevens and Nissen, 2011). I believe that the experience of learning from the black African social work students alerted those involved and awakened in me, a white woman, my inner political feminist stance that re-engaged with Carby's essay 'White Woman Listen!' In this essay Carby (1987) challenged white feminists to listen to the *herstories* of black women's lives past and present to understand the powerful systems of oppression that oncase them. She also called upon white feminists to acknowledge that they as a result of their 'race' have benefitted from the oppression of black women and consequently need to accept their involvement in constructing a feminist discourse that has ignored them. In the conclusion of her essay she argues strongly for white and black women to *construct alternatives* through the process of listening so that they can fully understand the ways in which black women have been oppressed (Carby, 1987, p 53). By reconnecting with the challenge posed by Carby in her essay, my listening to the black African students took on a critical edge that began to look closely at the words used by the men and women of the student group about their experience of social work education in the 'classroom' and in placement. What I found was that the black African students were using a range of generalised terms to describe the challenges they faced in their interactions with students, practice teachers and tutors. These terms were used when talking about painful experiences of being excluded from group exercises, told they could not be understood on the telephone or that their written work was not up to 'practice' standards. They had found new phrases and terms to describe their experiences – *it was a personality clash*, *it was miscommunication*, *it was a cultural misunderstanding*. From this interwoven discourse – the language and words – used by the students a distorted reality was hidden behind a blanket of 'silence'. For the students this telling was fraught with tensions. As students they were *subject to a range of institutional discourses* that regulate, assess and *approve ways to be* (Baxter, 2003, p 26) and as black students they were reluctant to bring attention to the subject of racism for fear of being considered troublesome or difficult. This event of listening challenged the belief within the social work programme that change was taking place. Although there had been positive changes within the programme it took a different event outside of the university to dramatically challenge and recover memories and be reminded of the reality of racism and in particular institutionalised racism within the profession of social work.

Hermeneutics in partnership with feminism as methods for 'tuning in'

Hermeneutics as an approach to understanding this event was chosen because in a modern sense it refers to relationships, interactions and communication and how these are interconnected through an understanding of each other in social contexts. Freeman (2011) refers to the term hermeneutics as *interpreting understanding and understanding that interpretation while situated in a world that is already interpreted* (p 545). In qualitative research it is used as a method of inquiry into understanding the human position and experience and ultimately poses questions about knowing (Ackerly and True, 2010). I feel the use of hermeneutics can help to support learning about the self and the situation of the self, and an intra-personal knowledge that Koprowska (2010) refers to as *tuning-in* that enables values to become 'live' for social work students.

The use of hermeneutics as an approach sits well with the overall ambitions of anti-oppressive, anti-discriminatory and anti-racist practice. They are connected by their location in a discourse that challenges social workers to look at society through a different lens and question the status quo (Frankenberg, 1993). As a method of inquiry it can help us to connect with the human position and the uniqueness of the individual. Hermeneutics will be used to understand the practice learning experience of Akua, a black African social work student, within the context of being assessed and how a range of interpretations about this experience by the white practice teacher and white academics led to a questioning of what was known and by whom. It is the critical inquiry of the event by exploring through Akua's narrative the relationships, interactions and communication that will be the focus of this chapter.

Feminism as a social work theory will also be used to support the learning and critical inquiry. This approach has been adopted because feminism offers a theoretical framework that helps to deconstruct and form new questioning approaches that help to understand the relationship between language and power (Baxter, 2003). Which feminist perspective is a question to be posed. I have chosen to draw upon a feminist approach that is united in a commitment to challenge inequality and firmly embedded in the principle that the *Personal is the Political*. Feminist social work as an approach covers a range of identities and debates. Over the years feminist social workers have argued for an approach that places relationships at the centre of a dialogue that explores different ways of *interpreting meaning* in the lives of women (White, 2006). As a feminist my position is about challenging the accepted and transgressing limits set on and around me and I will call upon feminist writers such as Helene Cixous (1998) to help us deconstruct the words and language used by Akua. The narrative will be used as a strategy to help us tune in to words and language that when constructed can *lead elsewhere than the place we were expecting them to* (Cixous, 1998, p xiii), encouraging you to make live your values and engage in deeper learning about your positioning in the debates about anti-racist social work practice. It may be helpful to demonstrate the partnerships using the following diagram

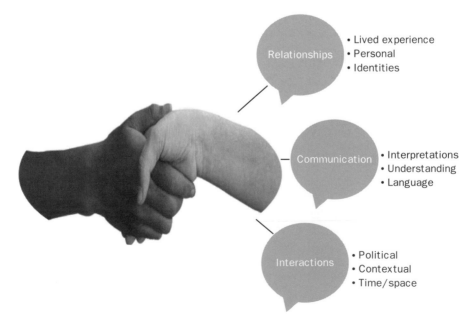

Relationships
• Lived experience
• Personal
• Identities

Communication
• Interpretations
• Understanding
• Language

Interactions
• Political
• Contextual
• Time/space

Studying the realities of relationships, communication and interactions from Akua's experience

AKUA'S NARRATIVE

I appear in this narrative in my role as a social work student in my second year. I have called myself Akua, a name that is meaningful but very distinct from my birth name. I am a Black African woman who has chosen social work as a professional career for all the reasons linked to my own life experience of wanting to help people and make a difference. In my second year a placement in Children's Services had been identified. I met with Jane the Practice Teacher in an introductory meeting. This first meeting appeared to go well. Jane explained the role and responsibilities of the team and welcomed me to the service. At this meeting Jane and I shared with each other our aims, expectations and what we both wanted to gain from this experience. I felt it important to share my experience as a child living in Austria and experiencing racism from school teachers and other children. I explained to Jane how this had impacted on my education and how I believed I had achieved despite this racist experience. Jane is a white woman and I shared this experience as a way of demonstrating that I wanted to learn and would work hard.

CRITICAL QUESTIONS

Refer to the partnership frame to aid critical thinking. How do you interpret what Akua told her practice teacher about her childhood experience? Did you question why Akua shared this experience with her practice teacher? What factors can you identify in the narrative that you think may shape how Akua is perceived by the white practice teacher? What do you think Akua's experience of racism was and how do you think this shaped her approach in this context?

In this narrative there are a range of interpretations set within the context and identities of those involved. If we focus on the different professional identities of the student and the practice teacher a common thread is the context of this relationship set within the activity that is social work. Expectations of social workers to meet academic and professional standards are charged with the demands of a profession that has seen a range of reforms and transformations aimed at ensuring that the profession of social work is better understood by the public and that social workers do not fail in their professional duties of protecting the most vulnerable in society. Change in social work education and practice has been rapid – a response fuelled by a media outcry that social workers needed to do better. This has seen the nature of social work become procedure driven in highly regulated systems constructed to eliminate error and that are preoccupied with assessment of service users, staff and students (Lonne *et al.*, 2009).

The world of the social work student is one of being assessed against standards and regulations within this context. If this was not enough for students, there is the added complexity of professional social work values and how these are made explicit, understood and assessed. The role of values in the context of social work practice and education has been contested. Clifford and Burke (2009) argue that values can mean anything to anyone depending on the human position. Values will be fluid, set within a time, a context, a faith, an experience and social interactions. They will also be open to interpretation and yet within social work there appears to be a view that values are *universally accepted and agreed* (p 51). It is helpful to remind ourselves about the social work values that underpin the profession and those that many students will have encountered. The National Occupational Standards (TOPPS, 2002) values and ethics for social work place the focus on the organisational context in which social work is practised, setting out practice standards under Key Roles – what is expected of the student, for example Key Role 1: *Prepare for, and work with individuals, families, carers, groups and communities to assess their needs and circumstances*. They also set out specific ethical expectations: that social workers must:

- respect;

- empower;

- be honest;

- challenge.

In the new regulatory landscape of the HCPC and PCF the above principles continue to be adopted. For example:

HCPC	PCF
Recognise that relationships with service users and carers should be based on *respect* and *honesty*.	Demonstrate *respectful* partnership work with service users and carers, eliciting and *respecting* their needs and views and promoting their participation in decision-making wherever possible.

(TCSW, 2012).

How each student navigates what has been referred to as the 'value maze' within social work is a challenge for the individual and those who have to assess a student's value base. What needs to be underlined is that social work values are based on the premise that those who join the profession do so because they are committed to bringing about change. Some do this from a political position of social justice and others from a helping, therapeutic position (Wilson *et al.*, 2008, p 75). Whatever position you adopt will come from within and be influenced by your lived experience, and may include your fears, prejudices, assumptions and attitudes about others. Consider the next narrative by the practice teacher:

PRACTICE TEACHER NARRATIVE

I am a new practice teacher, a young woman and a manager in Children's Services. I will refer to myself as Jane, a second name that I am rarely known by. I have been a qualified social worker for six years and in my current role I manage a busy intake team responsible for responding to referrals of concern about children and young people. As part of my post qualifying education I was enrolled on the module Enabling Others. As part of the learning I agreed to be 'matched' to a second year social work student. When Akua arrived I was in an emergency meeting. When we met Akua appeared anxious about being on placement in a statutory intake team. She told me that she was a little nervous but eager to learn. I could understand that she was nervous but when she told me about her childhood experiences of racism I also became nervous. I could not understand why she had raised this now. I questioned her reasons for doing so and felt that she had already made assumptions about me. I now felt cautious and unsure about how to develop a relationship with Akua.

CRITICAL QUESTIONS

What is your interpretation of Jane's caution and uncertainty? What links can you make to the context in which this event has taken place? Can you 'tune in' to the fears expressed by Jane? What assumptions did you make about Jane's description of herself?

Student in context: the impact of culture

The student experience of navigating a way through the placement successfully is fraught with challenges, with advice to students about how to survive their placement and ensure that the work they do is visible (Lomax *et al.,* 2010) being a demonstration of the language that is used to describe the context of this experience. The survival discourse can set a tone that emphasises a competency approach of completing and gathering hard evidence. It also alludes to the power imbalance that exists in the student/practice teacher relationship that is based on passing or failing. The pass/fail element is a powerful discourse that is often at the forefront of the student/practice teacher relationship. Behaviours and anxieties become amplified as the student and practice teacher negotiate relationships that are inextricably linked to a successful outcome that is driven by that scarce resource of time (Bryson, 2007). In this high spin cycle of expectations for student and practice teacher it can be hard to ensure that the learning experience is evenly distributed. It can feel from the beginning that the race is on and in the pressure to meet assessment and competency deadlines those soft elements associated with nurturing an honest relationship, developing open communication that shape our interactions with each other, become lost in the pressure of time. The impact of this on learning is that the *realm of necessity* takes over and all interactions are reduced to the minimum rather than expanded through critical inquiry and reflection (Bryson, 2007, p 36).

For Akua and Jane barriers were being constructed based on the binaries of black/white, student/practice teacher and pass/fail. Doors for understanding each other were closing. The language of setting tasks and deadlines became important and assessments became judgemental, based on assumptions about 'the other'. Both Akua and Jane found themselves not really knowing where this situation was taking them. As Cixous (1998) suggests, neither of them took the time to go outside and turn around to see the *face on* their *own door* (p 81). Read the following narrative and then consider the critical questions:

AKUA

I arrived at the placement and Jane had set aside time to make plans and organise dates and times for supervision. In this first meeting Jane told me again about the work that the team do. Jane told me how important the team are within Children's Services. She said that the duty team are responsible for receiving and acting upon concerns expressed about children. I wanted to reassure her that I was keen to learn and although I did not have experience of child protection or assessing risk I would draw upon my previous placement learning experience within adult services. Jane told me that this was a gap in my knowledge and in a busy duty team one that I would need to address. Jane said that I could join a group of other students that had been set up to offer 'peer' support to talk about assessment processes. I did attend this group but had to leave early because I do not drive and had to catch a bus home. I explained this to the group members who said they understood. Jane was aware that I did not drive and under the 6 ½ hours, which is the placement requirement, I agreed to make the time up. I was feeling more anxious about the placement. I was trying very hard but did not feel able to speak out so I remained silent. When I was with Jane and trying to learn from the case studies I did not feel confident enough to say what I really believed. I do understand the factors in child abuse and I tried to explain my thoughts about the child with bruising to her face. I felt that Jane was always disapproving or testing me. There were communication problems and I tried to explain that it was nothing to with my culture and that I would find questioning parents about their parenting style challenging. I felt that Jane had misunderstood what I was trying to say. Jane appeared tense all the time. I know she was very busy.

CRITICAL QUESTIONS

What do you think was happening to Akua? What factors do you think were having an impact on her relationship with Jane? What barriers do you think Akua was facing? How do you think Akua was perceived by Jane? Do you think assumptions were being made about Akua?

JANE

I was concerned when Akua told me that she had no experience of child protection or assessing risk. I knew this but wondered why she was telling me this now at such an early stage of the placement. I told Akua about the student peer support group and said that she would gain a lot of learning from attending this group. For now I wanted to ensure that we made time to go through childcare legislation and then using some case studies to talk about risk. Akua appeared enthusiastic and I was pleased to hear this. When we next met in supervision I had identified a range of cases for us to discuss. Akua appeared confused during this meeting about the role of social workers and said how difficult she believed it was to challenge parents about their care of their children. I became very anxious when she failed to understand the significance of bruising to a small child's face. I felt that Akua needed more help and support than I had first understood. I was very concerned when I heard that she had left the support group early and questioned her commitment to the placement and the learning. I set up more opportunities for her to work with social workers taking referrals and inputting the data into the Integrated Children's System. I spent time explaining legislation and what was expected of her. Other members of staff came to me saying that they were concerned that Akua was not able to communicate clearly on the telephone. During supervision I asked Akua about her work and we went through a recent referral that she had taken. I was concerned by the lack of accuracy in the work. I knew this family from previous referrals and Akua had got the children's names wrong. I did not know what to do and felt that I had to go back to the beginning with Akua. I felt there were cultural, communication problems and I was picking up a lack of commitment. Akua clearly did not fully understand the importance of getting referrals right. I gave Akua some work to do with clear instructions and asked her to repeat the instructions back to me. I was becoming increasingly worried about what work I could give Akua.

CRITICAL QUESTIONS

Do you think Jane held a neutral position in this context? Are there underlying assumptions held in this narrative? Do you think that there was an *insidious culture* being imposed on Akua that was regarded by *others as good or better* (Ryde, 2009, p 40)? What tensions in this relationship can you identify?

In both narratives you will have identified a range of factors that are having an impact on the relationship between Akua and Jane. Both narratives are filled with and will stir a range of emotions for the reader. Speer (2005) suggests that such emotions will have a power dimension linked to the role of identity. Both women appear caught up in their identities of black social work student and white practice teacher. For Jane this will bring with it contradictions. As a white woman who will have experienced sexism she may not be able to acknowledge her white privileged identity. She is working in a pressured environment and the concerns she has about Akua have raised emotions that are now *framing the issues and setting an agenda* (Todd and Abrams, 2011, p 354). The issues are set within an emotive and emotional context and the tensions are being expressed punitively. Jane sounds almost exasperated with Akua's performance and is possibly anxious about how this may reflect on her. Jane is now seeing Akua in her culture of 'third world other', interpreting her behaviour and communication through a racialised lens that she may be unaware of (Calliste and Sefa Dei, 2000). There are a range of oppressions evident in the two narratives that are impacting on both women's positions and lives. Akua has named her lived experience of racism and this has led to a response from Jane that is lacking in an awareness of her own white identity and the responsibilities that lie within this position.

Identities – Jane and me: living in a world of whiteness

In the practice teacher narrative Jane has not mentioned her whiteness when I have explicitly stated in the title of this chapter that I am a white woman listening. Some readers may view this as a statement of intent or a mixture of academic trickery that borders on the pretentious and/or arrogant (Ryde, 2009). Whatever the response the expression of whiteness or the mention of culture creates a range of emotions and deliberations for white people. White identity is complex. White people either do not see the importance of identifying their whiteness, demonstrating a lack of racial awareness of their dominant and privileged position (Frankenberg, 1993), or they retreat behind a 'no-culture' strategy based on guilt and defensiveness referred to as the 'not me, not now, not here' approach (Todd and Abrams, 2011). Both are positions of denial. The moment that transformed the hidden for me came through a process of realisation that led to a sense of belonging. By naming my whiteness I could no longer remain blind to the implications of the power that was held within my own whiteness. Ryde (2009) refers to this process as beginning to see beyond the nothingness of whiteness to a position of acceptance and understanding about privilege. Being involved in listening and talking to Akua and reading reports from Jane there was an awakening of a critical consciousness that began to ask questions of the white women involved – me and Jane.

1.   *Was Jane's approach to Akua intentionally racist and personal or had she behaved unconsciously, replicating the principles of the organisation?*

2.   *Had I failed to recognise the significance of 'race' in Akua's experience and had this led to me not seeing what was going on in the placement?*

I looked at the experience of Akua through a range of identities and within a context of representations and relationships (Calliste and Sefa Dei, 2000). I connected with the placement setting and I could understand the levels of anxiety presented by Jane in managing a team of social workers responsible for carrying out inquiries into allegations and claims of child abuse. This was a previous identity for me and I understood the challenges and the pressure. In my new identity I now had responsibilities for social work education and the student experience. I had not 'looked' at the experience from Akua's position. I was concerned that I had hidden behind these identities, failing to explore the significance of racism and the impact this was having on Akua. When I met and talked with Akua she told me about her childhood, her journey to England and her desire to become a social worker. Akua talked about the racism she had experienced and her family. She talked about how her father had supported her to go to university and become a social worker and to face the challenges of being a black woman in a white world. She also talked about the pressures of being a student in an environment that she described as full of stress. Akua talked about how Jane was always busy having to attend meetings, respond to staff and other agencies and how she did not want to add to these pressures. When Akua talked about her placement experience she appeared to choose her words and language carefully. She also presented as being reasonable and understanding about the position Jane had taken, which was to express considerable concern about Akua being 'safe to practise'. However, the weariness in her voice and eyes told me something different. hooks (2009) refers to this as *White People Fatigue Syndrome* (p 105). Akua was responding to her situation by trying to understand Jane through the range of identities and locations that kept shifting but were interconnected – practice teacher, manager, white woman – assessor, observer, provider of opportunities, opposite, powerful. She was also trying to make sense of her own situation, which was precarious because she knew how racism worked. How we gain an understanding about the workings of racism can begin through those smaller and more intimate interactions through the use of empathy. However, the use of empathy needs to go beyond the discourses of blaming and guilt through a process of exposure to *oppressed people's lives* and the ownership of whiteness and privilege (Abrams and Gibson, 2007).

The process of knowing and owning my 'whiteness' was the result of my relationship and interactions with Akua and Jane. Exploring and studying Jane's whiteness through her report and understanding how 'race' had happened in this event by listening and talking with Akua led to an understanding about how the different cultural and racial relations had been shaped by the invisibleness of whiteness (Calliste and Sefa Dei, 2000). By not owning my white position and privilege I had placed myself outside of being able to see the insidious presence of racism in the placement experience of Akua. Lorde (1984) reminds us that it is not always the differences of race that separate us but the refusal to acknowledge explicitly those differences and to examine *the distortions which result from our misnaming them and their effects on human behaviour and expectations* (p 115). Jane was already suspicious and fearful of Akua's black identity and although she may not have set out to be intentionally harmful to Akua she built barriers to her own learning and understanding that became insurmountable. The result was that someone was going to fail in this experience. This was Akua, who was assessed as not safe to practise. However, the failure was that of me and Jane to be conscious about our whiteness and the relative power located in this space and position.

Research carried out in 2005–06 by the University of the West of England, Bristol, into what it means to be white in Britain identified the range of white identities and how whiteness in Britain is articulated through class, with the notion of 'race' linked to minorities. This research also highlighted that one of the effects of living in a position of power for white people is that they deny that race has anything to do with the way in which they live their lives (Garner, 2007). In this situation I believe that Jane acknowledged that Akua was a black woman – she saw and knew the difference. For Jane this evoked feelings of fear and suspicion. Her dilemma was that if she identified the difference was she being racist or was she trapped in seeing Akua as the 'racialised' other rather than an individual – fearful of the collective denouncement of her as a practice teacher and unable to overcome her own history and institutionalised structures of oppression (Garner, 2007). My position was that I did and didn't see the difference. I saw Akua as different and I believed my anti-racist positioning of intent was enough. What I was not clear about nor did I consider was *whiteness in all its many layers in society* (Abrams and Gibson, 2007) and my structural position in relation to Akua as a student and Jane as a practice teacher.

The role of institutionalised racism that had been pervading this experience had gone unnoticed by me as I focussed on the individual intent of Akua and Jane. I had focussed on Jane, questioning her position and intent about anti-racism. I had then focussed on Akua as a failing student and the 'evidence' produced to support this. I had in the words of Calliste and Sefa Dei (2000) sought to know and manage the situation as an academic through knowledge of Akua as the 'third world other' – someone who needed to be known and managed underpinned by the norms of good and bad. These criteria were dictating the behaviour through a lens that was looking and doing white that did not take note of the structures or the way in which power was being used. How the social construction of whiteness is used to explore and understand racism is not new within the social sciences (Garner, 2007). However, within social work education and practice the use of white identity and white privilege as a tool for exploring anti-racism in the UK is relatively new (Abrams and Gibson, 2007). Todd and Abrams (2011) in their research with white students undertaking counselling programmes in the United States used a model of 'White Dialectics' to explore white privilege, colour blindness and minimisation of racism and how this framework was used to support a better understanding by white students about their white identity that increased learning and knowledge about racism.

Using whiteness in anti-racist social work education

I believed that I had unpacked my whiteness and privilege years ago, fully understanding my role as a social worker and now academic in challenging racism (Abrams and Gibson, 2007). However, as McIntosh (2009) suggests, academics in the seeing and not seeing do so as a way of self-preservation in a way of situating themselves in a position that says – 'I can analyse but not be analysed back' (p xiii). My eventual analysis of myself as a white woman through the experience of Akua has awakened in me a further desire to revisit those positions I have adopted – a white woman feminist who firmly positions herself in the *Personal is Political*. As a feminist I can connect with this statement as a political position of intent. It is also a way of seeking to achieve the 'ideal self', exploring what the personal is through those narratives that define me. It can be used to seek an understanding of the human position that helps us understand that not everyone has equal power in this creation of the self (Cixous, 2008). The unpacking of my whiteness led to a better understanding of the role of white privilege in the student life of Akua and how this had been used to situate her in a world that was already interpreted for her – a black woman who posed a problem to the white institution and the white practice teacher. How we move from the position of not seeing, not knowing and not understanding that produces fear and suspicion of each other will call for a positional shift in anti-racist social work education. hooks (2009) argues that a way of deconstructing racism is through the *disassociation of whiteness with terror in the black imagination* (p 105) that supports critical thinking and reflection that does not include guilt and denial.

How white theoretical approaches and frameworks are used to ensure that whiteness is made visible within social work education is a step that needs to be taken. Exploring anti-racism through a white privilege lens that adds to the debates and also ensures that social workers are equipped to recognise racism will take a range of tools and commitment from academics, practice teachers and the profession that is social work. There are cautionary approaches to mention before moving on. While Garner (2007) suggests that a way forward is to use whiteness as a tool for analysing racism within the power paradigms of white identities, Greenhalgh-Spencer (2008) argues that the white position is one of accessory and inequality and therefore a potentially binding script that many white people will be unable to step away from. Either because they want to remain invested in a structure that maintains white privilege, or stepping away means having to locate themselves in a different dialogue that betrays their white identities leaving them unconnected (Garner, 2007). While hooks (2009) makes a range of suggestions about how white people engage with the anti-racist debate, she calls upon writers such as Gayatri Spivak (1999) to suggest that one way of re-positioning racism is for those in positions of white privilege to live in the *subject position of the other* (p 105). However, my position refers back to that of Cixous (2008) drawing upon the construction of 'self', that before being able understand the experience of racism we need to deconstruct those narratives that have socially constructed white culture and identity. We need to ask those questions about whether the narratives have been formed on *real and verifiable events* (p 34) and look closely at how these 'truths' have been used to construct and interpret each other and ourselves. I would argue, like Lorde (1984), that we need to look deep inside our white identity to look closely at ourselves in order that the silence and invisibility is transformed in a *language of action* (p 40).

CRITICAL QUESTIONS

Who are you? Have you taken an anti-racist position that is cultural or political? Do you believe your position can be fluid? Using the partnership frame look closely at who you are and ask yourself the following questions:

- **What is your lived experience?**

- **How has this made a difference to you personally?**

- **How would you describe your identity?**

- **How do others describe you?**

- **What is your understanding of others' interpretation of you?**

- **What language do you use to describe yourself?**

- **What language do others use to describe you?**

- **Do you think you are political as a result of your experience and identity?**

- **How would you describe the context of your lived experience?**

- **Is your description defined by time and space? For example your childhood?**

Conclusion: the personal is political

Talking and listening to Akua was an important moment in time for me personally and for the social work programme. Reading the reports from Jane, I was concerned about the final analysis of Akua as a student who was considered 'unsafe', how this decision had been reached and the role of the university throughout the placement learning process. The multi-construction of boundaries through the process of seeing each other as opposites and the other produced the binary effect of black/white, good/bad, order/disorder and ultimately pass/fail. The role of power in this interaction was held by Jane. However, while Jane was aware of her power to pass or fail Akua I do not believe that she was fully aware of her white identity and the power inherent in this. She focussed on the problematic aspects of the placement learning opportunity and saw the problems belonging to Akua and not to her or the institution (Abrams and Gibson, 2007). The role of the university as a powerful white institution was not acknowledged through a colour-blind approach that failed to recognise institutional inequality and oppression ultimately colluding in the racist experience of Akua. The response by me and the programme team was to critically evaluate our role as a group of social work educators responsible for providing anti-oppressive and anti-discriminatory education. The challenge was to emerge from this experience with a commitment to collectively move out of the shadows in a way that addresses racism. The immediate need was to ensure that Akua did not suffer further; the outcome of the report was overturned and Akua continued and progressed to graduation. This decision opened up a new dialogue inside and outside of the university that has not been without tensions and anxieties. This was seen in the programme team when it became clear that within the social work curriculum at the University of Northampton there was a lack of consistency, specificity and focus about which frameworks to use when teaching about anti-oppression, anti-discrimination and anti-racism. There was a general belief that anti-oppressive, anti-discriminatory and anti-racism teaching was integrated in the curriculum, with some tutors feeling more confident than others about their knowledge and understanding. However, this belief was unsupported by the student experience, with black students talking about feeling safer with some tutors when the issue of racism was debated, white students saying that they felt 'got at' and some practice teachers saying that the university was overly zealous about racism, saying this supported segregation.

Helping student social workers to engage in the debates about anti-oppressive, anti-discriminatory and anti-racist practice in a way that helps them to connect with all forms of prejudice is the purpose of this chapter and an objective for the future of social work education. If we are to challenge students, tutors and practice teachers to move out of polemic positioning to a place that supports professional development in a world of social work where they will not be neutral or their decision-making will not be value-free needs to be done through the self. In this chapter I have referred to the self as a starting point for tuning into those values that define who we are. I believe this is the start of the learning and unlearning process that produces an understanding about all areas of oppression and discrimination through the political and or cultural lived experience – a practice that Flax (2010) refers to as *transforming both our understanding of and our ways of doing subjectivity, values, beliefs, power and politics* (p 129).

In my dialogue with Akua the role of whiteness and white privilege emerged as an important addition to the teaching and learning in the social work education. Through my internal dialogue I offer a contribution to the debate about how social work education can develop student learning and understanding about racism that helps to move beyond the slogan of the Personal is Political to using this statement as a framework of intent and action. Adopting a framework that places the focus on the personal will support white students and tutors to engage in the process of moving towards a self-understanding as a white person who is structurally constructed through white privilege and how this is communicated through language and behaviour. In this process there will be the opportunity for students and tutors to reflect on those wider social, structural and political influences that underpin oppression, discrimination and racism. Through this framework an understanding of the importance of race through a colour consciousness and a close and *personal and political* engagement with racism will evolve (Abrams and Gibson, 2007).

There is an acknowledgement within social work education that the language, theory and frameworks to teach and assess the knowledge and understanding of students about anti-oppressive, anti-discriminatory and anti-racist practice need to be reviewed (Boyce *et al.*, 2008). To ensure that there is more than one white woman listening, Carby (1987) argues for *concepts that allow for specificity* in anti-racist education (p 51) that support learning and understanding in safe environments that promote the self and identity. Key themes emerging in this chapter support the literature on anti-oppressive, anti-discriminatory and anti-racist social work education. They are concepts of:

*   self-identity;
*   whiteness;
*   racism;
*   oppression;
*   discrimination;
*   inequality.

Students undertaking a social work degree, who will be assessed against academic and professional regulatory standards, need to be reassured that those teaching them are comfortable in their own self-identity and secure in their knowledge and understanding of anti-oppressive, anti-discriminatory and anti-racist practice. There will be tensions in getting the checks and balances right. Ensuring that the dialogues, narratives and language support a new learning and understanding without exhausting black students, allowing white students to hide behind guilt and/or focussing attention on whiteness that perpetuates white privilege (Todd and Abrams, 2011) are just a few. There will also be resistance and controversy along the way and tutors and students need to prepare for this, ready to step out of the comfortable into the uncomfortable (hooks, 1994). The aim in this approach is to bring about change in social work education and practice, through the process of knowing oneself and reflecting upon oneself, that starts an internal dialogue that eventually leads to students daring to speak out. Cixous (2008) reminds us that this will be difficult as *students may speak poorly, with embarrassment, say things they shouldn't say or with tremendous reserve; it will happen and something will break loose* (p 64) and, as I have said to students from this experience, they will never be the same again – they will be different.

How social work educators join students in this dynamic process will be a key to the future of a service provision that is anti-racist, anti-oppressive and anti-discriminatory, filled with intent and actions that firmly adopt a stand against racism and fully engage in the wider struggle against all inequalities, oppressions and discriminations.

Where to next?

In this chapter I have identified key moments of learning that have added to the knowledge base about anti-oppression, anti-discrimination and anti-racism. I have drawn upon a wide range of writers with the aim of presenting different ways of thinking. These have been accompanied by critical questions aimed at helping you to engage in an internal dialogue that will be ongoing. As you begin to find the answer to one question you will be faced with another. Such is the nature of learning about the self. The question 'Where to next?' posed as a heading may be seen as a suggestion to look outwards. However, a central theme of this chapter is the need to look inwards to the self first. Learning about the self is I believe one of the biggest critical questions posed to challenge you. This may be something that is new to you and will take time and consideration. This is a journey of exploration and preparation for the work that you will do as a social worker and will be ongoing. Using the partnership frame will help you to begin the journey and help you develop your interpretation and understanding about what the statement the *Personal is Political* means for you.

Finding your position will also be important and in this chapter the role of feminism is the personal and political driving force. You will need to find your own position and platform from which to develop your critical thinking and questioning. The way forward begins with two basic steps to develop your intent and action:

1.   Begin the critical questioning of the self to understand what your intentions will become.

2.   Find a critical position to support turning your intentions into actions.

In all good social work you may want to critically reflect and review the self and your position. You will change and your position may change. Nawal El Saadawi, the Egyptian feminist, lawyer, doctor and teacher who has spoken out about and written about women's experiences of oppression in Egypt, has challenged governments and religions. For her intent and actions she has suffered imprisonment, exile and death threats. She has spoken of becoming more radical as she has grown older and from her lived experience says, *If I went back I would do it all again. That is what I have learned from my experiences, that I was on the right track* (Khaleeli, 2010, p 362). You now need to find out what track you want to be on.

6 Critical Race Theory and exploring 'whiteness'

PAUL CROFTS

Chapter aims

This chapter will take you on a journey into 'whiteness', a key concept providing a greater understanding of how racism is understood, especially by white students. It is a journey that is, at one level, personal, but at another level provides a basic map of the system of privileges, assumptions and perceptions behind *whiteness* that can evolve for a white person; and how it can influence the choices made in navigating the complexities of the terrain that it inhabits.

CRITICAL QUESTIONS TO BE ADDRESSED

* How might an exploration of Critical Race Theory (CRT) assist us to better understand *whiteness* and racism, particularly within the context of social work?

* Can CRT provide a structure or framework for taking ownership of racism by professionals that informs both understanding and practice?

  We will explore some of CRT's theoretical concepts and examine changes in attitudes and public policy from the 1980s to the present day, particularly in the context of meeting the diverse and specific needs of black and ethnic minority elders.

* Is there a need to promote positive images of white anti-racism activists and role models who take a stand in opposing racism alongside black people – either as professional colleagues or as service users? How might this support white anti-racist professionals working with and alongside black colleagues and service users in a complex, contradictory and challenging world?

* We will, in particular, draw upon work from the United States (Thompson *et al.*, 2003).

The term *black* will be used in the same way as the term *white*: as generic terms that in essence capture the *socially constructed* nature of race, racism and racial inequality. They are not terms that describe a distinct and unchanging culture or ethnicity of individuals, although people may be happy to describe themselves using these terms. However, occasionally the term *Black and Minorities Ethnic* (BME) will be used to signal when a more nuanced approach to the issue being discussed may be necessary.

Defining 'whiteness'

The word *white* has already been repeatedly used within this chapter, which is unusual, since it is a term that white people hardly use about themselves in everyday conversation. The word is virtually invisible and so is the social construction of the world that whiteness defines and acts within. However, the opposite, blackness, is often seen and spoken of. White people do not see their own colour and don't see race as socially constructed, but as natural, fixed and obvious. As a consequence, both historically and currently, this enables racism to continue, evolve and survive. The *problem* has always been defined with reference to *the other* (the minority black group); whilst the real problem, racism arising out of whiteness (the majority group), is ignored or not spoken of.

There is no shortage of literature where the lives of Black and Minority Ethnic (BME) communities are minutely examined and made into a problem. In 1903 the US black scholar and activist W.E.B. Du Bois in his book *The Souls of Black Folk* challenged white society with a question and reply: *How does it feel to be a problem*? *I answer seldom a word* (Du Bois, 1903, p 2). Is it not time for the unspoken to become the focus of attention and the world of *whiteness* to become explicit?

This chapter is written for white people and white social work students in particular. This is deliberate. This does not mean that black students are not involved in this discourse – far from it – but that the understanding of racism and its consequences can only be achieved by re-focussing attention onto the causes, rather than simply documenting the effects on those whom racism directly impacts by way of creating and perpetuating racial inequalities. Similar positions have been taken in respect of the role of men in opposing the sexual oppression of women:

men are the primary agents maintaining and supporting sexism and sexist oppression; they can only be eradicated if men are compelled to assume responsibility for transforming their consciousness and the consciousness of society as a whole. (bell hooks, 2000, p 83)

For white people it is very important we fully acknowledge that without our black critics, friends, colleagues, communities and historic black 'heroes' of resistance and civil rights/anti-racist struggles we would be floundering around. I fully acknowledge that without this help, support, friendship and guidance over the years the understanding of my whiteness would, *at best*, be limited and incomplete. This has taken a great deal of learning and reflecting.

Until I was in my mid twenties I had no knowledge of the long history and presence of black people in Britain. I assumed (incorrectly of course) that the current presence of black people in Britain mainly dated from the Second World War. It was not until the 1970s that I heard about the black presence in Britain dating back at least to Roman times (Duffield, 1981) and about the black nurse during the Crimean War who was a contemporary of Florence Nightingale: Mary Seacole (Alexander and Dewjee, 1984).

The often overlooked historic contribution of black people to the development of British history raises questions about the teaching of history in schools, the wider culture of British society and a sense of who we are as a people/nation. Such alternative readings of history challenge assumptions of white dominance and supremacy and also give black people a presence and, more importantly, a humanity that is often denied.

At least since the period of European colonial expansion, the institution of slavery and the exploitation of 'them', white researchers have been observing, documenting, photographing and measuring black people and their communities. This has always been on white people's terms and interests. Is it therefore not appropriate that a kind of *ethnography of whiteness* is explored that is informed by a black critique that white people can build upon and self-examine in an attempt to develop a greater understanding of racism? (Jackson, 1998).

This is not to deny agency to black people, or to marginalise them in the study of whiteness, but to ensure that white people take responsibility for whiteness and the consequences for black people, informed by what has been described as a 'black perspective'. For racism to be abolished whiteness needs to be acknowledged and understood as part of diversity and the power inherent in its invisibility.

CRITICAL QUESTIONS

Can you name any black *'heroes'* who have influenced your thinking about issues of race, racism or human rights?

Can you name any white *'heroes'* who have influenced your thinking about issues of race, racism or civil rights?

Is there a difference in the size of the lists? Why might that be?

Is the idea of an individualised 'hero' useful, or potentially misleading, when it comes to challenging racism? What roles do individuals play as part of collective endeavours in challenging injustice?

Introducing Critical Race Theory

Critical Race Theory (CRT) originated in the United States in the 1970s within the law faculties of some universities as a radical left movement of black academics and activists who started to think differently about how race and racism were being dealt with by both traditional liberal and more conservative thinkers, who had been involved in Critical Legal Studies. It challenged perceived liberal notions that the American civil rights movement had been a success and that there was linear or onward progress towards racial equality. CRT also raised concerns about how racism operated and was understood in relation to white power structures.

The leading US founder of CRT was Professor Derrick Bell of Harvard Law School, who wrote the deliberately provocative science-fiction work *The Chronicle of the Space Traders*, a story where aliens from outer space offer three gifts to the United States government (gold, cheap/ clean power and clean air) in exchange for handing over all the black people to an unknown fate. Bell summarises the message of the story:

Ever present, always lurking in the shadows of current events, is the real possibility that an unexpected coincidence of events at some point in the future – like those that occurred in the past – will persuade whites to reach a consensus that a major benefit to the nation requires an ultimate sacrifice of black rights – or lives. (Bell, 1992, p 13)

Bell's chronicle has been described as *a classic Jeremiad – a tale aimed at making a powerful group aware of its own iniquitous history and potential for more of the same. It aims at kindling conscience and jarring complacency* (Delgado and Stefancic, 1991, p 324).

CRT has sometimes been described as a rather pessimistic or depressing theory, and sometimes it can seem so as it does not present a rosy, liberal, easy, linear or comfortable view of progress in pursuit of racial equality. It also does not underestimate the resistance of white people to voluntarily give up their relative racial privilege and power. However, CRT can also be seen as liberating and providing hope in the realisation that the continued existence of racism is not a result of failures by anti-racists and racism can be defeated and overcome by collective endeavour. I have found CRT gives me a perspective on understanding racism that is both intellectually challenging, offers explanations of a complex phenomena and a theory for action, change and eventual liberation – both for white and black people.

An overview of some of the key themes of CRT has helpfully been supplied by Professor David Gillborn (Gillborn, 2008, p 40). Some of these will be considered in more detail later in this chapter.

Critical Race Theory: a conceptual map

Key themes

- *Racism as endemic*: racism as so extensive that it is normal (in the sense that it is often found – not normal in any moral or evaluative sense), not aberrant nor rare; 'race' is viewed as socially constructed and constantly changing.

- *Critique of liberalism*: views claims of neutrality, objectivity, colour-blindness and meritocracy as camouflages; formal equal opportunities laws as too limited in scope.

- *Revisionist critique of civil right laws*: identifying the limits of progress to date and the means by which apparent advances have been clawed back.

- *Call to context*: challenges ahistoricism and emphasises the importance of experiential knowledge.

Continuing debates

- *Intersectionality*: CRT recognises the importance of other areas of oppression (such as class, gender, sexuality, disability) but scholars are still working through possible ways of incorporating each successfully.

- *Essentialism and anti-essentialism*: there is ongoing debate about levels of group-identification/abstraction that are appropriate for different analytic and political purposes.

- *Action, optimism and despair*: detractors misread CRT as lacking hope. In fact a central feature of CRT is dedication to social action to bring about change, but CRT sees this as hard won and victories insecure.

Critical Race Theory: racism is endemic – white supremacy

The term *white supremacy* has been used by CRT to refer to an overall system of white *privilege* (racism) that is endemic, where the benefits accrue to white people whether they like it or not and irrespective of their intentions, desires or even actual knowledge of what is happening. Such privileges are the result of the normal way that a dominantly white society reproduces itself. Such privileges can often be banal and day to day, and thereby mainly go unrecognised or unseen by white people.

I became aware of just one of these 'hidden' benefits for myself when I went on holiday abroad for the first time in the mid-1970s. On my return I entered the 'British Passport' queue at immigration. I observed that every single white person in the queue was speedily dealt with by the immigration officer and waved through, yet nearly every single black person (albeit with the same passport and identical citizenship rights) was subject to more rigorous questioning and delay.

Racial profiling of black people by the police, store detectives, immigration officers, ticket inspectors, etc., is something that I suspect most white people are completely unaware of as we suffer no detriment – indeed it is a hidden benefit we enjoy as we go about our daily lives *without let or hindrance* (as is written in our passports). Not so for most black people! (Sveinsson, 2010).

I have come to see White privilege as an invisible package of unearned assets that I can count on cashing in each day, but about which I was 'meant' to remain oblivious. White privilege is like an invisible weightless knapsack of special provisions, assurances, tools, maps, codebooks, passports, visas, clothes, compass, emergency gear and blank checks (cheques). (McIntosh, 1989)

Also at the heart of CRT's understanding of white privilege is the concept of *institutional racism*, a term that was first used by the 1960s Black Power activists Stokely Carmichael and Charles Hamilton (Carmichael and Hamilton, 1967), but became widely used and recognised as a term in the UK from the 1990s:

[Institutional racism] ... can be seen or detected in processes, attitudes, and behaviour, which amount to discrimination through unwitting prejudice, ignorance, thoughtlessness, and racist stereotyping, which disadvantages minority ethnic people. (Macpherson, 1999, 6.34)

The notion that the actions of individuals and processes within the institutions and organisations of society which are 'unwitting' or based on 'ignorance' or 'thoughtlessness' can result in systematic racial inequalities and injustices is a powerful explanatory factor in why change is slow and uneven. If the very nature of how racism ('white superiority') is maintained and transmitted over time is invisible and unseen by most white people and white-dominated institutions, then is it really surprising that so little seemingly changes over time?

For those who are committed to change, this understanding offered by CRT points to multiple levels of intervention – at the level of the individual (micro) and the institutional/societal (macro) – and an appreciation that change may be difficult to achieve, particularly at the macro level. It also means that those of us who work at the micro level, as social workers or community advocates/campaigners, may begin to appreciate that fundamentally changing the life-chances or circumstances of those we work with will be difficult and challenging, as the wider racialised constraints are too endemic with powerful vested interests in maintaining the status quo. Nevertheless we can still make a real difference to the lives of those with whom we work on a day-by-day basis, particularly if we engage in collective action to challenge the injustices we come up against.

We can support and encourage critical engagement with these barriers to change and explore them together – with our clients/service users, our professional colleagues, community groups and organisation – how we might go round, under or over them. Together we can explore the pervasive but invisible assumptions, priorities, practices and policies maintaining racial inequality and injustice. In this way we firstly reject passive and 'unwitting' collusion or acquiescence with white superiority (racism), and secondly move on to empower both black and white people to challenge such systems of continued injustice.

CRITICAL QUESTIONS

Can you list up to ten ways in which white service users may be relatively privileged vis-à-vis black service users in similar situations? Try to list both those white privileges based around individuals and those that might relate to policies and practices within the institutional social work context.

Try the same exercise for white *social workers* vis-à-vis black and BME *social workers*.

A journey into exploring 'WHITENESS'

The journey about to be described is the author's own, which is not necessarily unique, but the routes followed are personal and so at times the first person will be used. My journey is a story, but it is not a simple straightforward narrative and it is certainly not completed.

Story-telling can be an important means of reflecting on how the world works; how our experiences, observations of others and the wider influences on what we do can be approached in a critical but non-threatening way. This is highly appropriate for the social work student, who will be well versed in reflective writing during practice learning experiences and analytical thinking throughout their studies. Similarly, story-telling has always been important for people who have experienced racism or injustice, keeping alive the history of struggles, maintaining communities and family life that are often undermined by dominant cultures and ideologies.

Writing a story (sometimes called a chronicle) is an important part of the methodology of CRT – using fictional and/or biographical scenarios set around real events as the material for the narrative and asking searching and sometimes difficult questions.

CRT scholars are not making up stories – they are constructing narratives out of the historical, socio-cultural and political realities of their lives and those people of colour. The job of the chronicle is to give readers a context of understanding the way inequity manifests in policy, practice and peoples' experiences. (Ladson-Billing, 2006, p xi)

The story within this chapter is not about the *black experience* but rather a *journey into an understanding of my whiteness*, whilst using a methodology common to CRT to document the experience of a white person (me, the chapter author) becoming critically aware of whiteness.

MY FIRST 15 YEARS

For the early years of my life my whiteness was invisible but I absorbed its influences. Children inhabit a world of socialisation in which they learn the *rules of the game* of life from the adults they encounter at home or school, the media they absorb or the groups they participate in (church, youth groups). As a white male I inhabited a world that never acknowledged its whiteness nor its patriarchy. I never encountered any abuse or hostility, discrimination or prejudice based on the colour of my skin. I slowly *learnt the rules of the game*, but was unaware how these were fixed in my (racialised) favour (see 'The Rules of Social Standing' in Bell, 1992, Chapter 6).

Attending school with only white students, with no black friends or family, I had no reference point as a child to understand whiteness until adolescence when I recognised racism in simplistic and abstract terms. Media reporting of Apartheid in South Africa and the Civil Rights movement in the United States confirmed that racism was not something about me in the here and now – it was something elsewhere, still largely invisible.

This all changed around 1968 when two Asian students joined my school class. I was 15 years old. It became apparent that they were different from *us*. They arrived in our class in the morning with torn shirts, grass and mud stains on their trousers and spittle running down the sleeves of their blazers and in their hair. There were sometimes blood and bruises on their faces: I was now introduced sharply and unexpectedly to *their* world and how it intersected with that of the white world that I was unaware of, but they were only too aware of.

They spoke of attacks that took place on the way to and from school and the verbal racist abuse hurled at them. Whilst not understanding the complexity of the hostility, as young people we knew the difference between *right* and *wrong*. As white classmates we had a choice, either to stand against these injustices or ignore them, knowing that the Asian students had no choice.

Racial attacks on black people are an extreme form of racism and the tip of a large racist iceberg; but most racism remains invisible beneath the surface and is not as crude or as obvious. When challenging racism as a white person it is important to acknowledge that a decision has been taken against racism and a human injustice. For many, the chance to *take a stand* against racism may be lost and may never be taken again. This is not a criticism per se, but an acknowledgement that white supremacy will continue if the overwhelming majority of white people remain silent and collude with it and in doing so there will be a continuing failure to recognise their own whiteness.

This notion of *taking sides* (Blair, 2004) is central to my story, because it is difficult and has costs attached to it. It is also the case that when taking sides and standing up for something we are also challenging our own preconceived and unquestioned worldview. Our internal voice is probably shouting *don't get involved*, remain a bystander, but another voice must be allowed to speak as well – to get involved and take a stand. The psychology of bystander behaviour is well documented and researched (Latene and Darley, 1970).

Implications for social work practice

These challenges will be a common feature of professional life as a social worker, particularly one who is committed to social justice and advocacy. This commitment *to challenge* injustice, and not remain a bystander, is also formally recognised as part of the Standards of Proficiencies for social workers issued by the Health and Care Professions Council (HCPC) who now regulate the profession:

6. be able to practise in a non-discriminatory manner

6.1 be able to work with others to promote social justice, equality and inclusion

*6.2 be able to use practice **to challenge** and address the impact of discrimination, disadvantage and oppression* (HCPC, 2012, emphasis added)

This is also echoed in the Professional Capabilities Framework (PCF) for social workers, with particular reference to:

DIVERSITY – Recognise diversity and apply anti-discriminatory and anti-oppressive principles in practice.

*Social workers understand that diversity characterises and shapes human experience and is critical to the formation of identity. Diversity is multi-dimensional and includes race, disability, class, economic status, age, sexuality, gender and transgender, faith and belief. Social workers appreciate that, as a consequence of difference, a person's life experience may include oppression, marginalisation and alienation as well as privilege, power and acclaim, and are able **to challenge** appropriately.*

RIGHTS, JUSTICE AND ECONOMIC WELLBEING – Advance human rights and promote social justice and economic wellbeing,

*Social workers recognise the fundamental principles of human rights and equality, and that these are protected in national and international law, conventions and policies. They ensure these principles **underpin their practice**. Social workers understand the importance of using and contributing to case law and applying these rights in their own practice. They understand the effects of oppression, discrimination and poverty.* (CoSW, 2012, emphasis added)

WHY?

One of first questions that my personal journey raised was '*Why?*'. Why was it that some pupils at my school decided to attack a group of Asian pupils (in the UK and at my school) and why was it that the authorities themselves only reluctantly recognised a problem? With hindsight the context in which these attacks occurred became more apparent and helped develop further understanding. The debates around the arrival of Asian communities sparked a wave of hostility to immigration and there was the political growth of the (then) National Front in local elections (Crewe, 1975). This was also the period when Enoch Powell made his infamous 'Rivers of Blood' speech (Powell, 1969) in which he predicted race wars and the domination of black people over white people as a result of the recently introduced legislation to outlaw race discrimination and the growth in the black population overtaking that of whites.

During the local elections in 1970 I was privileged to attend the count where the first Asian councillor was elected to Leicester City Council. Immediately after the announcement of his success the hall erupted with racist chants and shouting from the small but vocal National Front contingent. They also spat at the new councillor, who had to be protected from assault by the police. The hatred on the faces of those National Front members is something I will never forget.

It soon became apparent that the localised hatred that I had come across at school and the election count was linked to the national debates on black immigration from the Caribbean, East Africa, India, Pakistan and Bangladesh at that time; but they also continue to this day albeit in new circumstances and with new or revised groups to hate, despise, marginalise and discriminate against.

CRITICAL QUESTIONS

Can you recall situations in your life where a decision had to be made between standing up for what was right or remaining quiet? Can you think of an example of each choice made: doing something or remaining quiet? What were the consequences of each choice made both for you and others?

Understanding changes in social policy

The overt racial hatred displayed against my black school friends was an important, albeit painful, episode in my personal development and growing understanding of racism, but it was only *a start*. But for many white people who acknowledge or observe such personalised hostility their understanding and learning about racism *stops* at this point. We see such racism as nasty, visible and evil and this is how we come to see and define 'racism' – it's located in the actions of individuals who are ignorant or prejudiced. People who are *not quite like us*, who we can show disdain for, or even go as far as labelling them as another set of people not quite like us. We might even call them 'Chavs' as part of a wider demonising process of sections of working people who may also be discriminated against or marginalised in other ways (Jones, 2012). This is the visible racism that us white liberals see and can take comfort from challenging (as it should be).

But this is not the *real* racism that operates at the institutional or societal level, where the most pernicious and damaging forms of racial inequality are caused by structural and entrenched institutional indifference, which continues to remain invisible and thereby protected from recognition, scrutiny, challenge and action to address it.

The continuing controversies around immigration to the UK and the nature of the debates generated continue to this day and can act as a barometer of changes in overt racial hostility, through the passing of laws to restrict immigration and citizenship rights and debates around what it is exactly to be 'British' or public policy on 'community cohesion'. Behind all these issues stands the concept of white (British/English) privilege. Who is 'us' and who is 'them'.

Those who wished to advance white privilege based on overt racial hostility and discrimination were becoming increasingly marginalised during the 1970s and into the early 1980s. Had they continued or become more dominant they would have had serious destabilising effects within a society that was increasingly multiracial, with settled black and ethnic minority communities who were gradually asserting their rights as full British citizens to live with dignity and respect. The reality of British society as multiracial was slowly being recognised and starting to be celebrated; there was a growing consensus that racial discrimination was wrong and racial equality should be promoted.

Notions of racial superiority, based on overt racial hostility, segregation, apartheid and denial of human rights, were in direct conflict with a new international order of emerging independent, post-colonial countries and their growing economic and political strength.

White privilege was changing and making concessions in the face of a growing assertiveness nationally and internationally by black people and their organisations, but at the same time redefining itself and finding new means by which that same privilege might continue or be re-enforced albeit in new forms after a period of retreat. For CRT this ability for white supremacy to evolve reflects 'interest convergence', which will be looked at later in the chapter.

Two significant events also had profound effect on the nature of racial discourses in the UK during this period and acted as further imperatives for white supremacy to evolve in order to protect itself. Firstly, the major upheavals in inner city areas across the UK (Southall, Brixton and Liverpool) in 1981, which culminated in the Scarman Report (Scarman, 1982); the second was the murder of black teenager Stephen Lawrence in 1993 and the subsequent Macpherson Report (Macpherson, 1999). The effect of these incidents and subsequent official reports on them also contributed to the changes in the way race and racism was discussed.

For a brief period from the 1980s until the end of the twentieth century racial equality was on the agenda and there was a growth of anti-racism, multiracialism and support for race equality and black and ethnic minority community organisations. Progress appeared to be being made, albeit change was always slow and always contested.

CASE STUDY: SERVICES FOR BLACK COMMUNITY ELDERLY

Prior to the mid-1980s there was little discussion by professionals in social care areas on meeting the needs of black communities. Services were offered on a 'colour-blind' basis: predicated on a dominant white society. It was assumed service take-up would occur on an equitable basis simply because it was offered 'without discrimination'. But the reality belied these seemingly egalitarian and liberal assumptions.

Research (unpublished and now unfortunately unavailable) I conducted in the early 1980s into services for BME elders compared with white elderly in the area where I worked showed:

*   few were in residential care facilities;

*   few attended lunch-club or day-centres;

*   few received care at home, support or meals-on-wheels;

*   the absolute number and proportion of BME elderly would be rising considerably within the local community over the next 10–15 years as a result of the age demographics of the black community, but there was no evidence that public authorities were planning for these changes.

When these issues were raised with the relevant authorities with a view to engendering policy solutions to the inequalities identified, the responses ranged from:

*   BME do not need such services as they are cared for by their own families;

*   the current services are open to all therefore if they are not being used it is reflection of 'their' choices;

*   outright hostility, indignation and anger – how dare 'you' (the Racial Equality Council and black community organisations) challenge the democratically decided policies of the council(s) and advance narrow and sectarian interests ('isn't this apartheid?'; 'isn't this discriminating against white people?', 'this is racism', 'services are provided for all – we don't discriminate');

*   they are perhaps not using the facilities or taking up services because they will not 'fit-in' or be accepted.

At least the later explanation had the benefit of an awareness of diversity and prejudice but failed to see the logic of a solution to the 'problem': the need to change the nature of the service and to challenge the attitudes of those who currently used the services, planned them or ran them. But in reality there was little recognition of even a problem to address – the fact that BME elderly citizens were not accessing or using a considerable layer of social/housing/community services was seen as unproblematic.

The other reactions were based on un-evidenced and un-tested white assumptions and overt hostility.

This all began to change during the late 1980s and into the 1990s. Public authorities were increasingly challenged by a growing and articulate black community and their organisations (and a growing number of aware white professionals) who were asking questions such as:

- Why are we paying our taxes (local and national) for services that our community is not receiving on an equitable and fair basis?

- Why are our elderly effectively excluded from services that are available to white elderly?

- Why are the services provided not appropriate to the needs of elderly people from within our communities (for appropriate activities, food, language and cultural sensitivity)?

- Why are you assuming 'we' can or will care for 'our' elderly without public support?

Members of the black communities were also increasingly engaging with the political processes and getting elected as local and national politicians where these questions were being asked. Legal challenges under anti-discrimination law were being considered. Slowly, and not without opposition from many quarters, service providers began to change what they did.

In the area I was working, funding was found for new day-centres catering for the specific needs of both Asian and Afro-Caribbean elders, and an Elderly Asian Housing Association was founded that also worked closely with the local Afro-Caribbean Association to plan for a separate scheme for Afro-Caribbean elders. Campaigns were launched demanding that local political leaders and chief officers in both the county and borough councils met with community groups and listened to their needs. Legal advice was sought by the Racial Equality Council to potentially challenge the inequitable funding arrangements between meeting the needs of BME community elderly and funding provision for the (de facto) white elderly. Such a combination of challenges resulted in a shift in resources towards more equitable outcomes and a wider range of diverse services.

On the surface the changes in public policy during the 1980s and 1990s as illustrated, with progressive shifts in attitudes, policies and practices, appeared genuine and permanent. Such an assumption of slow but persistent improvements in racial attitudes, policies and practices is at the heart of a liberal approach to 'race relations', and one that I subscribed to at the time. But as we moved into the twenty-first century all the gains that were seemingly being made during this previous period started to unravel.

It could be argued that we are now leaping back in time to the 1960s and 1970s as a result of:

- The re-emergence of new colour-blind approaches wrapped up in the language of 'equality' in the area of social policy. Previous concern about meeting the specific and diverse needs of black communities and reducing or eliminating racial inequality are now criticised as being *politically correct* and a symptom of a *failure of multiculturalism* leading to a *divided and 'segregated' society* (Pilkington, 2012).

- A new assertive patriotic *Britishness* that challenges multiculturalism and seeks to assimilate black communities (Runnymede Trust, 2012) into a redefined citizenship (see as an example: Sandbrook, 2012) or increasing fears and Islamaphobia (Hitchins, 2012).

- Continuing populist hostility to immigration; further tightening of immigration controls.

- A weakening of the Equality Act 2010 and the significantly reduced effectiveness of the Equality and Human Rights Commission to perform its functions of: promoting equality, stopping discrimination and supporting victims of discrimination; all in the guise of reducing 'red-tape' and supporting businesses during difficult economic times (EDF, 2012).

- The withdrawal of funding to anti-racist groups, human rights advocates, advice agencies and black community groups – many of which may close completely as a consequence (eg some Equality Councils and Welfare Rights Groups). Across the UK there is a similar pattern of cuts to the voluntary sector disproportionately impacting against black communities (BARAC, 2012; REF, 2012).

CRITICAL QUESTION

How might CRT help to explain changes in policy and attitudes to 'race' between the 1960s/1970s, the 1980s/1990s and the early part of the twenty-first century?

Critical Race Theory (CRT): interest convergence

The concept of Interest Convergence is credited to one of the founders of CRT, Derrick Bell, and suggests that legal victories or changes in the law or government policies that advance the interests of black groups only really occur when racism has become excessive and/or exposes the contradiction between what society says about itself (free, democratic, equal) and the reality (overt racist practices, belief and significant racial inequalities). In essence, short-term changes are made that are necessary to serve and protect the long-term interests of white people as their authority is being challenged at both national and international levels. Bell states: *White elites will tolerate or encourage racial advances for blacks only when such advances also promote white self-interest* (quoted from Gillborn, 2008, p 32; Bell, 1980).

CASE STUDY: INTEREST CONVERGENCE AND THE BREAKTHROUGH OF BLACK PLAYERS INTO PROFESSIONAL FOOTBALL

By way of an exemplar, I wish to use the case of Ron Atkinson, who was manager of West Bromwich Albion between 1978 and 1981. Despite his relatively successful managerial career, Atkinson is most infamous for using the 'N word' when talking about Chelsea's black French defender, Marcel Desailly, during a television match commentary in 2004. While he believed that he was off-air, the broadcast was still going out live to viewers in the Middle East. My point, however, refers more to the subsequent reaction than to the incident itself. Atkinson, with a number of players he had managed (many of whom were black), stated that it was purely an aberration and out of character: put simply, he was 'not a racist'.

The significant factor that was recurrently cited in these mitigations was that Atkinson had been one of the first managers to regularly pick black players: namely Brendan Batson, Laurie Cunningham and Cyrille Regis. However this, and the selection of black players at other clubs, was not a deliberate anti-racist gesture, nor was it designed to promote minority ethnic inclusion in the game. These players were picked simply because they were all brilliant footballers. **The interest of black communities in gaining a foothold in the professional game converged with that of an average-performing, white-run football club that took full advantage of talented black footballers.**

(From Hylton *et al.*, 2011, p 53, emphasis added)

Critical Race Theory (CRT): contradiction closing cases

A CRT concept closely related to *Interest Convergence* is that of *Contradiction-closing Cases*. These are cases, such as the murder of Stephen Lawrence and the subsequent prolonged and difficult campaign for justice by his family (in the UK) or segregation (in the deep South of the United States) and the death of Dr Martin Luther King, where a racial injustice has been exposed so that it is *impossible* for white people to ignore without a serious threat to their credibility. However, CRT suggests that any changes made are of little significance for the advancement of equality *in the long term*, and as soon as possible after the event has ceased to be visible in the public imagination, there are policy reversals.

The election of Barak Obama as US president may also represent a contradiction-closing case. CRT may suggest that such cases can provide an opportunity for white elites to demonstrate that racism is no longer an issue. Justifications such as *if we can elect a black man as president then racism must have been solved* can be used to deny the continuation of racism and thereby close down further discussion, debate and action. Evidence from the United States suggests that since Obama's election as president racial inequality has not only worsened but policies are increasing being pursued that discriminate against black people or other ethnic groups (Kaiser *et al.*, 2009; Kochhar *et al.*, 2011; Stainback and Tomaskovic-Devey, 2012).

In the UK, the advances made following the Macpherson Report are now being rolled back. There is now growing evidence that levels of racial inequality in the UK are widening again and may return to previously unheard of levels: with white superiority and advantage being re-established after a short period of relative advance in racial equality.

Themes within CRT and changes in social policy

Period	Interest convergence [divergence]	Contradiction-closing [opening] cases	Changes in law, policy or practice
Pre-1970s	Rise in the number and relative size of black communities in the UK. Civil rights movement in the United States and growth of similar campaigns for racial equality in the UK (eg Campaign Against Racial Discrimination) exposes contradiction between ideology of equality and reality of racism and inequality. British colonialism being dismantled with newly independent countries.	1965 and 1968 Race Relations Acts	Encourages 'assimilation' of black people into white society. Colour-blind service provision that serves the needs of white society and effectively excludes black people, but under the cloak of 'equality' and non-discrimination. 'Race' is largely invisible not important.
1970s to early 1980s	Continuing civil rights struggles. Southall disturbances (1979) Brixton/Liverpool 'riots' (1981) Rise of policies to promote 'integration' (but combined with tough and racist immigration controls to restrict non-white immigration). Slow recognition of racial discrimination and the need for public policy to promote equality of opportunity.	Immigration Act 1971 (HMSO, 1971) Race Relations Act 1976 (HMSO, 1976) Scarman Report (Scarman, 1982) Swann Report (HMSO, 1985)	Growing black community confidence and political organisation and campaigning. New equality law. Legal action increasingly used or threatened. Rise of anti-racism, multiracialism/culturalism. Growing awareness of the effect of racism and requirement to meet black community's needs and to provide services on a more equitable basis based on evidence of inequality.
Late 1980s to twenty-first century	In response to murder of Stephen Lawrence, anti-racism gains some degree of credibility and moves more into the policy centre-stage. Recognition of 'institutional racism' and the legal policy response of new public sector duties to consider the needs of racial groups.	Macpherson inquiry and report into the death of Stephen Lawrence. (Macpherson, 1999) Race Relations (Amendment) Act 2000 (HMSO, 2000)	Changes in equality legislation that required public sector organisations to examine services to ensure non-discrimination and to have 'due regard' to promote equality (public sector equality duty).

Period	Interest convergence [divergence]	Contradiction-closing [opening] cases	Changes in law, policy or practice
2000 to 2012	Attacks by Al-Qaeda on twin-towers in New York (2001) and other attacks subsequently in London and elsewhere around the world. Rise of 'war against terror' and Islamaphobia as a new, additional, form of white superiority and creation of a new (non-white) 'other'. Riots following BNP provocation in Oldham in 2001 but blamed on Muslims.	Cantle Report into Oldham riots (Cantle, 2001). Attacks on a new 'segregation' caused by multiculturalism and liberal policies of equality. New Equality Act 2010 (HMSO, 2010), which *theoretically* is an advance on previous anti-discrimination legislation, but subsequently watered down; parts of the legislation are either not enacted or repealed.	Rise of new strategic initiatives of 'community cohesion'; attacks on multiculturalism, 'segregation' and 'political correctness'. Re-emergence of assimilationist and colour-blind policies hidden within ideological about 'equality for all' by providing generic services. Emergence of alleged white communities who are 'victims' of discrimination. Evidence of racial inequality growing in both new and old forms.

CRT and intersectionality

Thus far this chapter has focussed on the issues of racism and whiteness to ensure that these concepts remain central. However, our social world is not constructed in simply black/white divides. CRT fully acknowledges this complexity but remains focussed on racism as an important area of study and analysis in its own right. CRT has sometimes been criticised for being 'race' focused at the expense of other forms of oppression, particularly social class.

This overall criticism of CRT has been addressed as follows:

Although the word 'race' is in its title, CRT involves more than an unswerving focus on race and racism ... Critical race theorists often focus on how racism works with, against and through additional areas of differentiation including class, gender, sexuality and disability ... the multitude and changing interrelationships between racism and other axes of oppression is a complex area. (Gillborn, 2008, p 36)

CRT would also defend and support those who wish to study the specific nature of these other forms of oppression (who may have similar criticism made of them) and would wish to co-operate and share information and ideas that may be helpful.

A further danger of such arguments around intersectionality is that it simply becomes a way of ignoring complexity, which objectively ensures that relations of (white) power and privilege remain protected from scrutiny in their specific context, now and historically. For others, intersectionality may also be a way of deflecting discussion from consideration of racism to some other form of oppression, rather than having to deal with the complexity of looking at all areas of oppression equally and/or assessing the extent to which different forms of oppression operate in complex ways in different contexts and on different groups. For the less scrupulous (such as the populist media and politicians), such tactics can also be used quite deliberately to set one group of oppressed people against another or to develop notions of a hierarchy of oppressions.

Intersectionality can also be formally acknowledged and listed by policy-makers, but they then ignore or reduce it to a simple tokenistic tick-box exercise. we have done equalities now – let's move on to the real thing! (Troyna, 1994).

CRT is also a highly politicised theory in that it is engaged in the world (in order to change it) rather than just being about the world. At its core it is anti-racist; but most, if not all, its adherents are also aware of and against all other forms of oppression as well. It is through active *engagement* in the world, in challenging and overcoming such oppressions, that intersectionality becomes real, in *the absence of that chimerical entity, a unifying theory of race, class, gender oppression* (Mills, 1997, p 137).

CRT has also welcomed the development of other forms of 'Crit' thinking that have emerged from CRT in response to the diversity of the term 'race' to include other ethnicities and oppressed groups (eg LatCrit – Critical Latino Studies, Queer-Lit – looking at sexuality and Critical Race Feminism), as well as engaging in dialogue with Marxists around social class (Gillborn, 2008, pp 26 and 37–8). CRT is therefore a continuing and developing theory, which is not 'closed' or dogmatic and is constantly informed by activists who are confronting different forms of oppression on a daily basis.

CASE STUDY

Your service user is a 70-year-old man of black (Caribbean) origin. He lives alone in a large three-bedroom house and is of declining health with growing mobility difficulties. You are asked to undertake a social work assessment of his needs.

Identify the issues you may need to consider with him in relation to:

* his family circumstances and other forms of informal support; access to community services;

* access to care at home services;

* his financial situation; his current and future housing needs.

Identify those issues/barriers that may relate to his 'race' at an individual level *and* at a policy/practice level within the social work department or that of other agencies. How might these barriers be overcome?

What are the areas of intersectionality that you will need to examine? How might these complexities be 'resolved' to create 'win–win' outcomes? How might they possibly conflict?

Promoting white anti-racism role models

At the beginning this chapter you were invited to list white *heroes* who have influenced your thinking about issues of race, racism or human rights. Did you struggle to name any? At the start of my journey I would have had a similar difficulty, but after more than 30 years' involvement in the anti-racist movement this is less difficult, although still not easy. We don't have the white equivalents of Rosa Parks, Martin Luther King, Malcolm X, Nelson Mandela or Gandhi.

But, consider conquistador Bartolomé de las Casas who, in a trial held in 1542, argued that the native South Americans were full human beings and should not be enslaved: *All the peoples of the world are men, and there is only one definition of each and every man, and that he is rational* (quoted from Thompson, 2003, p xvii). Las Casas also challenged the prevailing treatment of the local people: *What we committed in the Indies stands out among the most unpardonable offenses committed against God and mankind, and this trade as one of the most unjust, evil, and cruel amongst them* (p xvi). At a time when the peoples of South America had no voices of their own Las Casas spoke out. He was white, Spanish and himself a conquistador. He didn't have to. He had a choice, but he did it anyway.

During the US civil war another white person spoke up, took action and died for racial justice. He has been immortalised in the famous song 'John Brown's body lies a mouldering in the grave'. But did you know he was white? – for most of my early life I thought he was black! John Brown was an anti-slavery campaigner who led a raid on an armoury intending to arm local slaves in revolt. After his capture he was put on trial for murder and encouraging slave insurrection. He was sentenced to death and hanged on 2 December 1859. At his sentencing hearing it is reported that he said:

If it is deemed necessary that I should forfeit my life for the furtherance of the ends of justice, and mingle my blood further with the blood of my children and with the blood of millions in this slave country whose rights are disregarded by wicked, cruel, and unjust enactments – I submit; so let it be done. (Brown, 1859)

In his book *American Negro Slave Revolts*, Herbert Aptheker challenged the prevailing notions that black slaves were essentially passive under slavery– but he also demonstrated that in most slave revolts white sympathisers, supporters and helpers were involved, many of them who, like John Brown, were killed alongside their black colleagues (Aptheker, 1993). Their names, unfortunately, are largely unknown.

This is not an argument that these white heroes should in any way replace or diminish black heroes – far from it, we need both. However, it interesting that even in their deaths in the struggle for racial justice white superiority (in its invisibleness) ensured that those white people who opposed it should also largely remain invisible.

Black people need black 'heroes' to counter the years of racism and white supremacy. It provides black pride and confidence and reasserts black people as part of humanity's rich pattern: through history, culture and the contributions to society that are so often ignored. Could white people also benefit from reading about the anti-racism of other white people? Would this help us – in conversation with our black colleague – navigate the journey into the world of whiteness we inhabit and demonstrate the possibilities of a future that can be different, without racism and racial inequality?

I came across an American publication, *White Men Challenging Racism* (Thompson *et al.,* 2003). The authors describe the reasons for the book as follows:

We wanted to break the isolation we sometimes feel when we speak up and act against racism and inspire and speak to others to stand up and act against racism. We wanted to find White men who could be mentors and teachers and supporters in our journey and others' journeys. We wanted to learn how other White men conceptualise and go about the task of challenging racism and then share that information so that others can benefit. There were so many questions we had. (Thompson et al., 2003, p xxxiii)

I found reading the stories of the white men in this book inspiring. They came from all walks of life, were motivated by religious conviction and humanist beliefs; they were policeman, historians, journalists, community activists, trade unionists, actors. What they shared in common was their whiteness and a commitment to racial justice and for standing up for what is right.

One contributor in particular – Bill Johnston – in many respects mirrored my own growing awareness of my whiteness and the need to do something about racism and get involved:

[I see] I was the victim, I was the bystander and I was the perpetrator ... we were extremely poor. The derogatory terms used to describe blacks, to describe Italians, to describe Jews – I heard them every day.

He subsequently became a police officer, as had been expected within his family, and he entered a new police family and joined the Tactical Control Force. The difficulty of challenging colleagues who were part of this new family, as his awareness of injustices grows, is fully acknowledged. But he nonetheless develops the courage to speak out within the police against racism, homophobia, and how women are treated in domestic violence situations.

*I remember the language they used to talk about the blacks. I realised that the department – and I – could make them less than me, less than human. And basically, we could do whatever we wanted to. There were times when my stomach told me, 'something is really wrong here. I mean really, really wrong'. But I didn't have the courage to stand up to my brother officers when they were using that language. In fact, I didn't have the courage for **me** not to not use that language. If you want to be part of the club, you use that language.*

... Am I a bad guy? No, I'm doing what the community wants, although I admit it's the community in power. I am also doing what my department wants. You have to realize we haven't even admitted we have a race problem ...

I guess dealing with families is what changed it for me. I remember one time going to see a family after an incident ... when all of a sudden eighteen windows are taken out ... And I stood there paralysed, not knowing what to do ... I think it was at that moment, when I looked in that guy's eyes and saw his fear and desperation, I understood ... What was stolen from that family was their dignity. The police department still classifies incidents like this as 'shattered windows'. They're looking at the wrong thing. It's not shattered windows. It's shattered families.

There was nothing he could do to protect his family ... his family was carrying the reason for their victimization around with them all the time: the color of their skin.

Finally, Bill talks about the necessity to challenge injustices and the price that he might have to pay for failing to do so:

I have a vision that when we come to the Pearly Gates, we're going to find out that God is everything that we're not. If God made us all, then he is all of us. At my moment of death, the God who comes to judge me will be young, gay, Jewish, African-American. And she is going to say, 'How the hell did you treat me?'

Ultimately I think that's the only sin that will keep you out of heaven.

(all quotes from Thompson *et al.*, 2003, pp 187–93, emphasis in original).

In Bill's discourse on intersectionalities (of race, sexuality and gender) they become at least partially resolved not at some theoretical level but *in the day-to-day specifics of challenging injustices as they manifest themselves*. Bill negotiated the complexities, took sides and had the courage to do so.

The nature of racism and white supremacy presents a social construction that sets 'black' against 'white'. Racism does this – it sets people apart. It therefore tries to close down opportunities to challenge racism across radicalised divides. *White Men Challenging Racism* presents another possibility – that black and white can throw away their constructed colours and work together for racial justice. It can provide opportunities for alliances and co-operation *in practice* – at work, professionally, in our local communities and in wider political arenas. If we want to build a non-racial, equal, society in the future we need to develop the skills and vision to see that it can work in the here and now. Ultimately white superiority depends on keeping black and white people apart and reproducing racialised inequality.

As a white social work student reading this book I hope you will be motivated to start a similar journey to myself, which is similar to many other white people's as well, as we become engaged with anti-racism and working for social justice.

If you are a black student, I hope you will also have found this chapter interesting and useful; if you come across racial or other injustices, whether involving yourself, your family, community or service users, I hope you will seek out and find black *and* white colleagues to join with you in challenging it, so that your and their journeys become shared. There's nothing like companions on a hard road, in difficult times, to share the load and provide comfort and sustenance.

Taking things further

After reading a chapter of a book like this you (particularly if you are white) may be left with a feeling of '*what do I do next?*'. I hope the following summary of some of the key intended learning points may be helpful.

- *Become self-aware of racism and other injustices around you*. If you are white, take ownership of your 'whiteness'. Do not be fearful of making this whiteness, and the power that underpins it, explicit. Talk about it, read about it, discuss it with other white colleagues and friends, observe it, challenge it.

- *Don't be a bystander* when you see injustice – make a stand and challenge; or at least ask questions.

- *Build into your professional practice an overt anti-racist, anti-oppressive practice stance.*

- *Empower and enable black service users* to have a voice. Ensure assessments and social work reports reflect the service user's voice and story.

- *Listen to the views of black colleagues and support them* if they raise issues about racism. So often their views can be dismissed or marginalised. Be aware that as a consequence you too may not be heard (you may even become 'black', in the socially constructed sense, and begin to experience the marginalisation as well).

- *Be ready to be challenged*, especially by black anti-racists: you will have to acknowledge mistakes and accept that there are things you do not know.

- *Identify and work with other white colleagues* who are committed to anti-oppressive practice, in collaboration with black colleagues.

- *Ask questions about diversity and racial equality*. Does the policy or practice within the organisation you are working *explicitly* take race equality into account? How?

- *What statistical, or other data, is available on who is using (or not using) the services the organisation you are working for is providing?* Is there quantitative evidence of over- or under-representation? If there is no data, how will anyone know if the service is accessible and available to all on an equitable basis?

- As a rule of thumb, which has served me well, you will *usually* find *over-representation* of black people in 'services' or areas that are punitive or negative (eg stop and search statistics, admission to secure mental health wards or other secure institutions, school exclusions, poor quality housing, poorly paid jobs with few prospects) and *under-representation* when services or areas are welcome, good, helpful and there is a degree of choice between different quality of provision (mental health counselling, quality day-care provision for the elderly, foster carers, admission to nursery and childcare provision, quality public housing, well paid jobs with career prospects). I always hoped that the rule of thumb did not work, but it rarely fails – and if it does fail I always asked why this was.

- *Can Critical Race Theory assist you in 'making sense' of white superiority and power* and in furthering understanding on how long-lasting social change may be difficult to achieve? Some victories may need defending almost as soon as they have been won. Be aware of the power of white elites to protect or re-establish their privileges in new ways and to redefine their privilege in ways that can sometimes be deceptive and might even use the language of equality.

Seek out or read about white role models and mentors who may be able to offer guidance and support.

CRT writers and researchers and recommended further reading

Powerful advocates for CRT in the United States include Kimberle Crenshaw, Richard Delgardo, Jean Stefancic, Adam Freeman, Angela Harris, Charles Lawrence, Mari Matsuda and Patricia Williams. Two good general introductions to CRT (but written with a clear focus on the United States) are:

Critical Race Theory: An Introduction (Delgado and Stefancic, 2001) and

Critical Race Theory: The Key Writings that Formed the Movement (Crenshaw *et al.,* 1995).

Leading authorities in the UK include:

- David Gillborn, Professor of Critical Race Studies at Birmingham University, has written extensively on racism and education. See *Racism and Education: Coincidence or Conspiracy* (Gillborn, 2008).

- Kevin Hylton, Professor of Social Sciences in Sport, Leisure and PE, Leeds Metropolitan University. See: *'Race' and Sport: Critical Race Theory* (Hylton, 2008).

- John Preston, Senior Lecturer in Citizenship and Education at the University of East London. See *Whiteness and Class in Education* (Preston, 2007).

For a general exposition of CRT, which draws together most of the key writers on CRT in the UK and activist(s)/scholars working internationally, as well as others relatively new or critical of CRT, see: *Atlantic Crossings: International Dialogues on Critical Race Theory* (Hylton *et al.,* 2011).

7 View from the workplace: practitioners speak out

CHARITY CHUKWUEMEKA

Chapter aims

This chapter will provide a reflective account of the intricacies around *blackness* and anti-racism in contemporary social work practice. It will explore a practitioner's personal understanding of the concept of anti-racist practice from the perspective of being black in a predominantly white social work setting. The effectiveness of current social work education about anti-racism will also be examined and some suggestions for future developments will be offered.

CRITICAL QUESTION TO BE ADDRESSED

To what extent does anti-racism feature in the contemporary social work agenda and what are the implications for education and practice?

Introduction

Anti-racist practice remains a highly contested topic that currently sits uncomfortably with the social work agenda. It is seen as *a perennial problem for the social work profession* (Heron, 2006, p 2) and one that has been subject to a weakening of its development as well as a loss of commitment to the wider issues of oppression in social work generally (Graham, 2007). Since the emergence of anti-racist social work in the 1980s and the expectation that it should form an integral aspect of social work education, some anti-racist writers have consistently questioned the meaning and place of anti-racism in the social work agenda (Dominelli, 1988, 2008; Singh, 2002; Turney, 1996; Graham, 2007; Thompson, 2006). Whilst the attempts to promote anti-racist practice in social work have been recently revisited, it is still unclear how anti-racist practice can be achieved in social work education and practice settings (Fook, 2002; Ferguson, 2008; Dominelli, 2008; Singh, 2006; Graham, 2007; Heron, 2006).

An exploration of the history of anti-racism in social work education can be found in Chapter 2 and this chapter will therefore explore the complexities around anti-racism and blackness in social work practice (Dominelli, 2008; Singh, 2002, 2006, Graham, 2007). This will be achieved by looking at the lived experience of black social workers in predominantly white social work settings and in respect to working relationships with colleagues, service users and other professionals as mandated by agencies' policies. The chapter will conclude by examining the relevance of anti-racist social work practice and suggestions for development regarding social work education.

Definition of key concepts

The key concepts discussed in this chapter are not new and have been defined differently by anti-racist authors. However, it will be useful to reflect on the meaning of racism, anti-racism and blackness in order to effectively communicate the author's message to the reader.

Racism and racial discrimination

The terms racism and racial discrimination are often used interchangeably but hold distinctive legal meanings (Heron, 2006). Racism is believed to be an ideology or practice through demonstrated power or perceived superiority of one group over others by reasons of race, colour, ethnicity or cultural heritage (Graham, 2007). Racial discrimination on the other hand is defined as a criminal act if proven. Anti-racist writers continuously acknowledge and recognise that racism within social work practice operates at the individual, cultural and institutional levels (Thompson, 2006; Dominelli, 2008).

Anti-racism/anti-racist practice

An anti-racist perspective offers a much more radical interpretation of discrimination within society and originated as a means to combat oppression experienced by Black Minority Ethnic (BME) people in the late 1970s and early 1980s (Penketh, 2000; Bonnett, 2000). It provides an understanding of how racism, oppression and discrimination impact on black people. Turney (1996) described anti-racist practice as a powerful and crusading attack on the whole edifice of white social work – the bureaucracy, the legal framework, the practice found at all levels as well as the education and training.

Blackness/black perspectives

The term blackness emerged in the 1970s, when many black professionals sought a common understanding. The word 'black' emerged as a unifying, collective term used to describe BME people united against racism and committed to challenging the behaviour and attitudes of racist individuals and institutions (Dominelli, 1988). 'Black' as a political colour provided a solution for some people; it simplified diversity and difference for others (Dominelli, 1997) and led to the development of Black Studies. Turney (1996) remarked that black perspectives in social work were seen as essential for both black and white workers to function effectively within a multi-ethnic society.

Authorial identity

It is essential to affirm who I am so as to give you an insight into my journey so far. I will do this from my perspective as a social work student, founder member of Padare student support group at the University of Northampton (see Chapter 4 for more about Padare) and now as a qualified and practising social worker. I believe this reflects the narrative of many black social workers in England who have been exposed to disabling experiences as a result of their ethnicity, race or colour.

As a black (African) social work student in a predominantly white institution of learning, I was somewhat conscious of my difference. Not only was I different in respect to my skin colour and accent, but also in respect to the different approaches to discussions and assessments, which can be attributed to my background and cultural orientation. Professor Stuart Hall once expressed that *the capacity to live with difference is in my view, the coming question of the twenty first century* (Hall, 1993, p 358). I often pondered on what he meant by this as being different in a society other than that of one's origin is a fact of life and did not need to come from any preconceived notions or perceptions. I knew that I was different and, as Britain was a culturally diverse nation, I expected to meet and interact with people with different languages, cultures and lifestyles. Whilst my previous higher education learning was more teaching intensive, with emphasis on note taking and closed book examinations, my social work programme was to focus more on individual study, research, essay writing and presentations. This difference was highlighted by Aymer and Bryan (1996) and Bartoli (2011) in terms of international students favouring examinations as assessment strategies and that learning is culturally situated. I was however prepared to integrate, learn and attain from my new learning environment and I believe it was that attitude and determination, amongst other positive factors, that saw me through the challenges.

At the point of qualifying, I experienced a mixture of relief and contentment with qualifying at last. I was well equipped for social work practice, having the knowledge base and competence to support those in need, whilst promoting social justice and the eradication of all forms of oppression. I had a good understanding of social work values, skills, methods, approaches and theories. Anti-oppressive and anti-discriminatory practice in respect to working with service users was part of my toolkit. I could not have been more prepared for the workplace. I was also aware of the momentum around anti-racism in society but I was not particularly bothered. I was only interested in getting on with the job and doing what I knew how to do best: giving a helping hand to those in need. I have now been qualified for over three years and although I have experienced overt and direct racism, it was only when I started writing this chapter that it occurred to me how oblivious and nonchalant I have been regarding this topic. Discussions with other black colleagues also highlight how issues about racism and anti-racism are taboo and sensitive topics that require high levels of care when addressing them. However, if our society is race-constructed and we decide not to look through the lens of racism, we will merely be perpetuating the disparities (Heron, 2006; Penketh, 2000).

Black or social worker

Appreciating the uniqueness of being black and a social worker entails critical reflection on social work's powerful role in eradicating oppression and the conceptualisation of the experiences of black people, as a marginalised group in society. However it is important to recognise that whilst there is a great deal of literature about the general experiences of Black Minority Ethnic (BME) service users, and BME students' experiences on social work courses, there is comparatively little written specifically about the experiences of black social workers in England. The few studies available are mainly descriptive and, although they demonstrate the many distinctive aspects of being black in predominantly white work settings, there has been very little research completed with regards to evaluating changes in this area. For instance, black social workers have related concerns around racism from the 1960s through to the 1980s but it is only recently that their apprehensions are being acknowledged.

A closer look at the social work values and the fundamental policies around challenging oppressive situations in service users' lives will be a starting point for this discussion. Social workers, unlike other professionals, have a mandate to address all forms of oppression and discrimination that compromise service users' needs, choice and well-being (Braye and Preston-Shoot, 2001). Maidment and Cooper (2002) highlight the need for social workers to be able to recognise and challenge oppressive structures and develop competence in working with diverse client groups irrespective of their race, culture, ethnicity, gender, disability or age. The Professional Capabilities Framework for Social Work (College of Social Work, 2012) went further, to emphasise the importance of social workers recognising diversity and demonstrating awareness and practice competence in understanding, evidencing and challenging oppressive practice in the modern social work settings.

The last three decades have also seen many other developments and positions around confronting racism amongst other forms of oppression in social work, with an emphasis being placed on the need to revisit anti-racism in social work education and practice. It is therefore demoralising that despite all these frameworks racism remains a persistent problem in social work. Black social workers continue to express concerns around overt and subtle racism experienced in the workplace and social work courses, and the impact it has on their career and professional development (Singh, 2002; Keating, 2000). Some black social workers are reluctant to challenge racial discrimination as a result of the anxieties around this topic (Ryde, 2009; Penketh, 2000; Channer and Doel, 2009; Graham, 2007) and the fear of the consequences and the impact it would have on their reputation and career progression. Gordon (2001) suggests that social workers are intimidated, become silent about their experiences and are often compelled to adopt the colour-blind approach, where they are expected to act and talk *white* in order to progress within the social work profession. In addition to other forms of oppression, racism not only affects black social workers' performance but also impacts on the output for service users. Thus colour frequently becomes a barrier to opportunities for professional development and career progression (Penketh, 2000).

Social work, although not always perceived as the most esteemed profession, especially by the media, still maintains some form of authoritarian position in society. Issues of power are real and entrenched in social work practice. Inequality and power imbalance between social workers and service users were examined by Thompson (2006). He suggests that the issues of inequality and disadvantage lie at the heart of social work practice and that there is the possibility of exclusion and unfair treatment. Being both a social worker and a black person can leave black practitioners feeling vulnerable and anxious about experiencing racism in the workplace. Black social workers therefore have to continually work hard to prove their competence whilst trying to promote healthy working relationships with colleagues, managers and service users.

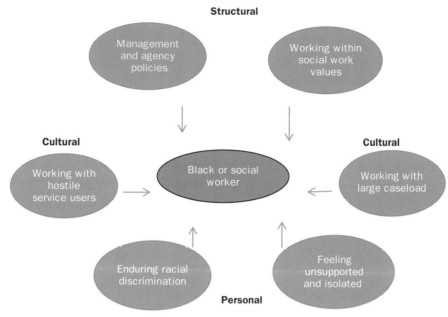

Figure 1 Adaptation of Thompson (2006) PSC model

In trying to explore the experience of BME students and workers, Bryan (2000) suggested that BME students and practitioners experience racism around the negative stereotypical perceptions regarding their limited 'intellectual' ability and that they are made to feel different when they come up against institutional discrimination, especially in the workplace (Dominelli, 2008). Brockmen *et al.* (2001) also suggest that black practitioners are not being valued and that they experience racism from service users and colleagues, and are often denied the opportunity for promotion (Johns, 2005; Stubbs, 1985). Singh (2006) argues that BME social workers and students are still undervalued, and that there has been a dislocation between the anti-racist movement from BME communities and the more sanitised version in social work organisations. There are also significant discussions around negative attitudes from other white colleagues when black social workers who are well experienced and qualified show interest in job opportunities and career progression.

Whilst there are some similarities and parallels in the general experiences of black and white social workers in Britain, there is also a fundamental difference. The figure above illustrates the complexities of being black *and* a social worker in an ever busy social work setting. Graham (2007, p 128) suggests that black social workers often *experience a marginal status within social work agency that is reflective of their experiences in the wider society.* The notion of structural racism was again revisited by Graham (2007) as she described the experiences of black social workers and the fact that they often find it difficult forming relationships with white colleagues and service users.

Perceptions of racism and anti-racism

Discussions around racism and anti-racism often incite extreme reactions depending on people's experience and conceptual understandings. Within a social work context, such debates can either lead to antagonistic or sensitive situations that leave individuals feeling vulnerable and uncomfortable about sharing their experiences let alone having the confidence to address racial differences appropriately. This has been the case ever since the introduction of an anti-racist framework in social work training. Graham (2007) highlighted that when this anti-racist approach came under scrutiny, concerns were raised in respect of the term 'race', its meaning and context. She also went further to highlight that even social work educators were uneasy about the theories underpinning anti-racist social work as they are not informed by sociological, political or economic theories or research.

There is a general consensus that diversity characterises and shapes human experience and that it is critical to the formation of identity. It is therefore fundamental to listen to the voices of black social workers and their experiences of inequality and racism in contemporary social work settings. Graham and Robinson (2004) suggest that *speaking about individual experiences of racism allows us to consciously engage in exploring our realities in sharing knowledge of lived experiences and ways to get through in and out of the world* (in Graham, 2007, p 25).

A colleague and social worker once stated that:

Being the only black worker in my Team, I was always aware of my difference and the fact that I was treated differently by my white colleagues. Some of them liked me and some didn't. The discernment became more apparent when pleasantries and greetings were deliberately ignored. Sometimes they walked past me like I didn't exist and went on to chat with their White Colleagues without even saying hello. This went on for several months and although I wanted to address it, I was concerned for my job, as some of these colleagues were in leadership positions. Sooner or later, I became indifferent to these attitudes and carried on doing my job even though it hurt badly. Eventually, I left the Team for another job but soon found out there's not much difference. I have now realised that I can't keep running away from racism; I need to be confident to challenge it.

Some of these concerns were re-echoed by some of the participants in Channer and Doel (2009) on how they had to compromise issues around racism because of the reaction they envisaged from their white colleagues. The discomfort of white social workers around black colleagues and the negative stereotypes held by white social workers have also been well documented. There are the ever present attitudes of white colleagues that extend from the wider society into the workplace. These underlying attitudes do not seem to have changed throughout the years. Ryde (2009) emphasised that it is complex to analyse whether the racism experienced is unconscious or unintentional on the part of their white colleagues but that a distinction is significant. Imagine being the only black person in a white social work setting and experiencing discrimination; there will come a time when the feeling of isolation overtakes the initial passion to make a positive and lasting difference in the lives of service users. Not having the opportunities to discuss with colleagues from similar backgrounds impacts on black social workers' practice and black students' performance in practice learning.

CRITICAL QUESTION

Imagine being isolated in the workplace due to a personal characteristic. How would you manage? Whom would you seek support from?

Most black social workers acknowledge that racism exists in the workplace but that one needs to be extremely careful about discussing issues around racism as it can have the tendency of impacting on progress in the profession.

One black colleague commented:

I need to be careful how racism is discussed as these colleagues have influence that could affect my career and reputation. At this point in time I don't think I am strong enough to play the games to enhance my career. So I would rather maintain my position, quietly in order to have peace of mind.

With respect to opportunities for professional development, a black colleague expressed:

I had discussed my professional development and goals to go for practice teaching trainings but my manager did not show any interest, rather the idea was dismissed immediately with an excuse that there was no funding. After several weeks, she came back to me and said that I could now go for it; by that time, it was already too late for applications.

One senior social work practitioner stated that:

racism is being disadvantaged due to the colour of one's skin or having an advantage over others due to the colour of the skin. I am very comfortable talking about racism with colleagues who have developed critical thinking around this concept. There are some colleagues whose own life experiences are limited and as such they do not appreciate issues around race as problems. For some of these people, they have adopted the denial approach as a coping strategy in order to survive the ever stressful profession.

Another colleague described it as:

a 'colour blind approach with a simplistic view that all people are the same and have equal opportunities'. A personal accommodation with the status quo such that they do not see themselves as directly personally affected by racism – a position that might in turn affect their ability to impart 'anti-racism'.

One colleague commented that:

as a black worker we are more challenged than ever to be able to maintain our professionalism at all times, always looking over your shoulder to cover every blind spot. I often hear fellow black workers commenting that they have to work 'harder than them'. It also appears that black workers are often given the most complex cases. Unfortunately not because they are seen as more competent but because they have high resistance level and low sickness and stress related absences from work. A critical look at the authority where I work highlights the fact that there are very few team managers with a black background. This is a poor reflection of how the authority nurtures its black workforce and supports them towards progressing to leadership positions.

Another colleague referred to the system in relation to class and social inequalities as a *glass ceiling* and stated that for the black worker *a concrete ceiling* applies.

Turney (1996) suggest that attempts to develop anti-racist practice have been pursued in a wide range of agency settings. At the same time, within social work education and training, there is a broad requirement for social workers to demonstrate understanding of and competence in anti-oppressive and anti-discriminatory practice whilst focusing on the theoretical and practical dimensions of anti-racism. Penketh (2000) argues that the failure to implement anti-discriminatory policies and the lack of awareness regarding racism and anti-racist strategies within social work agencies has led to difficult situations as demonstrated by the various experiences illustrated above.

Newly qualified and naïve

When newly qualified, there were times when I found it difficult to identify myself as a social worker. I tried not to dwell much on my difference but on my role as an agent of social change. This to an extent meant having the courage to overlook racial discrimination or attitudes that might suggest this. However, there are times when this has become difficult particularly when the racial comments or discrimination have been overtly addressed towards me. For instance, each time I picked up the phone to speak with a service user, I did not have to introduce myself as a black African woman with a background in architecture and now living out my passion for helping people. Instead my conversations began with, 'Hello, my name is …, social worker with children and families'. Consequently the caller/ service user is either able to establish my ethnicity from my accent or make a guess at it. Within this context, I can confidently and competently communicate my message to whoever the caller is. Why? Because my identity is to an extent shielded as a result of not coming into contact with the caller. However, during face to face meetings either with service users, colleagues or professionals from other agencies, I am consciously aware of my difference and how I am perceived by others particularly when my contributions are dismissed or paid little attention to.

Newly qualified and inexperienced

MY OWN CASE STUDY

The imperative to look back, reflect and learn is a prerequisite to positive action, progress and improvement for social workers, which is often driven by ethical standards. Looking back to when I was newly qualified and having overcome my first hurdle, I was full of aspirations and enthusiasm to enter the workplace. I wanted to practise what I felt I knew how to do best: helping people in need, promoting social justice and advocating on behalf of service users and their families. I was one of the privileged social workers who overcame a second hurdle by securing a job before receiving my degree award. I was therefore very grateful and issues around racism were the least of my worries. I had acquired the knowledge base and skills from my studies but did not see the need to request specific guidelines in respect of anti-racism during my induction period because it might have made me look rebellious, and I want to acquire a positive reputation. It was only when I experienced overt racism that I realised how limited and unprepared I was to address racial issues with service users. I had been allocated a 'difficult' case: a family that had a long-standing history with Children's Services where there were ongoing concerns about child neglect and hostility towards social workers. I picked up the case with a determination to make a difference. On meeting the family, I observed a high level of hostility, which I at first dismissed as 'typical' of some of the cases that social workers hold. However during my second visit to the family, it became very apparent that the parents did not want me to be their child's social worker. The father looked me straight in the eye, and with a look of disgust exclaimed: 'My child does not like black people; the other professionals working with him are all white and I don't think he will like to have a black social worker.'

If you were to step into my shoes, as a newly qualified black social worker, how would you feel?

This experience indirectly impacted on my relationship with the family, and although I mentioned it to the team manager, it was decided that there would not be a change of social worker. Yet, the racial issue was not addressed. Each time I approached the family's home, I had a feeling of tightness in my stomach and nausea in the anticipation of what I might be stepping into. On some occasions, I had wished that there would be no one there when I knocked on the door so that I could quickly return to the office and record that I had completed my statutory duty of visiting the family. I was however mindful of the impact that this feeling would have on my social worker career if this was not addressed immediately and so decided to share my fears in supervision. I requested that my manager made a joint visit with me to the family home. This became the turning point in the case; not only were the racial issues addressed appropriately but it also promoted a proactive approach to ensuring that the needs of the children in the family were adequately met.

The incident highlighted above illustrates how unequipped black social workers can be at the point of qualifying to challenge issues around racism and discrimination. As absurd as this may sound, it reflects the experience of many black social work students and other professionals within their personal and professional lives. Racism is experienced every day in social work agencies, ranging from the consistent failure to recognise and value the competence of this group of workers (Bryan, 2000) but also to the deliberate dismissal or lack of support with regards to their career progression and opportunities for professional development. This can often lead to black social work students and practitioners reverting to working in isolation or amongst other black people whom they are more comfortable and feel safe with.

A number of studies suggest that not only do practitioners feel uncomfortable about challenging racial discrimination; managers and practice educators are often not in the right positions to support black workers to tackle racial concerns (Penketh, 2000). As a student, I was hoping that I was going into a profession that had taken time to examine its anti-racist policies and practices but as the workplace is a reflection of society, it is clear that anti-racism is still not embedded within organisations and therefore mirrors the everyday experience for black social workers. Furthermore, Turney (1996) also suggests that not all black people are able or willing to challenge racism. He reiterated that it is possible that some black people will personally accommodate the status quo such that they do not see themselves as directly personally affected by racism – a position that might in turn affect their ability to make an impact on 'anti-racism'.

Step into my shoes: working with BME service users

The knowledge that BME service users face barriers and racism when trying to access and participate in the provision of services is not a recent phenomenon. In the late 1990s, research evidence noted the lack of awareness about available supportive services among parents of BME children (Beresford, 1995; Modood and Berthoud, 1997; Joseph Rowntree Foundation, 1999; Chamba *et al.,* 1999). Later, Coulshed and Orme (2006, p 241) argued that *most frequently being black significantly affects people's life experience and the way that they have been treated by health and social care services ... leads to unhelpful stereotyping or unjust practices.* Chamba *et al.* (1999) reported that black service users do not have equal access to services as white people. Several years later, the situation still remains the same. Research into the lives of BME people in England continues to highlight the need to improve accessibility to services and the promotion of participation in service provision for this group of service users (Bignall and Butt, 2000; Patel, 2002; Flynn, 2002; Joseph Rowntree Foundation, 2005; Barn, 2001, 2006; Begum, 2006).

Flynn (2002) reported that black communities are tired of taking part in research that asks them what they want from services, only to find nothing happens until five years later when they are asked the same questions all over again. It is therefore important to recognise exactly what factors constitute blocks to equality of opportunity for BME communities in England. In discussing the powerful influence research has in creating definitions of reality and in documenting disadvantage amongst black service users, Boushell (2000) identified that such people, who are already marginalised from the mainstream, are also found to be underrepresented in the participation and inclusion intended to develop services for them. Begum (2006) highlighted that BME participation has reduced over the past ten years and that although BME professionals and community leaders are consulted by policy-makers, they do not consult service users themselves. Shah and Priestley (2001) persuasively argued that there is no reason to believe that BME communities do not need or wish to use services, having evidenced that poor access to information, communication barriers, and lack of sensitivity for culture and traditions, and discrimination on the basis of race may prevent them from doing so. Much of the literature criticises service delivery for failing to meet BME people's needs (Stuart, 2006; Begum, 2006).

O'Neale (2000) identified that the quality of services delivered to BME service users was heavily dependent on the quality of the social work intervention. Graham (2007) argues that discussions on the barriers to accessing and participating in appropriate services by BME service users are a reminder of the nature of institutional racism and the multiple layers of oppression experienced by black people in UK, for example for black women facing domestic violence or black service users experiencing mental health issues.

Anti-racism: significant issues for social work education

Social work education and training have a significant role in promoting anti-racist social work practice. The recent Professional Capabilities Framework for social workers (College of Social Work, 2012) emphasises that social workers should be able to appreciate that, as a consequence of difference, a person's life experience may include oppression, marginalisation and alienation as well as privilege, power and acclaim. It also places emphasis on the need for social workers to demonstrate competence in working with diverse people and in eradicating all forms of oppression. Singh (1996) called on social work academics to ensure that responses to race are continually altered. Phillips (2010) suggests that since racism never stands still and affects different people in different ways, anti-racist responses must always be contingent in time and space. Macey and Moxon (1996) and Gould (1996) have also made a similar argument suggesting that any understanding of anti-racism requires an analysis of contemporary social relations.

Whilst on the social work degree programme, I can still recollect the segregation witnessed within the teaching environment. The predominantly white group, *who view themselves as superior or indeed as not having a 'race' and so perpetuating racialisation* (Ryde, 2009, p 15), had a special area where they sat, while the black students sat at the other end of the room (usually the front). This picture not only depicts division between black students and their white counterparts, but also reveals discrimination, which often occurs even in educational settings, such as a social work degree programme, which should be promoting social justice and anti-oppressive practice. I witnessed that the black students found it difficult to contribute to discussions and other collective activities as a result of the negative response and facial expressions from their white peers. On some occasions, the black students had made suggestions that nobody heeded, but later, a white student made the same comment and it was acknowledged. A high number of black students felt invisible and, in order to reduce their stress, learnt to be careless about the situation, which in turn led to decreased academic performance and confidence. This led to the formation of the support group, Padare, which is discussed in Chapter 4.

Promoting equality of opportunity for black social workers

The relevance of teaching anti-racism in social work practice cannot be over-emphasised. The past 20 years have seen a continuous imploration for the conceptualisation of anti-racism in social work practice, which necessitates an appreciation of black social workers' experience of oppression. According to Graham (2006), giving voice to the experiences of black workers has long been a call by black people in defining their own experiences. This chapter has demonstrated that black social workers are often marginalised and experience multiple layers of oppression in the workplace. There is therefore an urgent need to reintroduce appropriate measures to tackle racism in the workplace, not just to ensure that black social workers are not denied equal opportunities but also so that they are given the needed support that will eventually enhance the quality of work life.

However, it is important to acknowledge that racism, being a wider societal concern, cannot be eradicated through a 'quick fix'. Instead social work organisations will need to keep trying and altering what they do, and how accordingly, to ensure that racial issues are appropriately addressed. This might entail more consultation with social workers from black communities, ensuring adequate representation and cultural competence in social work education and practice learning, and promoting peer support groups such as Padare within the workplace (Dominelli *et al.*, 2001; Graham, 2007). Most importantly, social work and social work education will have to ensure that anti-racism remains a significant aspect of the social work agenda and social work education curriculum.

Suggestions for development

Radical social work values provided fertile ground for the social work profession to try to grapple with the complexities of 'race' and anti-racism (Turney, 1996). Macpherson (1999) highlighted that racism has resulted in the significant impairment of the life opportunities of black people in the UK. The experience of black social workers suggests that racism continues to operate in social work organisations despite all the great movements and campaigns to eradicate oppression based on race within the profession. This area of social work will therefore continue to require ongoing attention.

- Information and results from empirical studies and books regarding the experiences of black social work students and practitioners should be integrated into social work education curriculums and also shared with other social work institutions and organisations. For instance, the success of Padare support group.

- The importance of peer support for black students is well documented and should be promoted. However, care must be taken not to encourage division or a sense of segregation.

- A modern social work mentoring approach where students are linked up to a qualified social worker is highly recommended. The mentor is there to support the students with any issues that they might be struggling with in order to enhance their learning experience.

- Educators should continue to listen, encourage and demonstrate that they value the ideas of those who have a different narrative.

- In as much as emphasis is on 'equal opportunities' and the assumption that all social work students should have the ability and skills to practise in any setting, matching should also form an integral aspect of the process. Some 'matching', particularly in first placements, should allow students choice where possible and the selection of a setting where the student has some knowledge or experience, thus building confidence

- Good practice in respect of black social workers is clearly good practice for all (ie acknowledging and supporting the individual worker). Challenging agencies to recognise 'best practice' in respect of black social workers is therefore raising the bar for all.

- Social work educators and academics should have direct links with BME groups/projects. This connection will ensure that educators are well equipped in delivering education based on 'lived experience'. The students might also benefit from exposure to diverse communities and ways of living.

- Small group projects (integrated) with a cross-cultural dimension or theme will be beneficial to learning.

- A placement outside of Britain to experience the misconception that the historical accounts presented about other continents could help the future workforce to see how globalisation has become the equaliser for those who keep up with the modern trends. This might also expose student/educators to other forms of vulnerabilities that this has also created.

Conclusion: a forward looking journey

ANGIE BARTOLI, SUE KENNEDY AND PROSPERA TEDAM

Throughout this book a range of important debates about anti-racist social work have been identified and critical questions posed to you the reader. You have been asked to engage with the writers on a journey of self-discovery aimed at supporting new learning, a developed understanding of racism and the impact of this on everyone. Whether you are a newly qualified social worker or not this book demands at the very least a response that is filled with intent and purpose. We never said it would be easy. Then again social work is not an easy profession. It is hoped that those who have enrolled on social work education programmes have done so like all their predecessors because they believe that they can make a difference to people's lives.

Social work and social work education are facing a challenging time. As nostalgic social work students from the 1980s, our view is that social work is at a political standstill seemingly imprisoned by a level of amnesia that lacks the imagination to respond to a media backlash. The handover to the Health Care Professional Council (HCPC) as the new regulatory body for social work and the establishment of the College of Social Work have seen a range of consultations and outcomes aimed at *taking control of its own destiny* (TCSW, 2012). The introduction of the Professional Capabilities Framework with nine domains for benchmarking social work practice linked to a career pathway is an example of the many changes. The messages of reform and transformation are upbeat. However, in the language of change, social work must not lose sight of its cultural heritage and identity as a profession that emerged as the challenger of social injustices. That many of the contributors to this book have been shocked, reminded and reconnected with racism and its impact is a salient reminder that we now need a pit stop to reflect and recharge our thinking. Taking control of our professional destiny will be the responsibility of many and begins with the individual social work student. How social work educators shape the practitioners and managers for the future means engaging with the flip-side of the social work language that rallies for change. Engaging in the fears, uncertainty and messiness that are the lived experience of social work will need a response that ensures a more visible, diverse and explicit agenda that prepares students for practice. For black social work students education programmes will need to think about how to help them understand society's rules of engagement so that they can see the barriers for what they are and have the confidence to challenge them.

By being explicit about racism we ask you to critically think about the challenges that you will face, especially when we suggest that racism in this society has become like the wind. We know about it, we do not always see it, but we can all be touched by it. Throughout this book we have offered you a range of models, methods and theoretical frameworks to engage you in critical thinking. We ask you now to consider the wind as a metaphor for racism. In weather forecasts winds are often referred to in terms of the direction that they are blowing and their strength. From time to time, often dictated by the media, the impact or *force* of racism is more topical in a particular sphere of society. For example the *direction* of racism has focussed upon sport more recently (and in particular football) and the use of social media such as Twitter to promote racial hatred. Often fuelled by *unconsciously held beliefs and assumptions* that hooks (2010, p 98) reminds us result in students questioning the authority of a black lecturer, patients undermining the opinion of black doctors and service users refusing to have a black social worker. Racism, like the wind, may not always be seen but it becomes a movement ever present in the air. Race and wind are both four-letter words. Despite this, various terms and a number of names are associated with the word *wind* depending on the strength, direction and impact. At times it can be a slight *breeze* that briefly touches you or it can be unpredictable and stop you as you battle against sudden and short *gusts*. On other occasions its force, frequency and duration are such that it can have a devastating impact on humans and the environment, such as in thunderstorms, hurricanes, tsunamis and typhoons. Racism can be as subtle and insipid as a breeze or it can be destructive and catastrophic: from the black social work student who cannot be found a placement learning experience because their profile has been sent back from an employer provider; the overrepresentation of black children in the care system; the disproportionate numbers of black men in the mental health system because their symptoms are more likely to be pathologised; to the death of a young boy, Stephen Lawrence, stabbed to death because he was black. Racism, like the wind, cannot be touched or always understood. However, they can both touch us, changing lives and landscapes. Both racism and wind have inspired writers and poets to write about the horror they bring and the people they have inspired. Below, we offer you an adapted version of Aesop's fable of *The North Wind and the Sun*, to depict how the strength of the wind (racism) can be contested and challenged.

The North Wind, the Sun and the social work student

The North Wind considered itself strong. The Sun, fed up with the Wind constantly causing chaos, insisted that power lay in perseverance and gentleness. They argued for many years and decided to settle their differences by a contest. They looked down below and in the distance spotted a weary social work student carrying books and wearing a big coat, travelling along a road. 'Right, are you ready?' asked the Sun. 'Let us see which of us can take the coat off that social work student.' The wind was complacent. 'That's simple.

I will easily be able to force the coat off that student,' the Wind boasted. And so the North Wind blew as hard as possible; trees swayed and birds clung onto branches. The road was filled with dust, and leaves swirled. As the air became colder, ice began to form on the ground. The harder the Wind blew, the tighter the shivering social work student wrapped her coat around herself.

Appearing from behind a cloud came the Sun, who warmed the air and the frosty terrain below. The social work student looked up, and began to slowly unbutton her coat. The Sun grew brighter and its rays stronger. Soon, the student felt so hot that she took off her coat and sat under the shade of a tree.

The North Wind was tired and annoyed, and asked, 'How did you do that?' 'It was very easy,' said the Sun. 'I warmed the air and the soul of the student slowly. Through gentleness I got my way.'

Like the sun, we are not to be defeated and can see a way to challenge and bring about change. Yet, we are realistic too. Racism will not disappear and as Aesop's fable tells us it will be a constant element of life that will need different approaches to contest it. The relentless work of black and social justice activists has brought about change in laws, policies and attitudes. This approach has been like the sun burning brightly to warm the soul and sometimes having to cause a fire as a show of strength to stand up to the winds of racism. In Chapter 6 a critical question was posed to you the reader to identify a hero who has raised your awareness of racism. If you research this question you will come across a range of people to choose from – Martin Luther King, whose famous words 'I have a dream' from a speech given over 50 years ago are frequently seen on posters in academic rooms and in some social work offices as a demonstration of awareness. You may draw upon those writers who have been cited in this book, for example bell hooks and Stuart Hall, to help you develop your awareness and knowledge. We have drawn your attention to a range of writers in the hope that you will be inspired by their thoughts and views and motivated to take up the challenge to find out more or to know that you are not isolated in the challenge.

Taking up the baton

Throughout this book references have been made to time-lines in UK history when racism in society social work education and practice has been challenged. You have been introduced to Critical Race Theory as a theoretical framework for understanding the why in developing knowledge and awareness about racism. The time-lines show us that in the UK events have taken place that have led to changes in law, from the Race Relations Act 1965 to the Equality

Act 2010, all aimed at ensuring racial equality. The changes are reflected in social work education, which has moved with the time-line, and now through the introduction of the Professional Capabilities Framework (PCF), which asks that:

- Social workers understand that diversity characterises and shapes human experience and is critical to the formation of identity. Diversity is multi-dimensional and includes race, disability, class, economic status, age, sexuality, gender and transgender, faith and belief. Social workers appreciate that, as a consequence of difference, a person's life experience may include oppression, marginalisation and alienation as well as privilege, power and acclaim, and are able to challenge appropriately.

- Recognise the importance of diversity in human identity and experience, and the application of anti-discriminatory and anti-oppressive principles in social work practice. (TCSW, 2012)

What we begin to recognise is that legislation and new frameworks have not diminished or eradicated racism and that there will always be the need for new generations of social work students to become involved in what for black people is becoming a marathon event. This is because there will always be an event or events that will shake people out of thinking that society is tolerant and safe to live in. What the writers of this book recognise is that global events in Africa have meant that people fleeing social and political intolerance have arrived in the UK hoping to be safe, healthy, to enjoy and achieve, make a contribution and achieve economic independence. For some this has meant seeking a social work education so that they can provide services aimed at making a difference in a society that is acknowledged by legislation and social policy as diverse and multicultural. However, the experience of black African social work students has been one of segregation and exclusion as a result of suspicion and racism in the classroom, which is then experienced when they become employed as professional social workers. The writers of this book acknowledge the contribution that black African students have made to social work education at this university. As a result of the global events that have brought them to this country and to social work education, their experience has reignited a passion for finding a social work voice that says these are the concerns and this is the challenge.

- Racism exists and has not gone away.

- It is a static reality but the experience is dynamic.

- Racism exists alongside sexism, homophobia, ageism and disablism.

- Racism imprisons those who are subjected to it.

- Racism captures and paralyses thinking, producing one-dimensional social workers.

Taking up the baton at this point in social work education will be important for the next generation of social work students. At a time when the public sector equality duty that sits within the Equality Act 2010 and is the *mechanism by which government policies are assessed to ascertain the impact they will have on minorities* (Muir, 2012) is being challenged by the current Home Secretary Teresa May for being overly time consuming and bureaucratic, social work needs to be ready for the challenge. If a hero should be identified for you then it has to be Doreen Lawrence, whose life was devastated by racism when her son was murdered in a racially motivated attack over 20 years ago and who has campaigned for justice ever since. She has said she is tired and is now looking to the next generation of activists who will challenge a government and system that continues to ignore racism. She has asked that educational establishments do more to change society's negative attitudes to ethnic minorities by promoting more positive images and stories that acknowledge lived experiences of black people living in the UK (Dodd, 2012; Muir, 2012). This is now the time for social work education to align itself with a social work identity equipped to face the challenge that racism presents.

In Chapter 7 the experience of the black social worker was highlighted with critical questions posed about being prepared for social work practice and facing covert and overt racism within the profession from white colleagues and outside from white service users. Feeling unprepared for social work practice is not a new experience. The transition from social work student to qualified and employed professional social worker is an exciting and frightening experience. Many newly qualified social workers will face expectations from employers that they can 'hit the ground running' in an ever demanding profession that, despite attempts to introduce projects for supporting newly qualified social workers, is moving at an unprecedented pace of change. In those first few months of employment social work education can feel like a lifetime away and the relevance of assignments and debates about social work values and theories questioned. This is now the time that you are expected to deliver services in line with agency eligibility criteria and service thresholds and finding the time to consider any stance – anti-oppressive, anti-discriminatory and anti-racist – from which to practise is lost in the demands and pressures of providing services. This loss is significant in its multiplicity of losses and impact on outcomes for social workers, services and service users. The loss of a black identity, white identity and a Practice stance in those first few months in professional practice can and will lead to the development of a dominant perspective that lends itself to the language and practice of oppression, discrimination and racism – a language that is careless, defeatist and unchallenging, which leads to behaviour that isolates black social workers and does not serve black service users – and the production of one-dimensional social workers who are unable to form an attachment to a specific practice stance – Feminist, Anti-Racist, Anti-Oppressive, Anti-Discriminatory – as a term of self-identity and self-identification because by doing so may be considered too challenging or too tiring (White, 2006).

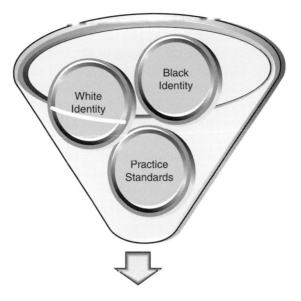

One-Dimensional Social Work

The call for social work education to take up the baton to inform the next generation of social workers about racial injustice is the challenge. It is an opportunity to reclaim a professional identity that is associated with speaking out and being active in the pursuit of social justice. How social work education does this in a way that does not exclude, isolate or disengage students is a matter for consideration. In Chapters 4 and 6 the authors identify the lack of a white dialogue in a social work curriculum that engages white students in an external and internal dialogue about their white identity. If there is to be a response from social work education that involves all students in learning about racism and their role in combating it then black *and* white social work academics, practitioners and students individually and collectively all play a part in passing on the baton through insistent perseverance. For social work education this may mean taking a long hard look at what we do and who we are. As Ryde (2009, p 197) points out, *If we are to really tackle racism we need to stop looking through binoculars and look in the mirror instead.*

White social work education

Currently this is what is in place. What the writers have identified and supported through research (Chapter 4) is that social work education is white in content and has a *framework of assimilation* that reinforced the racialisation of black students as the other (Hickman and Walter, 1995, p 5). The absence of white identities in the teaching and learning has meant that white students and tutors have not had to have an internal dialogue about who they are in a way that helps them critically understand the social construction of their white privilege. This has led to denial, 'colour' blindness, segregation in class and an over-reliance on black students to deal with it.

There is a need to deconstruct whiteness that enables all students to learn about the range of racist ideologies that exist without creating a hierarchy of racism that becomes counterproductive. The challenge to social work education will be to include teaching and learning about white identities that acknowledge that whiteness does not mean the same or that it should be equated with a homogenous way of life. Using the culturagram identified in Chapter 3 will help white students to examine their social experiences of being white in the UK and the impact this has had on developing an identity that takes into account gender, sexuality, attainments, class, religion, values, language and traditions. This will help students to understand the social and family scripts that have been handed down to them that have made them who they are. How they undo these scripts or draw upon them is part of the journey that the writers in this book refer to. The journey should impress upon white students that an understanding of who they are and where they have come from will support an understanding of where they want to be and what type of social worker they are aiming to be – ordinary or extraordinary? It will always need an extraordinary social worker to work with and make sense of the complexities of people's lives.

Is there a balance to be struck in this education process? Introducing white identities into the social work curriculum will raise suspicions from within the white student group and outside questioning what this is about. There may be fear that the focus on white identities may be a way of using a 'Get Whitey' approach to challenge white students, or a level of suspicion from black social work students that this approach is one that lets them 'off the hook' because it lacks critical challenge. This is the challenge and if we are to take a stand against racism then these debates need to be had in the classroom. The absence of whiteness will only encourage exclusion and negative attitudes based on assumptions and stereotypes. Racialised invisibility needs to be avoided. We need to find the space, time and narratives that ensure that those discriminatory and oppressive barriers are identified so that those in the margins can come together through diversity to find a way through. Where the white debate takes place is a question that is already being asked of this social work programme. However, when it takes place is now and this is the start of another journey. There should be no hesitation and we will find ways to build on the tools for learning identified in this book. All those involved in producing chapters for this book have demonstrated the strength of a collective approach and it is this that will be used to take action for the future. There will be disagreements and this is what will bring about progression. We will use a *grammar of light* (Duffy, 1993, p 33) to set out what we mean by white identities and how these should be deconstructed. By using imagination and insights into the intersectionality of race, class, gender and sexuality to help students understand their *modes of existence* we may come up with an approach that ultimately means the end of one-dimensional social work (Power, 2009, p 69).

A way forward

As suggested earlier in this concluding chapter, a collective response to engaging and challenging racism has proved to be beneficial for the authors and the social work students. Maintaining the levels of engagement in a way that keeps moving forward will demand something of all those involved. For social work the way forward begins with education and within the curriculum. Opportunities need to be made for students to have the time and space to be able to tune-in to those fears, beliefs, family and cultural scripts that define who they are. Identifying a personal value base-line from the *Personal is Political* that helps us understand our role in challenging racism and the interconnected relationships of power, inequality, oppression and discrimination is a way of setting down a foundational block strong enough for further building.

Creating learning opportunities outside of the curriculum through support groups is one way forward and for the black African social work students they say this has been an empowering experience for them. Setting up a group called Padare for black African social work students has also raised the profile and identity of this particular student group within the university. In many ways this group has now become a movement in which the group members come together to share experiences, raise specific issues, engage in research and host biennial conferences. It is hoped that this movement will continue to set the pace in social work education.

We also know that within social work education we need to develop strategies that unite the student group through transformative learning from one another about diversity, with the aim of reclaiming a professional social work identity that is organised around a common commitment to challenge all forms of discrimination and oppression. There will be tears of anger, frustration and empathy in this process. The outcome of such a personal and collective journey will be to produce social workers with a firm personal and professional identity who can confidently challenge racism and become the leaders and managers of the future. It will be down to these social workers to ensure that the lessons they have learned throughout their social work education are taken into the workplace. This will call upon a level of bravery that you may not feel you have. However, if professional social work is to step out of the margins and become a progressive movement then maybe one of the final critical questions is for you to identify a hero within your current student group, or a qualified social worker who inspired you during your practice learning experience or a tutor who has been a role model and helped you to think differently.

The aim of this book has been to add to the current literature on anti-racist social work and what we have found is that there remain gaps in what is available for social work students to learn about anti-racist social work in the UK. This may be a first action point in a plan for the way forward. This is not to dismiss those wonderful authors that have inspired the contributors of this book. For some of us they were a starting point in learning about oppression, discrimination, inequality and racism. However, by establishing social work as the lead discipline in writing about anti-racism sends a strong message about the position of social work and the intent of those who practise.

Finally, you may want to take up a critical challenge to plan your own way forward:

The Personal Plan:

1.   Make a statement about how your identity will shape your social work practice.

2.   Set out your social work positioning and stance.

3.   Read the books identified by the authors of this book.

4.   If you have read them already then identify new authors.

5.   Look for organisations that are fighting against racism.

Add to the plan, go back to it and/or share it with others and, when you feel like hiding in the margins, behind words, leaving the challenge to others or relaxing in the belief that it is not your problem, then remember the words of Doreen Lawrence:

I would love to get back to where I could just walk out and not be recognised. There is an expectation of me constantly. The quiet life I had before is what I want again. But I know that is never going to happen. So I have to make the best of what I have now. (Lawrence, 2012 cited in Muir, 2012)

References

Introduction

BBC News (2012) Rotherham Foster Couple want Council Apology. Available at: www.bbc.co.uk/news/uk-20517514 [accessed on 29 November 2012].

Bhatti-Sinclair, K. (2011) *Anti-racist Practice in Social Work*. Basingstoke: Palgrave Macmillan.

The College of Social Work (2012) *The Professional Capabilities Framework*. Available at: www.collegeofsocialwork.org/pcf.aspx [accessed on 29 November 2012].

Dominelli, L. (2008) *Anti-racist Social Work*. Basingstoke: Palgrave Macmillan.

Graham, M. (2007) *Black Issues in Social Work and Social Care*. Bristol: Policy Press.

Laird, S.F (2008) *Anti-Oppressive Social Work: A Guide for Developing Cultural Competence*. London: Sage.

Leveson, J. (2012) *An Inquiry into the Culture, Practices and Ethics of the Press Report*. London: The Stationery Press. Available at: www.official-documents.gov.uk/document/hc1213/hc07/0780/0780_ii.pdf [accessed on 3 December 2012].

Lourde, A. (2007) *Sister Outsider*. Toronto: Crossing Press.

Marsden, S. (2012) Foster Parents 'Stigmatised and Slandered' for being Members of UKIP, *Daily Telegraph*, 23 November 2012. Available at: www.telegraph.co.uk/news/politics/ukip/9700001/Foster-parents-stigmatised-and-slandered-for-being-members-of-Ukip.html [accessed on 29 December 2012].

Sinclair, K.B., Adams, R., Dominelli, L. and Payne, M. (2011) *Anti-Racist Practice in Social Work: Reshaping Social Work*. Basingstoke: Palgrave Macmillan.

Travis, A. (2012) Net Migration to UK Falls by a Quarter: ONS Figures Show Net Migration Fell from 242,000 to 183,000 in Past Year, Driven in Part by Fewer Overseas Students. Available at: www.guardian.co.uk/uk/2012/nov/29/net-migration-falls-quarter [accessed on 30 November 2012].

Chapter 1

BBC (1999) Top Secret Papers Reveal 1968 Truth. Available at: http://news.bbc.co.uk/1/hi/special_report/1999/01/99/1968_secret_history/244380.stm [accessed on 20 November 2012].

Brown, D. (2001) A New Language of Racism in Politics, *Guardian*. Available at: www.guardian.co.uk/uk/2001/apr/27/race.world2 [accessed on 21 November 2012].

Castles, S., Crawley, H. and Loughna, S. (2003) *States of Conflict: Causes and Patterns of Forced Migration to the EU and Policy Responses*. London: IPPR.

The College of Social Work (2012) *The Professional Capabilities Framework*. Available at: www.collegeofsocialwork.org/pcf.aspx [accessed on 29 November 2012].

Department of Health (2006) Our Health, Our Care, Our Say: A New Direction for Community Health Services, Cm 6737. Norwich: The Stationery Office.

Dominelli, L. (2008) *Anti-racist Social Work*. Basingstoke: Palgrave Macmillan.

Equality Act (2010) London: Stationery Office. Available at: www.legislation.gov.uk/ukpga/2010/15/contents [accessed on 20 November 2012].

Friedman, E. (2008) Britain as Refuge: The Real Story, *The Jewish Chronicle On-Line*. Available at: www.thejc.com/comment/essays/britain-refuge-real-story [accessed on 26 November 2012].

Gough, I., McGregor, A. and Camfield, L. (2007) Theorising Wellbeing in International Development, in Gough, I. and McGregor, A., *Wellbeing in Developing Countries: From Theory to Research*. Cambridge: Cambridge University Press, pp 3–43.

Graham, M. (2004) Empowerment Revisited: Social Work, Resistance and Agency in Black Communities. *European Journal of Social Work*, 7(1): 43–56.

Granada (1978) *World in Action*, Margaret Thatcher TV interview. Off-air recording. 27 January 1978. Available at: www.margaretthatcher.org/document/103485 [accessed on 21 November 2012].

Hall, S. (1992) The Question of Cultural Identity, in Hall, S., Held, D. and McGrew, A. (eds) *Modernity and Its Futures*. Cambridge: Polity Press, pp 274–316.

Hall, S., Critcher, C., Jefferson, T., Clarke, J. and Roberts, B. (1978) *Policing the Crisis*. London: Macmillan.

Harris, J. (2008) State Social Work: Constructing the Present from Moments in the Past. *British Journal of Social Work*, 38(4): 662–79.

Home Office (2007) *Accession Monitoring Report: A8 Countries*. London: Home Office.

Jacobs, S. (1985) Race, Empire and the Welfare State: Council Housing and Racism. *Critical Social Policy*, 13. Cited in Williams, F. (1989) *Social Policy: A Critical Introduction*. London: Polity.

Karpf, A. (2002) We've Been Here Before, *Guardian*, 8 June

Knox, K. and Kushner, T, (1999) *Refugees in an Age of Genocide: Global, National and Local Perspectives during the Twentieth Century*. London: Frank Cass.

Lipsky, M. (1980) *Street-level Bureaucracy, Dilemmas of the Individual in Public Services*. New York: Russell Sage.

Macpherson, W. (1999) *The Stephen Lawrence Inquiry: Report of an Inquiry by Sir William Macpherson of Cluny*. London: The Stationery Office.

Mullin, C. (2011) *Decline and Fall: Diaries 2005–2010*. London: Profile Book.

Ní Laoire, C., Bushin, N., Carpena-Méndez, F. and White, A. (2008) *Negotiating Belonging: Migrant Children and Youth in Ireland*. Cork, University Cork College. Available at: http:// migration.ucc.ie/children/working%20paper%201.pdf.

Pain, R. and Hopkins, P. (2009) *Common Ground: A Space of Emotional Well-being for Young Asylum Seekers*. Available at: www.dur.ac.uk/resources/beacon/Report_to_Common_ Ground_FINAL.pdf [accessed on 26 November 2012].

Parrott, L. (2010) *Values and Ethics in Social Work*. Exeter: Learning Matters.

Powell, E. (1969) *Freedom and Reality*. Kingswood: Elliot Right Way Books.

Refugee Council (2012) *Separated Children & Young People in the Asylum System, 10th October 2012* Expert Session 3 – Preparing a Human Rights Assessment for refused young people with Zubier Yazdani, Solicitor Deighton Pierce Solicitors. Available at: www. refugeecouncil.org.uk/eventsandtraining/conferences/archive/conference2012 [accessed on 26 November 2012].

Rhodes, C.J. (1902) *The Last Will and Testament of Cecil John Rhodes*. Edited by W.T. Stead. London: Review of Reviews Office.

Robinson, V. and Segrott, J. (2002) *Understanding the Decision-Making of Asylum Seekers*. Home Office Research Series Paper 243 (74pp).

Scarman, Lord (1981) *The Brixton Disorders 10–12 April 1981*. Special Report. London: HMSO.

Shaw, J. and Durkin, N. (2003) Unsafe Countries, Unlawful Proposals. *Amnesty*, July/August, pp 6–7.

Soysal, Y.N. (1994) *Limits of Citizenship: Migrants and Postnational Membership in Europe*. Chicago: University of Chicago Press.

Thompson, N. (2007) *Power and Empowerment*. London: Russell Housing.

Runnymede Trust (2012) *The Struggle for Race Equality: An Oral History of the Runnymede Trust, 1968–1988*. Available at: www.runnymedetrust.org/histories/race-equality/109/ runnymede-lectures.html [accessed on 20 November 2012].

Williams, F. (1989) *Social Policy: A Critical Introduction*. London: Polity.

Chapter 2

Ahmad, B. (1990) *Black Perspectives in Social Work*. Birmingham: Venture Press.

Alexander, C. (2007) Cohesive Identities: The Distance between Meaning and Understanding, in Wetherell, M., Laflèche, M. and Berkeley, R. (eds) *Identity, Ethnic Diversity and Community Cohesion*. London: Sage, pp 115–25.

Al-Krenawi, A. and Graham, J. (2000) Islamic Theology and Prayer: Relevance for Social Work Practice. *International Social Work*, 43(3): 289–304.

Anthias, F. (1999) Institutional Racism, Power and Accountability. *Sociological Research Online*, 4(1): 1–12. Available at: www.socresonline.org.uk/4/lawrence/anthias.html [accessed 11 November 2012].

Anthias, F. (2002) Diasporic Hybridity and Transcending Racisms, Problems and Potentials, in Anthias, F. and Lloyd, C. (eds) *Rethinking Anti-Racisms*. London: Routledge, pp 22–43.

Anthias, F. and Lloyd, C. (2002) Introduction: Fighting Racisms, Defining the Territory, in Anthias, F. and Lloyd, C. (eds) *Rethinking Anti-Racisms*. London: Routledge, pp 1–21.

Black, L. (2004) Writing In and Against Time, in Bulmer, M. and Solomos, J. (eds) *Researching Race and Racism*. London: Routledge, pp 203–13.

Balbo, L. (1998) Talking of Racism: The Project of a Society of Diversity. *European Journal of Social Work*, 1(1): 83–5.

Ballard, R. (1992) New Clothes For the Emperor: The Conceptual Nakedness of the Race Relations Industry in Britain. *New Community*, 18(3): 481–92.

Banks, N. (1999) *White Counsellors – Black Clients: Theory Research and Practice*. Aldershot: Ashgate.

Barn, R. (2007) 'Race', Ethnicity and Child Welfare: A Fine Balancing Act. *British Journal of Social Work*, 37(8): 1425–34.

Becker, H. (1967) Whose Side Are We On? *Social Problems*, 14: 239–47.

Bhatt, C. (1997) *Liberation and Purity, Race, New Religious Movements and the Ethics of Postmodernity*. London: Routledge.

Bhatti-Sinclair, K. (2011) *Anti-Racist Practice in Social Work*. Basingstoke: Palgrave.

Bonnet, A. (2000) *Anti-Racism*. London: Routledge.

Bonnett, A. and Carrington, B. (1996) Constructions of Anti-Racist Education in Britain and Canada. *Comparative Education*, 32(3): 271–88.

Bourne, J. (2007) *In Defence of Multiculturalism*. London: Institute of Race Relations.

Brah, A. (1996) *Cartographies of Diaspora: Contesting Identities*. London: Routledge.

Brah, A. (2005) Difference, Diversity and Differentiation, in Donald, J. and Rattansi, A. (eds) *Race, Culture and Difference (Third Edition)*. London: Sage, pp 126–48.

Brah, A. (2007) Non-Binarized Identities of Similarity and Difference, in Wetherell, M., Laflèche, M. and Berkeley, R. (eds) *Identity, Ethnic Diversity and Community Cohesion*. London: Sage, pp 136–46.

Braye, S. and Preston-Shoot, M. (2006) Broadening the Vision: Law Teaching, Social Work and Civil Society. *International Social Work*, 49(3): 376–89.

Burke, B. and Harrison, P. (2002) Anti-Oppressive Practice, in Adams, R., Dominelli, L. and Payne, M. (eds) *Social Work Themes, Issues and Critical Debates (Second Edition)*. Basingstoke: Palgrave, pp 222–36.

Burnett, J. (2007) Britain's 'Civilising Project': Community Cohesion and Core Values. *Policy and Politics*, 35(2): 353–7.

Butler, A., Elliot, T. and Stopard, N. (2003) Living up to the Standards We Set: A Critical Account of the Development of Anti-Racist Standards. *Social Work Education*, 22(3): 271–82.

Cantle, T. (2001) *Community Cohesion: A Report of the Independent Review Team*. London: HMSO. Available at: www.communities.gov.uk/archived/publications/communities/communitycohesionreport [accessed 12 November 2012].

CCETSW (Central Council for Education and Training in Social Work) (1991) *Requirements and Regulations for the Diploma in Social Work* (Paper 30) (Second Edition). London: CCETSW.

The College of Social Work (2012) *The Professional Capabilities Framework*. Available at: www.collegeofsocialwork.org/pcf.aspx [accessed on 29 November 2012].

Collins, S., Gutridge, P., James, A., Lynn, E. and Williams, C. (2000) Racism and Anti-Racism in Placements Reports. *Social Work Education*, 19(1): 29–43.

Commission on Integration and Community Cohesion (CICC) (2007) Our Interim Statement. Available at: http://resources.cohesioninstitute.org.uk/Publications/Documents/Document/Default.aspx?recordId=64 [accessed on 12 November 2012].

Connolly, P. (2000) Racism and Young Girls' Peer-Group Relations: The Experiences of South Asian Girls. *Sociology*, 34(3): 499–519.

Crabtree, S.A., Hussain, F. and Spalek, B. (2008) *Islam and Social Work: Debating Values Transforming Practice*. Bristol: Policy Press.

Dalrymple, J. and Burke, B. (2006) *Anti-Oppressive Practice: Social Care and the Law (Second Edition)*. Maidenhead: Open University Press.

Danso, R. (2007) Emancipating and Empowering De-Valued Skilled Immigrants: What Hope Does Anti-Oppressive Social Work Practice Offer? *British Journal of Social Work*, 1–17.

Dominelli, L. (1988) *Anti-Racist Social Work: A Challenge for White Practitioners and Educators*. Basingstoke: Palgrave.

Dominelli, L. (2002) Changing Agendas: Moving Beyond Fixed Identities in Anti-Oppressive Practice, in Tomlinson, D.R. and Trew, W. (eds) *Equalising Opportunities, Minimising Oppression: A Critical Review of Anti-Discriminatory Policies in Health and Social Welfare*. London: Routledge, pp 56–71.

Dominelli, L. (2008) *Anti-Racist Social Work (Third Edition)*. Basingstoke: Palgrave Macmillan.

Downing, J. and Husband, C. (2005) *Representing 'Race': Racisms, Ethnicities and Media*. London: Sage.

Dunne, M., Pryor, J. and Yates, P. (2005) *Becoming a Researcher*. Berkshire: Open University Press.

Dwyer, P. (2004) *Understanding Social Citizenship*. Bristol: Policy Press.

Fanon, F. (1970) *Towards the African Revolution*. Hamondsworth: Penguin.

Fernando, S. (1989) *Race and Culture in Psychiatry*. London: Routledge.

Fook, J. and Askeland, G.A. (2006) The 'Critical' in Critical Reflection, in White, S., Fook, J. and Gardner, F. (eds) *Critical Reflection in Health and Social Care*. Maidenhead: Open University Press, pp 40–55.

Fook, J., Ryan, M. and Hawkins, L. (2000) *Professional Expertise: Practice, Theory and Education for Working in Uncertainty*. London: Whiting & Birch Ltd.

Fook, J., White, S. and Gardner, F. (2006) Critical Reflection: A Review of Contemporary Literature and Understandings, in White, S., Fook, J. and Gardner, F. (eds) *Critical Reflection in Health and Social Care*. Maidenhead: Open University Press, pp 3–21.

Fredman, S. (2002) *Discrimination Law*. Oxford: Oxford University Press.

Fryer, P. (1984) *Staying Power: The History of Black People in Britain*. London: Pluto.

Gillborn, D. and Ladson-Billings, G. (2004) Introduction, in Ladson-Billings, G. and Gillborn, D. (eds) *Multicultural Education*. London: Routledge, pp 1–5.

Gilligan, P. and Furness, S. (2006) The Role of Religion and Spirituality in Social Work Practice: Views and Experiences of Social Workers and Students. *British Journal of Social Work*, 36(4): 617–37.

Goldstein, B.P. (2005) Introduction: A Context to the Review, in Thoburn, J., Chand, A. and Proctor, J. (eds) *Child Welfare Services for Minority Ethnic Families*. London: Jessica Kingsley, pp 13–25.

Goldstein, B.P. (2008) Black Perspectives, in Davis, M. (ed) *The Blackwell Companion to Social Work (Third Edition)*. Oxford: Blackwell, pp 415–22.

Graham, M. (2000) Honoring Social Work Principles: Exploring the Connections between Anti-Racist Social Work and African-Centred Worldviews. *Social Work Education*, 19(5): 421–36.

Graham, M. (2002a) *Social Work and African-Centred Worldviews*. London: Venture Press.

Graham, M. (2002b) Creating Spaces: Exploring the Role of Cultural Knowledge as a Source of Empowerment in Models of Social Welfare in Black Communities. *British Journal of Social Work*, 32(1): 35–49.

Graham, M. (2004) Empowerment Revisited – Social Work, Resistance and Agency in Black Communities. *European Journal of Social Work*, 7(1): 43–56.

Graham, M. (2007) *Black Issues in Social Work and Social Care*. Bristol: Policy Press.

Gray, A. (2003) *Research for Cultural Studies*. London: Sage.

Gunaratnam, Y. (2003) *Researching Race and Ethnicity, Methods, Knowledge and Power*. London: Sage.

Hall, S. (1992) New Ethnicities, in Donald, J. and Rattansi, A. (eds) *Race, Culture and Difference*. London: Sage, pp 252–9.

Hall, S. (2000) Who Needs 'Identity'? in du Gay, P., Evans, J. and Redman, P. (eds) *Identity: A Reader*. London: Sage, pp 15–30.

Healy, K. (2005) *Social Work Theories in Context: Creating Frameworks for Practice*. Basingstoke: Palgrave Macmillan.

Heron, G. (2004) Evidencing Anti-Racism in Student Assignments: Where has all the Racism Gone? *Qualitative Social Work*, 3(3): 277–95.

Heron, G. (2006) Critical Thinking in Social Care and Social Work: Searching Student Assignments for the Evidence. *Social Work Education*, 25(3): 209–24.

Hugman, R. (1996) Professionalization in Social Work: The Challenges of Diversity. *International Social Work*, 39(2): 131–47.

Humphries, B. (1999) Feminist Evaluation, in Shaw, I. and Lishman, J. (eds) *Evaluation and Social Work Practice*. London: Sage, pp 118–32.

Humphries, B. (2004) An Unacceptable Role for Social Work: Implementing Immigration Policy. *British Journal of Social Work*, 34(1): 93–107.

Husband, C. (2000) Recognising Diversity and Developing Skills: The Proper Role of Tran-cultural Communication. *European Journal of Social Work*, 3(3): 225–34.

Husband, C. (2007) Social Work in a Ethnically Diverse Europe: The Shifting Challenge of Difference. *Social Work and Society, International Online Journal*, 5(3). Available at: www.socwork.net/sws/article/view/138/507 [accessed on 12 November 2012].

Johnson, N. (2007) Building an Integrated Society, in Wetherell, M., Laflèche, M. and Berkeley, R. (eds) *Identity, Ethnic Diversity and Community Cohesion*. London: Sage, pp 24–33.

Karner, C. (2007) *Ethnicity and Everyday Life*. London: Routledge.

Keating, F. (2000) Anti-Racist Perspectives: What are the Gains for Social Work? *Social Work Education*, 19(1): 77–87.

Keating, F., Robertson, D., McCulloh, A. and Francis, E. (2002) *Breaking the Circles of Fear*. London: The Sainsbury Centre for Mental Health.

Khan, O. (2007) Policy, Identity and Community Cohesion: How Race Equality Fits, in Wetherell, M., Laflèche, M. and Berkeley, R. (eds) *Identity, Ethnic Diversity and Community Cohesion*. London: Sage, pp 40–58.

Kumar, K. (2008) Core Ethnicities and the Problem of Multiculturalism: The British Case, in Eade, J., Barrett, M., Flood, C. and Race, R. (eds) *Advancing Multiculturalism, Post 7/7*. Cambridge: Cambridge Scholars Publishers, pp 116–34.

Lacroix, M. (2003) Culturally Appropriate Knowledge and Skills Requested for Effective Multicultural Practice with Individuals, Families and Small Groups, in Al-Krenawi, A. and Graham, J.R. (eds) *Multicultural Social Work in Canada, Working with Diverse Ethno-Racial Communities*. Ontario: Oxford University Press, pp 23–46

Law, I., Phillips, D. and Turney, L. (2004) Tackling Institutional Racism in Higher Education: An Antiracist Toolkit, in Law, I., Phillips, D. and Turney, L. (eds) *Institutional Racism in Higher Education*. Stoke on Trent: Trentham Books, pp 93–104.

Lloyd, C. (2002) Anti-Racism, Social Movements and Civil Society, in Anthias, F. and Lloyd, C. (eds) *Rethinking Anti-Racisms*. London: Routledge, pp 60–77.

Lorenz, W. (1996) The Education of the Nation: Racism and the Nation State, in Aluffi Pentini, A. and Lorenz, W. (eds) *Anti-Racist Work with Young People*. Dorset: Russell House Publishing, pp 1–25.

Macey, M. and Moxon, E. (1996) An Examination of Anti-Racist and Anti-Oppressive Theory and Practice in Social Work Education. *British Journal of Social Work*, 26(3): 297–314.

Mac an Ghaill, M. (1999) *Contemporary Racisms and Ethnicities: Social and Cultural Transformations*. Buckingham: Open University Press.

Macpherson, W. (1999) *The Stephen Lawrence Inquiry*. London: HMSO.

Mason, D. (2003) Changing Ethnic Disadvantage: An Overview, in Mason, D. (ed) *Explaining Ethnic Differences, Changing Patterns of Disadvantage in Britain*. Bristol: Policy Press, pp 9–20.

May, S. (1999) Critical Multiculturalism and Cultural Difference: Avoiding Essentialism, in May, S. (ed) *Critical Multiculturalism, and Anti-Racist Education*. Abingdon: Routledge, pp 11–42.

McGhee, D. (2005) *Intolerant Britain? Hate, Citizenship and Difference*. Maidenhead: Open University Press.

McGhee, D. (2008) *The End of Multiculturalism: Terrorism, Integration and Human Rights*. Maidenhead: Open University Press.

McLaughlin, K. (2005) From Ridicule to Institutionalization: Anti-Oppression, the State and Social Work. *Critical Social Policy*, 25(3): 283–305.

Miles, R. (1989) *Racism*. London: Routledge.

Mirza, H.S. (2003) 'All the Women are White, all the Blacks are Men – But Some of Us are Brave': Mapping the Consequences of Invisibility for Black and Minority Ethnic Women in Britain, in Mason, D. (ed) *Explaining Ethnic Differences, Changing Patterns of Disadvantage in Britain*. Bristol: Policy Press, pp 121–38.

Modood, T. (1992) *Not Easy Being British: Colour, Culture and Citizenship*. London: Runneymede Trust and Trentham Books.

Modood, T. (2001) British Asian Identities: Something Old, Something Borrowed, Something New, in Morley, D. and Robinson, K. (eds) *British Cultural Studies*. Oxford: Oxford University Press, pp 67–78.

Modood, T. (2007) *Multiculturalism*. Cambridge: Polity Press.

Modood, T. (2008) Remaking Multiculturalism after 7/7, in Eade, J., Barrett, M., Flood, C. and Race, R. (eds) *Advancing Multiculturalism, Post 7/7*. Cambridge: Cambridge Scholars Publishing, pp 135–48.

O'Donnell, M. (2006) Researching Students on a 'Race' and Ethnicity Module, in Farrar, M. and Todd, M. (eds) *Teaching 'Race' in Social Sciences: New Context, New Approaches* (C-SAP), The Higher Education Academy Network: University of Birmingham, pp 32–52.

O'Hagan, K. (2001) *Cultural Competence in the Caring Professions*. London: Jessica Kingsley Publishers.

Owusu-Bempah, K. (2005) Race, Culture and the Child, in Hendrick, H. (ed) *Childwelfare and Social Policy*. Bristol: Policy Press, pp 177–90.

Parekh, B. (2000) *The Future of Multi-Ethnic Britain*. London: Profile Books.

Patel, N. (2002) The Campaign against Anti-Racism in Social Work: Racism Where? You See it … You Don't, in Tomlinson, D.R and Trew, W. (eds) *Equalising Opportunities, Minimising Oppression: A Critical Review of Anti-Discriminatory Policies in Health and Social Welfare*. London: Routledge, pp 30–40.

Penketh, L. (2000) *Tackling Institutional Racism, Anti-Racist Policies and Social Work Education and Training*. Bristol: Policy Press.

Pierson, J. (2008) *Going Local, Work in Communities and Neighbourhoods*. London: Routledge.

Pilkington, A. (2003) *Racial Disadvantage and Ethnic Diversity in Britain*. London: Sage.

Pilkington, A. (2004) Institutional Racism in the Academy? in Law, I., Phillips, D. and Turney, L. (eds) *Institutional Racism in Higher Education*. Stoke on Trent: Trentham Books, pp 15–26.

Platt, L. (2007) *Poverty and Ethnicity in the UK*. Bristol: The Policy Press.

Porter, S. (2002) Critical Realist Ethnography, in May, T. (ed) *Qualitative Research in Action*. London: Sage, pp 53–72.

Quality Assurance Agency for Higher Education (QAA) (2008) Subject Benchmark Statement: Social Work. Available at: www.qaa.ac.uk/Publications/InformationAndGuidance/Pages/Subject-benchmark-statement-Social-work.aspx [accessed on 12 November 2012].

Ratcliffe, P. (2004) *'Race' Ethnicity and Difference, Imagining the Inclusive Society*. Berkshire: Open University Press.

Rattansi, A. (1999) Racism, 'Postmodernism' and Reflexive Multiculturalism, in May, S. (ed) *Critical Multiculturalism, and Anti-Racist Education*, Abingdon: Routledge, pp 77–112.

Rattansi, A. (2005) Changing the Subject? Racism, Culture and Education, in Donald, J. and Rattansi, A. (eds) *Race, Culture and Difference (Third Edition)*. London: Sage, pp 11–48.

Requirements for Social Work Training (2002) Department of Health. Available at: www.dh.gov.uk/en/Publicationsandstatistics/Publications/PublicationsPolicyAndGuidance/DH_4007803 [accessed on 11 November 2012].

Robinson, L. (1995) *Psychology for Social Workers*. London: Routledge.

Robinson, L. (1999) Racial Identity Attitudes and Interracial Communication: Implications for Social Work Practice in Britain. *European Journal of Social Work*, 2(3): 315–26.

Sakamoto, I. and Pitner, R. (2005) Use of Critical Consciousness in Anti-Oppressive Social Work Practice; Disentangling Power and Structural Levels. *British Journal of Social Work*, 35(4): 435–52.

Sharma, S. (2006) *Multicultural Encounters*. Basingstoke: Palgrave Macmillan.

Singh, G. (1996) Promoting Anti-Racist and Black Perspectives in Social Work Education and Practice Teaching. *Social Work Education*, 15(2): 35–55.

Singh, G. (2002) The Political Challenge of Anti-Racism in Social Care and Health, in Tomlinson, D.R. and Trew, W. (eds) *Equalising Opportunities, Minimising Oppression: A Critical Review of Anti-Discriminatory Policies in Health and Social Welfare*. London: Routledge, pp 72–82.

Singh, G. (2006) *Developing and Supporting Black and Minority Ethnic Practice Teachers and Assessors*. Leeds: Practice Learning Taskforce.

Singh, G. and Cowden, S. (2010) From 'Anti-racist' to 'Post-racist' Education: Problems and Possibilities, in Amsler, S., Canaan, J.E., Cowden, S., Motta, S. and Singh, G. (eds) *Why Critical Pedagogy and Popular Education Matter Today*. Birmingham: CSAP, pp 28–33.

Sirna, C. (1996) The Significance of Language in Socio-Cultural Marginalisation, in Aluffi-Pentini, A. and Lorenz, W. (eds) *Anti-Racist Work with Young People*. Dorset: Russell House Publishing, pp 73–89.

Sivanandan, A. (1983) Challenging Racisms: Strategies for the 80s. *Race and Class*, 25(2): 1–11.

Solomon, B. B. (1976) *Black Empowerment: Social Work in Oppressed Communities*, Columbia, Columbia University Press.

Solomos, J. (2003) *Race and Racism in Britain (Third Edition)*. Basingstoke: Palgrave Macmillan.

Spalek, B. (2005) A Critical Reflection on Researching Black Muslim Women's Lives Post September 11th. *International Journal of Social Research Methodology*, 8(5): 205–418.

Spencer, S. (2006) *Race and Ethnicity: Culture, Identity and Representation*. London: Routledge.

Taher, A. (2008) *British Muslim Students*, The Sunday Times, 27 July.

Thompson, N. (2012) *Anti Discriminatory Practice (Fifth Edition)*. London: Palgrave.

Tomlinson, D.R. (2002) The significance of Anti-Discrimination and Social Advocacy, in Tomlinson, D.R. and Trew, W. (eds) *Equalising Opportunities, Minimising Oppression: A Critical Review of Anti-Discriminatory Policies in Health and Social Welfare*. London: Routledge, pp 149–59.

Turney, D. (1996) *The Language on Anti-Racism in Social Work: Towards a Deconstructive Reading*. London: University of London Press.

Turney, L., Law, I. and Phillips, D. (2002) Institutional Racism in Higher Education Toolkit Project: Building The Anti-Racist HEI, Centre for Ethnicity and Racism Studies, University of Leeds. Available at: www.sociology.leeds.ac.uk/assets/files/research/cers/the-anti-racism-toolkit. pdf [accessed 13 November 2012].

Walker, S. (2005) *Culturally Competent Therapy: Working with Children and Young People*. Basingstoke: Palgrave Macmillan.

Wetherell, M. (2007) Community Cohesion and Identity Dynamics: Dilemmas and Challenges, in Wetherell, M., Laflèche, M. and Berkeley, R. (eds) *Identity, Ethnic Diversity and Community Cohesion*. London: Sage, pp 1–14.

White, S. (2006) Unsettling Reflections: The Reflexive Practitioner as 'Trickster' in Interprofessional Work, in White, S., Fook, J. and Gardner, F. (eds) *Critical Reflection in Health and Social Care*. Maidenhead: Open University Press, pp 21–9.

Williams, F. (1989) *Social Policy: A Critical Introduction*. Oxford: Blackwell.

Williams, C. (1999) Connecting Anti-Racist and Anti-Oppressive Theory and Practice: Retrenchment or Re-appraisal? *British Journal of Social Work*, 29(2): 211–30.

Williams, C. and Soydan, H. (2005) When and How Does Ethnicity Matter? A Cross-National Study of Social Work Responses to Ethnicity in Child Protection Cases. *British Journal of Social Work*, 35(6): 901–20.

Williams, C., Hold, M. and Kimani, S. (2009) *Race Equality and 'Cultural Competency' in Qualifying Social Work Education in Wales*. Wales Ethnicity Research Collaboration, Wales.

Wilson, A. and Beresford, P. (2000) 'Anti-Oppressive Practice': Emancipation or Appropriation? *British Journal of Social Work*, 30(5): 553–73.

Women Living Under Muslim Laws (2006) *Knowing Our Rights: Women, Family Laws and Customs in the Muslim World*. Nottingham: The Russell Press.

Woodward, K. (2003) *Social Sciences: The Big Issues*. London: Routledge.

Zahl, M., Furman, L., Benson, P. and Canda, E. (2007) Religion and Spirituality in Social Work Practice and Education in a Cross-Cultural Context: Findings from a Norwegian and UK Study. *European Journal of Social Work*, 10(3): 295–317.

Chapter 3

Armour, M.R., Bain, B. and Rubio, R.J. (2006) *Education for Cultural Competency: Tools for Training Field Instructors*. Alexandria, VA: Council on SocialWork Education.

Boyle, D.P. and Springer, A. (2008) Towards a Cultural Competence Measure for Social Work with Specific Populations. *Journal of Ethnic and Cultural Diversity in Social Work*, 9(3–4): 53–71.

College of Social Work (2012) Professional Capabilities Framework. Available at: www.collegeofsocialwork.org [accessed on 5 December 2012].

Connolly, M., Critchon-Hill, Y. and Ward, T. (2006) *Culture and Child Protection: Reflective Responses*. London. Jessica Kingsley Publishers.

Congress, E. (1997) Using the Culturagram to Assess and Empower Culturally Diverse Families, in Congress, E., *Multicultural Perspectives in Working with Families*. New York: Springer, pp 3–16.

Cross, T.L. (2007) What is a Culturally Competent Professional? *Pathways Practice Digest*, pp 10–11.

Cross, T.L. (2008) Cultural Competence, in Mizrahi, T. and Davis, L.E. (eds)*The Encyclopedia of Social Work*. National Association of Social Workers and Oxford University Press, Inc. Richard Stockton College of New Jersey.

Cross, T., Bazron, B., Dennis, K. and Isaacs, M. (1989) *Towards a Culturally Competent System of Care Volume I*. Washington, DC: Georgetown University Child Development Center, CASSP Technical Assistance Center.

Dean, R.G. (2001) The Myth of Cross-Cultural Competence. *Families in Society: The Journal of Contemporary Human Services*, 82(6): 623–30.

Department for Education (2012) National Action Plan to Tackle Child Abuse Linked to Faith or Belief. Available at: www.education.gov.uk/publications/standard/publicationDetail/Page1/DFE-00094–2012 [accessed 8 January 2013].

Fumanti, M. (2010) 'Virtuous Citizenship', Ethnicity and Encapsulation among Akan-speaking Ghanaian Methodists in London. *African Diaspora*, 3: 13–42.

Furness, S. (2005) Shifting the Sands: Developing Cultural Competence. *Practice: Social Work in Action*, 17(4): 247–56.

Furness, S. and Gilligan, P. (2010) Social Work, Religion and Belief: Developing a Framework for Practice. *British Journal of Social Work*, 40: 2185–02.

Geron, S.M. (2002) Cultural Competency: How is it Measured? Does it Make a Difference? *Generations*, 26: 39–54.

Gilligan, P. and Furness, S. (2006) The Role of Religion and Spirituality in Social Work Practice: Views and Experiences of Social Workers and Students. *British Journal of Social Work*, 36: 617–37.

Gutierrez, L., Zuniga, M. and Lum, D. (2004) *Education for Multicultural Social Work Practice: Critical Viewpoints and Future Directions*. Alexandria, VA: CSWE.

Harrison, G. and Turner, R. (2011) Being a Culturally Competent Social Worker: Making Sense of a Murky Concept in Practice. *British Journal of Social Work*, 41(2): 333–50.

Holland, K. and Hogg, C. (2001) *Cultural Awareness in Nursing and Health Care*. London: Arnold.

Hoopes, D.S. (1979) Intercultural Communication Concepts and the Psychology of Intercultural Experience, in Pusch, M.D. (ed) *Multicultural Education: A Cross-Cultural Training Approach*. Yarmouth, ME: Intercultural Press.

International Federation of Social Workers (IFSW) (2001) Definition of Social Work.

Johnson, Y.M. and Munch, S. (2009) Fundamental Contradiction in Cultural Competence. *Social Work*, 54(3): 220–31.

La Fontaine, J.S. (ed) (2009) *The Devils' Children: From Spirit Possession to Witchcraft*. Farnham: Ashgate. Laird, S. (2008) *Anti-Oppressive Social Work: A Guide for Developing Cultural Competence*. London: Sage.

Laird, S. (2008) *Anti-oppressive Social Work: A Guide for Developing Cultural Competence*, London: Sage.

Laird, S. (2010) *Practical Social Work Law: Analysing Court Cases and Inquiries*. London: Pearson.

Long, T.B. (2012) Overview of Teaching Strategies for Cultural Competence in Nursing Students. *Journal of Cultural Diversity*, 9(3): 102–8.

Lord Laming (2003) *The Victoria Climbié Inquiry*. London: HMSO.

Lum, D. (2007) *Culturally Competent Practice: A Framework for Understanding Diverse Groups and Justice Issues*. Belmont: Brooks/Cole.

Macpherson, W. (1999) *The Stephen Lawrence Inquiry*. London: Home Office.

Maiter, S. and Stalker, C. (2010) South Asian Immigrants' Experience of Child Protection Services: Are We Recognising Strengths and Resilience? *Child and Family Social Work*, 16: 138–48.

Mama, R.S. (2001) Preparing Social Work Students to Work in Culturally Diverse Settings. *Social Work Education*, 20(3): 373–82.

McKie, L. and Cunningham-Burley, S. (2005) *Families in Society: Boundaries and Relationships*. Bristol: Policy Press.

McPhatter, A. (1997) Cultural Competence in Child Welfare. What is it? How Do We Achieve it? What Happens Without it? in S. Jackson and S. Brissett-Chapman (eds) *Serving African American Children: Child Welfare Perspectives*. New Jersey: Child Welfare League, pp 255–78.

NASW (2001) *Standards for Cultural Competence in Social Work Practice*. Washington, DC.

Norton, D.G. (1978) *The Dual Perspective: Inclusion of the Ethnic Minority Content in the Social Work Curriculum*. New York: Council on Social Work Education.

Obadina, S. (2012) Witchcraft Accusations and Exorcism: A Form of Child Abuse. *British Journal of School Nursing*, 7(6): 287–91. Available at: www.teachernet.gov.uk/publications [accessed on 5 November 2012].

O'Hagan, K. (2001) *Cultural Competence in the Caring Professions*. London: Kingsley

Parker, J. and Bradley, G. (2010) *Social Work Practice: Assessment, Planning, Intervention and Review (Third Edition)*. Exeter: Learning Matters.

Parrott, L. (2009) Constructive Marginality: Conflicts and Dilemmas in Cultural Competence and Anti-oppressive Practice. *Social Work Education*, 28(6): 617–30.

Raghallaigh, M.N. (2011) Religion in the Lives of Unaccompanied Minors: An Available and Compelling Coping Resource. *British Journal of Social Work*, 41: 539–56.

Safeguarding Children from Abuse Linked to a Belief in Spirit Possession, DCSF (2007) Available at: www.teachernet.gov.uk/publications [accessed on 5 November 2012].

Serious Case Review (Kyra Ishaq). Available at: www.lscbbirmingham.org.uk/downloads/Case+14.pdf [accessed on 1 October 2012].

Stobart, E. (2006) Child Abuse Linked to Accusations of 'Possession' and 'Witchcraft'. Research Report 750. Department for Education and Skills.

Sue, D.W. (1981) *Counselling the Culturally Different: Theory and Practice*. New York: Wiley.

The Children Act 1989. HMSO.

The Education Act 1996. HMSO.

The Housing Act 1996. HMSO.

The Human Rights Act 1998. HMSO.

The Housing Act 2004. HMSO.

The Children Act 2004. HMSO.

The Equality Act 2010.HMSO.

Thyer, B., Wodarski, J., Meyers, L. and Harrison, D. (2010) *Cultural Diversity in Social Work.* Springfield, IL: Charles C. Thomas Publisher.

Walker, S. (2005) *Culturally Competent Therapy: Working with Children and Young People.* Basingstoke: Palgrave Macmillan.

Yan, M.C. and Wong, Y.R. (2005) Rethinking Self-awareness in Cultural Competence: Toward a Dialogic Self in Cross-Cultural Social Work. *Families in Society: The Journals of Contemporary Social Services*, pp 181–7.

Chapter 4

Aymer, C. and Bryan, A. (1996) Black Students' Experience on Social Work Courses: Accentuating the Positives. *British Journal of Social Work*, 26: 1–16.

Bartoli, A. (2011) Assessment and International Students – Black African Social Work Students. *Enhancing the Learner Experience in Higher Education*, e-journal.

Bartoli, A., Kennedy, S. and Tedam, P. (2008) Who is Failing to Adjust? Black African Student Experience of Practice Learning in a Social Work Setting. *Journal of Practice Teaching in Health and Social Work*, 8(2): 75–90.

Bartoli, A., Kennedy, S. and Tedam, P. (2009) Learning from African Students. *Enhancing the Learner Experience in Higher Education*, 1(1), e-journal.

Bernard, C., Faritlough, A., Fletcher, J. and Ahmet, A. (2011) *Diversity and Progression among Social Work Students in England.* London: Goldsmiths University of London. Available at: www.kcl.ac.uk/sspp/departments/sshm/scwru/dhinitiative/projects/bernardetal2011 diversityfinalreport.pdf [accessed on 14 May 2012].

Brown, A. (1994) *Groupwork (Third Edition).* Hampshire: Ashgate.

Brown, S. and Joughin, G. (2007) Assessment and International Students: Helping Clarify Puzzling Processes, in Jones, E. and Brown, S. (eds) *Internationalising Higher Education.* Oxon: Routledge, pp 57–71.

Carroll, J. and Ryan, J. (eds) (2005) *Teaching International Students: Improving Learning for All.* Oxon: Routledge.

Connor, H., Tyres, C., Modood, T. and Hillage, J. (2004) *Why the Difference? A Closer Look at Higher Education Minority Ethnic Students and Graduates*. Institute for Employment Studies.

Coulshed, V. and Orme, J. (2006) *Social Work Practice (Fourth Edition)*. Basingstoke: Palgrave Macmillan.

Cree, V.E. (ed) (2003) *Becoming a Social Worker*. Oxon: Routledge.

Department for Education and Skills (DfES) (2003) *Aiming High: Raising Achievement of Minority Ethnic Pupils*. London: HMSO.

Doel, M. (2006) *Using Groupwork*. Oxon: Routledge in association with Community Care.

Doel, M. and Sawdon, C. (1999) *The Essential Groupworker: Teaching and Learning Creative Groupwork*. London: Jessica Kingsley.

Dominelli, L. (2008) *Anti-Racist Social Work (Third Edition)*. Hampshire: Palgrave.

Garvin, C.D., Gutierrez, L.M. and Galinsky, M.J. (2006) *Handbook of Social Work with Groups*. New York: The Guilford Press.

General Social Care Council (GSCC) (2009) *Raising Standards in Social Work Education in England 2007–8*. London: GSCC.

Gray, M. and Fook, J. (2004) *The Quest for Universal Social Work: Some Issues and Implications. Social Work Education*, 23(5): 625–44.

hooks, b. (2010) *Teaching Critical Thinking: Practical Wisdom*. London: Routledge.

Hussein, S., Moriarty, J. and Manthorpe, J. (2009) *Variations in Progression of Social Work Students in England: Using Student Data to Help Promote Achievement: Undergraduate Full-Time Students' Progression on the Social Work Degree*. London: Social Care Workforce Research Unit, King's College London and General Social Care Council.

Hussein, S., Moriarty, J., Manthorpe, J. and Huxley, P. (2006) *A Report on Progression among DipSW Students*. London: The General Social Care Council.

Hussein, S., Moriarty, J., Manthorpe, J. and Huxley, P. (2008) Diversity and Progression among Social Work Students Starting Social Work Qualifying Programmes in England between 1995 and 1998: A Quantitative Study. *British Journal of Social Work*, 38(8): 1588–609.

Hyland, F., Trahar, S., Anderson, J. and Dickens, A. (2008) *A Changing World: The Internationalisation Experiences of Staff and Students (Home and International) in UK Higher Education*. Bristol: Higher Education Academy.

Koutsantoni, D. (2006) Paper 1: Definitions: What is Internationalisation, in *Leadership Summit 2006: The Leadership and Development Challenges of Globalisation and Internationalisation*. London: Leadership Foundation for Higher Education, pp 10–12.

Kurta, L.F. (2006) Support and Self-Help Groups, in Garvin, C.D., Gutierrex, L.M. and Galinsky, M.J. (eds) *Handbook of Social Work with Groups*. New York: The Guildford Press, pp 139–59.

Mayadas, N.S., Smith, R. and Elliott, D. (2006) Social Group Work in a Global Context, in Garvin, C.D., Gutierrex, L.M. and Galinsky, M.J. (eds) *Handbook of Social Work with Groups*. New York: The Guildford Press, pp 45–57.

McGregor, K. (2011) Social Work Student from Ethnic Minorities Face Struggle. Available at: www.communitycare.co.uk/Articles/02/03/2011/116371/social-work-students-from-ethnic-minorities-face-struggle.htm [accessed on 12 November 2012].

Nagy, G. and Faulk, S. (2000) Dilemmas in International and Cross-Cultural Social Work Education. *International Social Work*, 43(1): 49–60.

Razack, N. (2009) Decolonizing the Pedgogy and Practice of International Social Work. *International Social Work*, 52(9): 9–21.

Singh, G. (2011) *Black and Minority Ethnic (BME) Students' Participation in Higher Education: Improving Retention and Success*. York: The Higher Education Academy.

Stevenson, J. (2012) *Black and Minority Ethnic Student Degree Retention and Attainment*. The Higher Education Academy. Available at: www.heacademy.ac.uk/assets/documents/retention/Summit/bme_summit_final report.pdf [accessed on 20 November 2012].

Tomlin, C. and Olusola, M. (2006) *An Analysis of High Attaining Black Students: Factors and Conditions That Effect Their Achievement Levels*. University of Wolverhampton.

Trahar, S. (2007) *Teaching and Learning: The International Higher Education Landscape*. Bristol: The Higher Education Academy.

Welikala, T. and Watkins, C. (2008) *Improving Intercultural Learning Experiences in Higher Education: Responding to Cultural Scripts for Learning*. London: Institute of Education, University of London.

Chapter 5

Abrams, L.S. and Gibson, P. (2007) Reframing Multicultural Education: Teaching White Privilege in the Social Work Curriculum. *Journal of Social Work Education*, 43(1): 147–59.

Ackerly, B. and True, J. (2010) *Doing Feminist Research in Political and Social Science*. Basingstoke: Palgrave Macmillan.

Bartoli, A., Kennedy, S. and Tedam, P. (2008) Who is Failing to Adjust? Black African Student Experience of Practice Learning in a Social Work Setting. *Journal of Practice Teaching in Health and Social Work*, 8(2): 75–90.

Baxter, J. (2003) *Positioning Gender in Discourse: A Feminist Methodology*. Basingstoke: Palgrave Macmillan.

Boyce, P., Harrison, G., Jelley, M., Jolley, M., Chukumeka, M., Soper, S., Wattam, E. and White, G. (2008) *Review of the Anti-Racist Standards within Anti-oppressive Practice*. University of Plymouth: Centre for Excellence in Professional Placement Learning (CEPPL).

Bryson, V. (2007) *Gender and the Politics of Time: Feminist Theory and Contemporary Debates*. Bristol: Policy Press.

Calliste, A. and Sefa Dei, G.J. (2000) *Anti-Racist Feminism*. Nova Scotia: Fernwood Publishing.

Carby, H.V. (1987) White Woman Listen, in Mirza, H.S. (ed) *Black British Feminism: A Reader*. London: Routledge, pp 45–53.

CCETSW (1991) Rules for Regulations for the Diploma in Social Work, Dip S.W. CCETSW, Paper 30, Second Edition.

Cixous, H. (1998) *Stigmata*. London: Routledge.

Cixous, H. (ed) (2008) *White Ink: Interviews on Sex, Text and Politics*. Stocksfield: Acumen.

Clifford, D. and Burke, B. (2009) *Anti-Oppressive Ethics and Values in Social Work*. Basingstoke: Palgrave Macmillan.

The College of Social Work (2012) *Professional Capabilities Framework*. London: The College of Social Work (TCSW).

Curry-Stevens, A. and Nissen, L. (2011) Reclaiming Futures Considers and Anti-Oppressive Frame to Decrease Disparities. *Children and Youth Services Review*, 33(1): 54–9.

Dominelli, L. (2002) *Anti-Oppressive Social Work Theory and Practice*. Basingstoke: Palgrave Macmillan.

Flax, J. (2010) *Resonances of Slavery in Race/Gender Relations: Shadow at the Heart of American Politics*. Basingstoke: Palgrave Macmillan.

Fook, J. (2004) Some Considerations on the Potential Contributions of Intercultural Social Work. *Social Work Society*, 2(1): 83–6.

Frankenberg, R. (1993) *The Social Construction of White Women, Whiteness Race Matters*. Minneapolis: University of Minnesota Press.

Freeman, M. (2011) Validity in Dialogic Encounters with Hermeneutic Truths. *Qualitative Inquiry*, 17(6): 534–8.

Garner, S. (2007) *Whiteness and Introduction*. Oxon: Routledge.

General Social Care Council (2002) *Accreditation of Universities to Grant Degrees in Social Work*. London: General Social Care Council (GSCC).

Greenhalgh-Spencer, H. (2008) Audience and Author: The Reading of the 'White Expert'. *Borderlands e-journal*, 7(3): 1–17.

Hall, S. (ed) (1997) *Representations: Cultural Representations and Signifying Practices*. London: Sage.

Health and Care Professions Council (HCPC) (2012) *Standards of Proficiency: Social Workers in England*. London: HCPC.

hooks, b. (1994) *Outlaw Culture*. London: Routledge.

hooks, b. (2009) *Belonging: A Culture of Place*. London: Routledge.

Humphries, B. (2004) An Unacceptable Role for Social Work: Implementing Immigration Policy. *British Journal of Social Work*, 34(1): 93–107.

International Federation of Social Work (IFSW) (2004) Available at: http://ifsw.org/policies/definition-of-social-work.

Jones, K., Cooper, B. and Ferguson, H. (2008) *Best Practice in Social Work: Critical Perspectives*. Basingstoke: Palgrave Macmillan.

Jordan, B. (2000) *Social Work and the Third Way*. London: Sage.

Jordan, B. (2004) Emancipatory Social Work: Opportunity or Oxymoron. *British Journal of Social Work*, 34: 5–19.

Jordan, B. (2006) *Social Policy in the Twenty-First Century: New Perspectives, Big Issues*. Cambridge: Polity Press.

Khaleeli, H. (2010) I Have the Rebel Gene, in: Cochrane, K. (ed) (2012) *Women of the Revolution: Forty Years of Feminism*. London: Guardianbooks, pp 361–6.

Koprowska, J. (2010) *Communication and Interpersonal Skills in Social Work (Third Edition)*. Exeter: Learning Matters.

Lomax, R., Jones, K., Leigh, S. and Gay, C. (2010) *Surviving Your Social Work Placement*. Basingstoke: Palgrave Macmillan.

Lonne, B., Parton, N., Thompson, J. and Harries, M. (2009) *Reforming Child Protection*. London: Routledge.

Lorde, A. (1984) *Sister Outsider: Essay and Speeches*. London: The Crossing Press.

MacDonald, C. (2006) *Challenging Social Work: The Context of Practice*. Basingstoke: Palgrave Macmillan.

McIntosh, P. (2009) Foreword, in: Weeks, K., *Privilege and Prejudice: Twenty Years with the Invisible Knapsack*. Newcastle upon Tyne: Cambridge Scholars Publishing.

McLaughlin, K. (2005) From Ridicule to Institutionalisation: Anti-oppression, the State and Social Work. *Critical Social Policy*, 25(3): 283–305.

Mutokori, M. (2012) Student Verbal Feedback – *Global Communities*, Lecture, 24 October.

Nakagawa, A. (2012) Available at: http://racefiles.wordpress.com.

Padare (2012) Beyond Horizons: 'Black African Social Work Students Look to the Future' Conference June 2012, Northampton, University of Northampton.

Pon, G. (2009) Cultural Competency as New Racism: An Ontology of Forgetting. *Journal of Progressive Human Services*, 20: 59–71.

Ryde, J. (2009) *Being White in the Helping Professions*. London: Jessica Kingsley.

Singh, G. (2011) Social Work's Anti-racist Journey. *Community Care*. Available at: www. communitycare.co.uk/Articles.02.03/2011/116358/social-works-anti-racist.

The Social Work Task Force (SWTF) (2010) *Building a Safe and Confident Future: Implementing the Recommendations of the Social Work Task Force*. London: HMSO.

Speer, S. (2005) *Gender Talk: Feminism, Discourse and Conversation Analysis*. Hove: Routledge.

Spivak, G. (1999) *A Critique of Postcolonial Reasoning: Toward a History of the Vanishing Present*. Cambridge, MA: Harvard University Press.

Todd, R.N. and Abrams, E.M. (2011) White Dialectics: A New Framework for Theory, Research, and Practice with White Students. *The Counseling Psychologist*, 39(3): 353–95.

TOPPS (2002) *The National Occupational Standards for Social Work*. UK Partnership: TOPPS.

Webb, S.A. (2006) *Social Work in a Risk Society*. Basingstoke: Palgrave Macmillan.

White, V. (2006) *The State of Feminist Social Work*. London: Routledge.

Wilson, K., Ruch, G., Lymbery, M., and Cooper, A. (2008) *Social Work: An Introduction to Contemporary Practice*. Essex: Pearson Education Limited.

Chapter 6

Alexander, Z. and Dewjee, A. (1984) *The Wonderful Adventures of Mrs Seacole in Many Lands*. London: Falling Wall Press.

Aptheker, H. (1993) *American Negro Slave Revolts*. New York: International Publisher.

BARAC (2012) No to Cuts, No to Racism. Black Activists Against the Cuts. Available at: www. blackactivistsrisingagainstcuts.blogspot.co.uk/2012/07/rise-mobilise-organise-tackling-racism.html (accessed on 5 November 2012).

Bell, D. (1980) Brown v. Board of Education and the Interest Convergence Dilemma. *Harvard Law Review*, 93: 518–33.

Bell, D. (1992) *Faces at the Bottom of the Well: The Permanence of Racism*. New York: Basic Books.

Blair, M. (2004) The Myth of Neutrality in Educational Research, in Ladson-Billings, G. and Gillborn, D. (eds) *The RoutledgeFalmer Reader in Multicultural Education*. London: RoutledgeFalmer, pp 243–51.

Brown, J. (1859) Final Speech. The Guilder Lehrman Institute of American History. Available at: www.gilderlehrman.org/history-by-era/failure-compromise/resources/john-brown%E2% 80%99s-final-speech-1859 (accessed on 10 December 2012).

Cantle, T. (2001) *Community Cohesion – A Report of the Independent Review Team*. London: Home Office.

Carmichael, S. and Hamilton, C.V. (1967) *Black Power: The Politics of Liberation in America*. New York: Vintage.

CoSW (2012) *Domains within the Professional Capabilities Framework*. London: College of Social Work.

Crenshaw, K., Gotanda, N., Peller, G. and Thomas, K. (eds) (1995) *Critical Race Theory: The Key Writings that Formed the Movement*. New York: The New Press.

Crewe, I. (ed) (1975) *British Political Sociology Yearbook Volume 2: The Politics of Race*. London: Croom Helm.

Delgado, R. and Stefancic, J. (1991) Derrick Bell's Chronicle of the Space Traders: Would the U.S. Sacrifice People of Color if the Price were Right? *University of Colorado Law Review*, 62: 321. Available at: www.papers.ssrn.com/sol3/papers.cfm?abstract_id=2097937 [accessed on 9 December 2012].

Delgado, R. and Stefancic, J. (2001) *Critical Race Theory: An Introduction*. New York: New York University Press.

Du Bois, W.E.B. (1903) *The Souls of Black Folk*. Chicago: A.C. McClurg& Co.

Duffield, I. (1981) Black People in Britain: History and the Historians. *History Today*, 31(9).

EDF (2012) EDF briefing on the Enterprise and Regulatory Reform Bill. Equality and Diversity Forum. Available at: www.edf.org.uk/blog/?p=21517 [accessed on 5 November 2012].

Gillborn, D. (2008) *Racism and Education: Coincidence or Conspiracy*. Oxford: Routledge.

HCPC (2012) *Standards of Proficiency: Social Workers in England*, Health and Care Professions Council. London: HCPC.

Hitchens, P (2012) Dragging Nick Griffin into it, *Mail on Sunday*, 20 August. Available at: www. hitchensblog.mailonsunday.co.uk/2012/08/dragging-nick-griffin-into-it/comments/ page/2/[accessed on 5 November 2012].

HMSO (1976) *The Race Relations Act 1976*. London: Her Majesty's Stationery Office.

HMSO (1985) *The Swann Report: Education for All. Report of the Committee of Enquiry into the Education of Children from Ethnic Minority Groups*. London: Her Majesty's Stationery Office.

HMSO (2000) The *Race Relations (Amendment) Act 2000*. London: Her Majesty's Stationery Office.

HMSO (2010) *The Equality Act 2010*. London: Her Majesty's Stationery Office.

Hooks, B. (2000) *Feminist Theory: From Margin to Center*. Cambridge, MA: South End Press.

Hylton, K (2008) *'Race' and Sport: Critical Race Theory*. London: Routledge. Available at: www.bl.uk/sportandsociety/exploresocsci/sportsoc/sociology/articles/hylton.pdf [accessed 10 December 2012].

Hylton, K., Pilkington, A. Warmington, P. and Housee, S. (eds) (2011) *Monograph 15. Atlantic Crossings: International Dialogues on Critical Race Theory*. Birmingham University: Sociology, Anthropology, Politics (C-SAP), The Higher Education Academy Network.

Jackson, P. (1998) Constructions of 'Whiteness' in the Geographical Imagination. *AREA*, 30(2): 99–106.

Jones, O. (2012) *Chavs: The Demonization of the Working Class*. London: Verso.

Kaiser, C., Drury, B., Spalding, K., Cheryan, S. and O'Brien, L. (2009) The Ironic Consequences of Obama's Election: Decreased Support for Social Justice. *Journal of Experimental Social Psychology*, 45: 556–9.

Kochhar, R., Fry, R. and Taylor, P. (2011) *Wealth Gaps Rise to Record Highs Between Whites, Blacks, Hispanics*. Pew Research Center, 26 July.

Ladson-Billing, G. (2006) They're Trying to Wash us Away: The Adolescence of Critical Race Theory in Education, in Dixson, A. and Rousseau, C. (eds) *Critical Race Theory in Education: All God's Children Got a Song*. New York: Routledge.

Latene, B. and Darley, J. (1970) *The Unresponsive Bystander: Why Doesn't He Help?* New York: Appleton-Century-Croft.

Macpherson, W. (1999) *The Stephen Lawrence Inquiry: Report of an Inquiry by Sir William Macpherson of Cluny*. London: Home Office.

McIntosh, P. (1989) *White Privilege: Unpacking the Invisible Knapsack*. Peace and Freedom. Available at: www.library.wisc.edu/edvrc/docs/public/pdfs/LIReadings/InvisibleKnapsack.pdf [accessed on 4 December 2012].

Mills, C.W. (1997) *The Racial Contract*. London: Cornell University Press.

Pilkington, A. (2012) *Beyond the Radical Hour: The Changing Discourse on Race and Ethnicity*, 28 October. Available at: www.leftcentre.org.uk [accessed on 29 October 2012].

Powell, E. (1969) *Freedom and Reality*. Kingswood: Elliot Right Way Books.

Preston, J. (2007) *Whiteness and Class in Education*. London: Springer.

REF (2012) *Disproportionate Impact of Cuts on Black and Ethnic Minority Groups is 'No Surprise'*. Race Equality Foundation. Available at: www.raceequalityfoundation.org.uk/news/dis proportionate-impact-cuts-black-and-minority-ethnic-groups-no-surprise [accessed on 5 November 2012].

Runnymede Trust (2012) *Runnymede Trust Response to the Government's Integration Strategy: 'A Dangerous and Ill-Advised Reversion to Assimilationist Policy'*. Available at: www.runnymedetrust.org/uploads/Integrationstrategypressresponse.pdf [accessed on 22 October 2012].

Sandbrook, D. (2012) How Glorious, After Years of Our National Identity being Denigrated, to see Patriotism Rekindled, *Daily Mail*, 10 August.

Scarman, L. (1982). *The Scarman Report:The Brixton Disorders 10–12 April 1981*. London: Penguin.

Stainback, K. and Tomaskovic-Devey, D. (2012) *Documenting Desegregation: Racial and Gender Segregation in Private Sector Employment Since the Civil Rights Act*. Russell Sage Foundation. Available at: www.russellsage.org/publications/documenting-desegregation [accessed on 22 October 2012].

Sveinsson, K.P. (ed) (2010) *Ethnic Profiling: The Use of 'Race' in UK Law Enforcement*. Runnymede Trust.

Thompson, C., Schaefer, E. and Brod, H. (2003) *White Men Challenging Racism*. Durham and London: Duke University Press.

Troyna, B. (1994) The 'Everyday World' of Teachers? Deracialised Discourses in the Sociology of Teachers and the Teaching Profession. *British Journal of Education*, 15(3): 325–39.

Chapter 7

Aymer, C. and Bryan, A. (1996) Black Students: Experience on Social Work Courses: Accentuating the Positives. *British Journal of Social Work*, 26: 1–16.

Barn, R. (2001) *Black Youth on the Margins: A Research Review*. York: Joseph Rowntree Foundation.

Barn, R. (2006) *Improving Services to Meet the Needs of Minority Ethnic Children and Families*. Department of Education and Research in Practice. Available at: www.rip.org.

Bartoli, A. (2011) Assessments and International Students: Black African Social Work. *Enhancing the Learner in Higher Education*, 3(1): 45–58.

Begum, N. (2006) *Doing It for Themselves: Participation and Black and Minority Ethnic Service Users*. Participation Report 14. Bristol: Policy Press.

Beresford, B. (1995) *Experts' Opinion: A National Survey of Parents Caring for a Severely Disabled Child*. London: HMSO.

Bignall, T. and Butt, J. (2000) *Between Ambition and Achievement, Young Black Disabled People's Experiences and Views of Independent and Independent Living*. York: Joseph Rowntree Foundation.

Bonnett, A. (2000) Anti-Racism, in Wainright, J. (2009) Racism, Anti-Racist Practice and Social Work: Articulating the Teaching and Learning Experiences of Black Social Workers. *Race, Ethnicity and Education*, 12(4): 495–512.

Boushell, M. (2000) What Kind of People Are We? Race, Anti-Racism and Social Welfare Research. *British Journal of Social Work*, 30: 71–89.

Braye, S. and Preston-Shoot, M. (2001) Social Work Practice and Accountability, in Cull, L.A. and Roche, J. (eds) *The Law and Social Work*. Basingstoke: Palgrave.

Brockman, M., Butt, J. and Fisher, M. (2001) The Experience of Racism: Black Staff in Social Services. *Research Policy and Planning*, 19(2): 1–10. Available at: http://ssrg.org.uk/wp-content/uploads/2012/02/rpp192/article1.pdf.

Bryan A. (2000) *Exploring the Experiences of Black Professionals in Welfare Agencies and Black Students in Social Work Education*. PhD Thesis, University of Bath. Available at: http://people.bath.ac.uk/mnspwr/doc_theses_links/a_bryan.html.

Chamba, R., Ahmad, W., Hirst, M., Lawton, D. and Beresford, B. (1999) *On the Edge: Minority Ethnic Families Caring for a Severely Disabled Child*. Bristol: Policy Press.

Channer, Y. and Doel, M. (2009) Beyond Qualification: Experiences of Black Social Workers on a Post-Qualifying Course. *Social Work Education*, 28(4): 396–412.

Coulshed, V. and Orme, J. (2006) *Social Work Practice (Fourth Edition)*. Basingstoke: Palgrave Macmillan.

Dominelli, L. (1988) *Anti-racist Social Work: A Challenge for White Practitioners and Educators*. Basingstoke: Macmillan Education Limited.

Dominelli, L. (1997) *Anti-Racist Social Work*. London: Macmillan Press.

Dominelli, L. (2008) *Anti-Racist Social Work (Third Edition)*. Basingstoke: Palgrave Macmillan.

Dominelli, L., Lorenz, W. and Soydan, H. (2001) *Beyond Racial Divides*. Aldershot: Ashgate.

Ferguson, I. (2008) *Reclaiming Social Work: Challenging Neo-liberalism and Promoting Social Justice*. London: Sage.

Flynn, R. (2002) *Short Breaks: Providing Better Access and More Choice for Black Disabled Children and Their Parents*. Bristol: Policy Press.

Fook, J. (2002) *Social Work: Critical Theory and Practice*. London: Sage.

Gordon, G. (2001) Transforming Lives: Towards Bicultural Competence, in Reason, P. and Bradbury, H. (2001) *Handbook of Action Research*. London: Sage.

Gould, N. (1996). Introduction: Social Work Education and the 'Crisis of the Professionals', in Phillips, C. (2010) White Like Who? Temporality, Contextuality and Anti-racist Social Work Education and Practice. *Critical Social Work*, 11(2).

Graham, M. (2006) Giving Voice to Black Children: An Analysis of Social Agency. *British Journal of Social Work*, 37: 1305–17.

Graham, M. (2007) *Black Issues in Social Work and Social Care*. Bristol: The Policy Press.

Graham, M. and Robinson, G. (2004) The Silent Catastrophe: Institutional Racism in the British Educational System and the Underachievement of Black Boys. *Journal of Black Studies*, 34(5): 653–71.

Hall, S. (1993) Culture, Community, Nations. *Cultural Studies*, 7(3): 349–63.

Heron, G. (2006) Using Students' Written Feedback on 'Race' Issues to Enhance Self-Regulated Learning. *British Journal of Social Work, 38(2): 376–94.*

Johns, N. (2005) Positive Action and the Problem of Merit: Employment Policies in the National Health Service. *Critical Social Policy*, 25(2): 139–63.

Joseph Rowntree Foundation (1999) *Supporting Disabled Children and Their Families*. York: Joseph Rowntree Foundation.

Joseph Rowntree Foundation (2005) *Making Change Happen for Black and Minority Ethnic Disabled People: Findings*. York: Joseph Rowntree Foundation.

Keating, F. (2000) Anti-Racist Perspectives: What are the Gains for Social Work? *Social Work Education*, 19(1): 77–87.

Macey, M. and Moxon, E. (1996) An Examination of Anti-Racist and Anti-Oppressive Theory and Practice in Social Work Education. *British Journal of Social Work*, 26: 297–314.

Macpherson, W. (1999) *The Stephen Lawrence Inquiry*. London: The Stationery Office Ltd.

Maidment, J. and Cooper, L. (2002) Acknowledgement of Client Diversity and Oppression in Social Work Student Supervision. *Social Work Education*, 21(4): 399–407.

Modood, T. and Berthoud, R. (1997) *Ethnic Minorities in Britain: Diversity and Disadvantage*. London: Policy Studies Institute.

O'Neale, V. (2000) *Excellence Not Excuses: Inspection of Services for Ethnic Minority Children and Families*. London: Department of Health.

Patel, V. (2002) *Not More But the Same: The Voices and Views of Disabled Children from Black Minority Ethnic Communities in Scotland*. York: Joseph Rowntree Foundation.

Penketh, L. (2000) *Tackling Institutional Racism: Anti-Racist Policies and Social Work Education and Training*. Bristol: The Policy Press.

Phillips, C. (2010) White Like Who? Temporality, Contextuality and Anti-racist Social Work Education and Practice. *Critical Social Work*, 11(2).

Ryde, J. (2009) *Being White in the Helping Professions: Developing Effective Intercultural Awareness*. London: Jessica Kingsley.

Shah, S. and Priestley, M. (2001) *A Research Report for Leeds Involvement Project*.

Singh, G. (1996) Promoting Anti-racist and Black Perspectives in Social Work Education and Practice Teaching. *Social Work Education*, 15(2): 35–56.

Singh, G. (2002) The Political Challenge of Anti-Racism in Social Care and Health, in Tomlinson, D.R. and Trew, W. (eds) *Equalising Opportunities, Minimising Oppression: A Critical Review of Anti-Discriminatory Policies in Health and Social Welfare*. London: Routledge.

Singh, G. (2006) Postmodernism, Anti-Racism and Social Work, in Wainright, J. (2009) Racism, Anti-Racist Practice and Social Work: Articulating the Teaching and Learning Experiences of Black Social Workers. *Race Ethnicity and Education*, 12(4): 495–512.

Stuart, O. (2006) *Will Community-Based Support Services Make Direct Payments a Viable Option for Black and Minority Ethnic Service Users and Carers?* SCIE Race Equality Discussion Paper 01. London: Social Care Institute for Excellence.

Stubbs, P. (1985) The Employment of Black Social Workers: From 'Ethnic Sensitivity' to Anti-racism. *Critical Social Policy*, 12(85): 6–27.

Thompson, N. (2006) *Anti-Discriminatory Practice (Fourth Edition)*. New York: Palgrave Macmillan.

Turney, D. (1996) *The Language of Anti-Racism in Social Work: Towards a Deconstructive Reading*. London: Goldsmiths College, University of London.

Conclusion

The College of Social Work (2012) *The Professional Capabilities Framework*. Available at: www.collegeofsocialwork.org/pcf.aspx [accessed on 29 November 2012].

Dodd, V. (2012) Doreen Lawrence: I Don't Think I've Anymore to Give, *Guardian*, 27 January.

Duffy, C.A. (1993) *Mean Time*. London: Anvil Press Poetry.

Hickman, M.J. and Walter, B. (1995) Deconstructing Whiteness: Irish Women in Britain. *Feminist Review*, 50: 5–19.

hooks, b. (2010) *Teaching Critical Thinking: Practical Wisdom*. London: Routledge.

Muir, H. (2012) Doreen Lawrence: Stephen is Always in My Thoughts, *Guardian*, 18 December.

Power, N. (2009) *One Dimensional Woman*. Winchester: O Books.

Ryde, J. (2009) *Being White in the Helping Professions*. London: Jessica Kingsley.

White, V. (2006) *The State of Feminist Social Work*. London: Routledge.

Index